D1536494

General Editors: J. R. MULRYNE
and J. C. BULMAN
Associate Editor: Margaret Shewring

Hamlet

Already published in the series

Scott McMillin *Henry IV, Part One*
Bernice W. Kliman *Macbeth*
Hugh M. Richmond *King Henry VIII*
Geraldine Cousin *King John*
Anthony B. Dawson *Hamlet*
James N. Loehlin *Henry V*
Margaret Shewring *King Richard II*

Volumes on most other plays in preparation

Of related interest

Kate Chedgzoy *Shakespeare's queer children: sexual politics and contemporary culture*

Jonathan Dollimore and Alan Sinfield, eds *Political Shakespeare: new essays in cultural materialism, 2nd edition*

Alison Findlay *Illegitimate power: bastards in Renaissance drama*

John J. Joughin, ed. *Shakespeare and national culture*

Michele Marrapodi, A. J. Hoenselaars, Marcello Cappuzzo and L. Falzon Santucci, eds *Shakespeare's Italy*

Ann Thompson and Sasha Roberts *Women reading Shakespeare 1600–1900: an anthology*

Hamlet

ANTHONY B. DAWSON

Manchester
University Press

Manchester and New York

Distributed exclusively in the USA by St. Martin's Press

Copyright © ANTHONY B. DAWSON 1995

Published by
Manchester University Press
Oxford Road, Manchester M13 9NR
and Room 400, 175 Fifth Avenue,
New York NY 10010, USA

Distributed exclusively in the USA by
St. Martin's Press, Inc., 175 Fifth Avenue,
New York, NY 10010, USA

Distributed exclusively in Canada by
UBC Press, University of British Columbia,
6344 Memorial Road,
Vancouver, BC, Canada V6T 1Z2

British Library Cataloguing-in-Publication Data
A catalogue record for this book is available
from the British Library

Library of Congress Cataloging-in-Publication Data
Dawson, Anthony B.
  Hamlet / Anthony B. Dawson.
     p. cm. — (Shakespeare in performance)
  Includes bibliographical references and index.
  ISBN 0-7190-3933-9
  1. Shakespeare, William, 1564-1616. Hamlet. 2 Shakespeare,
William, 1564-1616—Film and video adaptations, Shakespeare,
William, 1564-1616—Stage history. I. Title. II. Series.
PR2807.D35 1996
822.3'3—dc20   95-5556
                                                         CIP

ISBN 0 7190 4625 4 *paperback*

First published 1995, reprinted in paperback 1997, 2000

Typeset by
Koinonia Limited, Manchester
Printed in Great Britain by Biddles Ltd,
www.biddles.co.uk

CONTENTS

To Claire, Emma, Matthew and Jeremy

LIST OF PLATES

SERIES EDITORS' PREFACE

In the past two decades, the study of Shakespeare's plays as scripts for performance in the theatre has grown to rival the reading of Shakespeare as literature among university, college and secondary-school teachers and their students. The aim of the present series is to assist this study by describing how certain of Shakespeare's texts have been realised in production.

The series is not concerned to provide theatre history in the traditional sense. Rather, it employs the more contemporary discourses of performance criticism to explore how a multitude of factors work together to determine how a play achieves meaning for a particular audience. Each contributor to the series has selected a number of productions of a given play and analysed them comparatively. These productions – drawn from different periods, countries and media – were chosen not only because they are culturally significant in their own right, but also because they represent something of the range and variety of the possible interpretations of the play in hand. They illustrate how the convergence of various material conditions helps to shape a performance: the medium for which the text is adapted; stage design and theatrical tradition; the acting company itself; the body and abilities of the individual actor; and the historical, political and social contexts which condition audience reception of the play.

We hope that theatre-goers, by reading these accounts of Shakespeare in performance, may enlarge their understanding of what a play-text is and begin, too, to appreciate the complex ways in which performance is a collaborative effort. Any study of a Shakespeare text will, of course, reveal only a small proportion of the play's potential meaning; but by engaging issues of how a text is translated in performance, our series encourages a kind of reading that is receptive to the contingencies that make theatre a living art.

J. R. Mulryne and J. C. Bulman, General Editors
Margaret Shewring, Associate Editor

ACKNOWLEDGEMENTS

Librarians in Britain, the United States and Canada have helped me enormously, especially Sylvia Morris, Mary White and their co-workers at the Shakespeare Centre in Stratford, and the extremely helpful staff members at the Folger Shakespeare Library in Washington, at the Theatre Museum in London, and at the Birmingham Shakespeare Library; a special word of thanks also to the long-suffering staff of the interlibrary loans department at the University of British Columbia. Susan Brock at the Shakespeare Institute in Stratford provided me with invaluable information and materials, and I am indebted to various other members of the Institute as well: Stanley Wells made me welcome when I was in Stratford, Russell Jackson gave me a number of excellent leads, and Claire Cochrane provided me with a copy of her thesis on the Birmingham Repertory Theatre and told me about the wonderful array of photographs of the BRT 1925 production. I am particularly grateful to the Social Sciences and Humanities Research Council of Canada, which awarded me a grant to travel to England to do the necessary research and which has supported my writing of the book in numerous ways. James Bulman and J. R. Mulryne, the general editors of this series, have been unflagging in their support and in the care with which they combed the manuscript, at various stages, for errors and solecisms. Jim, with meticulous precision and enthusiastic encouragement, helped me stay on track; Ronnie tried, successfully I hope, to keep me from seeming unduly provincial. Barbara Hodgdon gave me all kinds of useful advice and also commented acutely on parts of an early draft, Joel Kaplan and Sheila Stowell offered consistent support and a London roof, and Paul Yachnin, who read several early versions of various chapters and discussed a whole range of questions with me, was unfailingly generous with both his time and assistance. Finally, I want to thank Gabi Helms, who helped me with German translations, and Julie Walchli, whom I was extremely lucky to have as my very able research assistant.

All references are to *The Riverside Shakespeare*, edited by G. B. Evans (1974).

CHAPTER I

Performing *Hamlet*'s meanings

Announced by the watchful Rosencrantz and Guildenstern, actors arrive unexpectedly at Elsinore, and Hamlet seizes on their presence as a weapon. As someone deeply concerned with drama, acting, and theatrical representation, Hamlet is hyper-alert to the meanings circulating around him, aware of the power of the interpretations that he will be able to generate in and through theatre. The actors, he knows, are 'the abstract and brief chronicles of the time' (II.ii.524-5); they can help him sort out his world, detect the 'form and pressure' of the milieu he must perforce inhabit. He thinks of Trojan Hecuba, the grieving wife and mother, as a dramatic image of what his own mother ought to be. He is beginning too to devise 'The Murder of Gonzago' as a theatrical mirror of the situation he seeks to test. Elated by the possibilities of what he can do by 'playing', he asks the Player for a speech on Priam and Hecuba, but the fiction that follows generates unlooked-for problems. Rather than clarity, new enigmas emerge. He, who has spoken earlier of having 'that within that passes show', is struck anew by the question of the truth of his own, and everyone else's, interior motions. How can the actor, in only a 'dream of passion', wind his body and soul to such a pitch that his play-acted feelings are indistinguishable from Hamlet's own *real* ones? Perhaps, despite his earlier protestations, Hamlet's feelings are merely an illusion. In his typically inquiring way, he pushes the mystery further. What, he wonders, if the actor were to play *him*? 'He would drown the stage with tears ... Make mad the guilty ... amaze indeed / The very faculties of eyes and ears' (II.ii.562-6). If the actor can play *him*, Hamlet, and be both more stirred in his own person than Hamlet and more effective with his audience, drowning the stage with tears, then where does that leave the Prince? Who is he anyway? Is he any more than an actor?

[1]

As audience, we are faced with an odd spectacle: an actor playing a part is telling us how his truth (or that of his 'character') is threatened by his encounter with an actor who, were *he* to play the part assigned to the first actor (i.e. the part of Hamlet, who even in his own persona is much given to acting), would do a much more commanding job. Hamlet's reality becomes at this moment something inseparable from the enacted; indeed, the entire scene exerts constant pressure on the distinction between the performed and the authentic, since Hamlet is using performance as a way of trying to get at his own authentic feelings. In the face of such an enterprise, an abyss of receding images seems to gape.

When a modern actor approaches the part of Hamlet, he has somehow to confront that abyss, even if he never consciously names it to himself. Current acting theory prompts him to seek the 'inner truth' of the character – a truth that is more or less stable and fixed. The very term 'character', which modern actors use to define that elusive being that they seek to find in the text, suggests something fixed and written – more knowable than what the Elizabethans, with fruitful ambiguity, called 'person'. At the same time, in approaching a role like Hamlet, an actor could hardly not be aware of inconsistency and indeterminacy. The moment we have begun with is a perfect example of how the 'reality' of the character can slide into a maze of reflections and enactments. So the actor, aware too of a whole history of Hamlets that have preceded him, knows that what he offers an audience is provisional, his own interpretation, and that 'Hamlet' is merely an effect of his encounter with the text. My point is that these oppositions between stability and indeterminacy, being and acting, truth and interpretation, are built right into the experience of reading, playing or indeed seeing *Hamlet*.

And what exactly *is* this thing called '*Hamlet*'? First and foremost, of course, it is a text; but even such a simple statement is misleading, as we shall see. And what is the relation between a text and a 'performance' of that text? How prescriptive is the script? Should we regard the text mainly as a pre-text for performance of whatever sort, or as something separate, with perhaps more far-reaching authority than performance?[1] It is a commonplace these days to say that Shakespeare's plays were written to be performed, but this too is an oversimplification. In order to be performed, they first have to be read.

Besides, our current familiarity with *Hamlet* is generally a consequence of reading, and certainly our study of it, as well as our judgment of performances, depends on reading, which is always what drives interpretation. Because of the play's intense concern with theatricality and performance, we could even say that reading it *is* performing it. Beyond that, the text comes to us now via a long history of reception that conditions any performance or indeed any reading. So one of the first things *Hamlet* does is to complicate the very assumptions behind writing a book like the present one.

My task is to provide some sense of the performance history of *Hamlet,* differences among interpretations, and the multiplicity of possible ways of reading and enacting this most famous and slippery of plays. I am writing as part of a series called Shakespeare in Performance, published by a well-established university press. This context automatically confers an air of authority on the book that may be misleading because it suggests that 'Shakespeare', '*Hamlet*' and 'performance' are all stable entities; plus it assumes that when I describe a production I am somehow able to convey what really took place. But there is something crucial left out of such an assumption, something that is foregrounded in the text of *Hamlet* itself. And that is that all such certainties are to some degree illusory – or at least that they are the result of an elaborate network of interpretations and constructions. I do not want to be disingenuous here – I do claim a certain authority as author of the book, and I claim as well to be able to convey a set of meanings launched into circulation by the meeting of *Hamlet* and a wide variety of actors and directors. But all meanings, as the play reminds us, are provisional and temporary, a result of negotiation and cultural struggle as well as individual effort and creativity. I am engaged in reconstructing the meanings generated by past performances of a text that makes the play of meaning one of its primary subjects. And 'reconstructing' is itself a slippery process, since it depends on documentary sources, such as reviews and promptbooks, that are themselves culturally mediated. The result is an approximation that I want to make accurate, but which itself derives from a constraint associated with the responsibility of writing a book like this one – the need to produce a meaningful narrative, to offer more than just a lot of loose details to my readers.

Just as director and actors are bound to produce a 'reading' of *Hamlet* to present to their audience, I am bound to produce a reading of their reading for mine. So too a reader of this book has certain expectations about meaning and coherence, about the relationship between histories of performance and performances themselves and what both might mean in a culture. These expectations work to condition both the writing and the reception of the book, just as audience expectations condition the way performances are put together and received. Given this concentration on the construction of meaning, which is a concern in *Hamlet* that our present cultural moment makes eminently visible in the text, I want to draw attention to the fact that making meanings is a cultural practice inseparable from performance in whatever arena. Writing this book, or even reading it, can thus be seen, within the context I am sketching, as itself a kind of performance. Further, both writing and reading are taking place within a highly developed educational system in which literature, and pre-eminently Shakespeare, plays a prominent ideological role. And the project is linked both to the evolution of Shakespeare studies itself (not to mention the accompanying commercial initiatives) and to the cultural changes that have affected the study of Shakespeare. Only relatively recently have scholars begun to emphasize the performance aspects of his work. This in turn is related to cultural changes in which the idea of performance in all its senses (encompassing politics, teaching, communications and information exchange as well as theatre) has become dominant. In our post-modern world, selfhood itself has come to be seen as primarily a matter of performance, rather than as something 'real'.

If ideas about an autonomous and unified selfhood that grounds and authenticates action are scoffed at in advanced intellectual circles nowadays, *Hamlet* has changed with the times. One clear manifestation of the undermining of stability has been the demise of the unified text. It used to be that *Hamlet*, like other Shakespeare plays, was a single, recognizable object. This is no longer so. We now have a number of competing texts, none of which is 'authentic', i.e., none of which represents exactly 'what Shakespeare wrote'; furthermore, the grounds on which a text may be said to be authentic are themselves in dispute. The idea that a particular early text may be closer to Shakespeare's hand or his intention than another is no longer a guarantee of its superiority or value. Indeed, the idea of intention implies something like a unified subjectivity, a stable 'Shakespeare' as source of the text, a notion that is no longer taken for granted. It is evident that there are analogies here between the autonomous text and the autonomous self. Each is now viewed as a construction rather than something merely given. Old assumptions about the possibility and/or desirability of the unified text (or self) have crumbled away, victims of an intellectual onslaught that has sought to expose them as fabrications of the bourgeois order, weapons in an ideological struggle whose outcome ensured the ascendancy of individualist values, and the dominance of a whole host of cultural imperatives that went with that ascendancy: capitalism, European imperialism, a reconstituted family structure together with new forms of patriarchy, etc. Or so many of the more radical critics would have us see the issue.

So the failure of the unified text is not an isolated phenomenon. But it might help to describe it in a little more detail, since it provides a clear and comprehensible example of what we might call the crisis of indeterminacy. And it focuses the problem of the relation of text and performance, since, if the text is unstable, what does this do to the prescriptive notion that performance should be 'true' to the text? The text of *Hamlet* is not simply an unchanging entity, an object that is the same now as it was in 1601; it has a history of its own, and what we today think of as *Hamlet* is a result of that history. There are three important early texts of *Hamlet*, which differ from each other in significant ways. There are the two quartos (Q1, 1603 and Q2, 1604) and the folio version (F), published in the volume of Shakespeare's plays that came out in 1623. Q1 is a 'reported' edition, presumably patched together by a bit player in a travelling production of the play (the evidence suggests that it was the actor who played Marcellus and Lucianus), who wrote down what he could remember, made up what he could not, and then sold his reconstruction to an unscrupulous printer. That at least is one version of its origin, currently the most widely accepted one. But note how such a scholarly narrative seeks to put a distance between the corruptions of illegitimate transmission and what is regarded as the true text. Another theory would see Q1 as an early draft of the play; still a third regards it as a script used by a travelling troupe in need of a short text for provincial consumption. Q2, published a year or so later, was designed to correct Q1's many 'errors' and present a 'true and perfect Coppie' to its readers. 'Newly corrected and enlarged' to a length almost twice that of its predecessor, it has often been considered the most authoritative early text. (The promises of the title page are of course not neutral – equivalent to the modern 'blurb' they have designs on the prospective buyer.) The folio version lacks about 230 lines found in Q2, and adds about 80 not in Q2, some of which are parallel to lines in Q1. There are as well many smaller differences of vocabulary, punctuation, stage directions, speech headings, even names of characters. For many years, accepted editorial practice has been to conflate the different early versions, using one, usually Q2, as the 'copy text' but making free use of the others. But Q2, formerly regarded as Shakespeare's 'original' version, no longer has the priority it once had. There is an important new version based on F (the Oxford edition of G. R. Hibbard, who argues effectively that F derives from a copy that Shakespeare revised on the basis of theatrical considerations) and there is a movement afoot, as with the Oxford *King Lear,* to publish separate texts, based respectively on Q2 and F.[2]

The precise relations between these various *Hamlet*s and early performance is something I will take up in Chapter II. For now, it is enough to note that contemporary directors usually select, often quite arbitrarily, a particular modern edition as their basis, and then proceed to trim and shape it according to their overall conception. Modern editions are themselves the product of complex editorial procedures with a history of their own, a history that makes plain their implication in a web of cultural assumptions; the belief in a true and authoritative text somehow present behind the different historical manifestations, for example, bespeaks a cultural investment in the idea of stable origins that is at present under fire. No modern text simply passes on one of the early texts in new form. They all conflate, transpose, change – they all add stage directions, straighten out confusions, or make educated guesses about 'correct' readings when the original does not make sense. When editors conflate Q2 and F, for example, they create a composite text that has no historical precedent or authority; or, more precisely, such versions derive their authority from editorial tradition rather than from a putative connection with the 'original'. Thus we frequently get modern editions longer than either F or Q2, with readings that appear in neither, some taken from Q1, some culled from the long history of editorial revision, and some devised by the current editor. Thus is generated this mythological creature known as *Hamlet*.

Despite such uncertainty, or perhaps because of it, *Hamlet* is one of the – if not *the* – most frequently performed of Shakespeare's plays and indeed the most written-about text (with the exception of the Bible) in all of western literature. What has made it such a potent test of cultural meaning? One possibility is its mysterious indeterminacy. It has generated a never-ending supply of interpretations and has become in the process a kind of sacred text, one that is constantly being reinvented by a vast range of ingenious exegetical commentary. It seems always to tease us with the promise of meanings that in the event turn out to be just out of reach. Questions abound ('Who's there?' are the very first words spoken); speech curls around on itself; madness gnaws at the edges of meaning. In order to find method in the madness, any given interpretation, whether on stage or in books, has to freeze the flow of possible significances, to build a meaning in the face of indeterminacy; even a deliberate refusal to answer the play's questions constitutes a kind of meaning.

More important even than this in accounting for the play's cultural centrality may be the prominence the text and its performances confer on the individual self. Born at a time when the emerging forces of Protestant theology, capitalist enterprise and humanist individualism were combining to form what has come to be called the 'modern subject', Hamlet seems to embody the struggles and aspirations of the individual soul set afloat in a sea of troubles and uncertainties. The play exemplifies more fully than any other the unfolding of one man's mind, the assailable but uniquely independent spirit forming itself in opposition to, but also in conjunction with, the forms and pressures of the time and its deeply entrenched structures of power. Out of this struggle comes a sense of a fragmented and subjected self, but one which is also improvisatory and questing, very much its own. This self, discernible too in the *Essais* of Montaigne, in the unmoored satirist-commentators of Jacobean tragedy, and in a host of other late Renaissance texts, finds its fullest expression in *Hamlet*. And as years and centuries passed, and the primacy of the individual came more and more to dominate political as well as philosophical agendas, as the interior life became the common focus of literary texts and even generated its own special literary form, the novel, Hamlet moved ever more assuredly to centre stage. The Romantic writers adopted his melancholic alienation as their own; the Victorians saw in him a man who retained his princely integrity and sense of values in the face of a deteriorating and false society; our own century has been drawn to his search for authenticity in a world devoid of certainties and governed by the arrogance of power.

Productions have marked these transitions and been instrumental themselves in the process of cultural transmission whereby notions of what constitutes selfhood are generated and reproduced. One thing that is immediately noticeable about both the centuries-old English performance tradition, and the much-cut text that has served as the basis of that tradition, is an excision of politics – an emphasis in no way inevitable given the various possibilities of the early texts. British Hamlets (unlike, say, Russian ones) have in general turned away from political matters to explore an inner, or a domestic, landscape. *Hamlet* performance can thus be seen as an important element of cultural history – not just a passive record, but part of a formative process. It has contributed to the making of the modern self, that sense of an inner space, protected from the socio-political realm, where the individual finds fulfilment. Obviously, this process of fashioning selfhood is not ideologically neutral – it is part of a larger network within which laws, moral values, political exigencies, and psychological understanding all claim a place.

In this regard, too, the prominent cultural position of certain actors, such as David Garrick in the eighteenth century, Henry Irving in the nineteenth, or Laurence Olivier in the twentieth, makes itself felt. In all three cases, we have renowned actors who appealed to their public because of the way they combined the histrionic with cultural assumptions about 'natural' behaviour and its psychological underpinnings. Garrick, for instance, was celebrated for his 'naturalness', and for his remarkable ability to convey rapid shifts of feeling. His interest in the interior life, in complex psychology, and in what

[8]

his contemporaries called 'sentiment', all coalesced around his admiration for Shakespeare; his Hamlet was a sensitive man of feeling, masculine in his vigour, sympathetic in his sorrow and filial devotion. As I suggest in Chapter II, it is no exaggeration to say that Garrick's acting did much to form an image of what his age regarded as the ideal man. So too his approach to acting mirrored his age in that its commitment to 'nature' drew on an interest in contemporary theories concerning the relations between the psychological and the physical, or, to put it in eighteenth-century language, between the 'passions' and bodily motion; nature could, that is, be represented in mechanical terms, the body regarded as an animate machine (see Roach, 'Garrick', and below, Chapter II). Hence what the age understood by both 'man' and 'human nature' found corroboration in its leading actor.

In the Victorian period, Henry Irving brought an intense focus on individual psychology to the staging of Shakespeare, marked by a concentration on small but telling details. Despite his lack of the actor's usual graces of voice and movement, his theatre became a veritable temple of art, one that among other things reflected his age's interest in *character*. Irving found in Hamlet, with his bent for intelligent and speculative introspection, a figure who perfectly matched his own propensities. His prince was disjointed and edgy, intense and idiosyncratic. He sought to represent through sharp physical and vocal detail the unique and inalienable features of one particular man. Where Garrick stressed the typical and the representative (for him the 'natural' was what made him *like* other men), Irving went the opposite way, seeking those special tonalities that made him different, utterly individual. This too was a version of 'natural', but one that responded to the idea that what is most natural about a person is her or his unique interiority. And, of course, this way of conceptualizing subjectivity carried over into the twentieth century, with its stress on the particularity of individual experience.

Laurence Olivier's flirtations with Freudianism on both stage and screen (see Chapters IV and VII) provide our own century's clearest example of the intersection of theatrical representation with ideas about the self and psychological theory. The Oedipus complex, in fact, offers a kind of blend of the differing notions of 'natural' just discussed: all men (the gender bias of Freud's theory is by now well established) are alike in that they share in the Oedipal struggle, but each is unique in how he feels and manages it. Oedipal interpretations of *Hamlet* have become so commonplace in our century that we now routinely expect a bed to be present in the closet scene, a bit of furniture that would have shocked Garrick. Olivier, though not the first to explore this territory, has certainly been the most influential. One of the advantages that his approach offered was the possibility of representing a self that was both riven with conflict *and* integrated. Hamlet's vitality as well as his celebrated delay could both be accommodated by such a theory, as could the idea of a man's authentic self being somehow not fully accessible to his own conscious explorations. This gives full play to the twentieth-century concern with fragmentation and uncertainty, without undermining the notion of an essential, if embattled, selfhood.

Despite his commitment to the psychoanalytic model of a deeply layered subjectivity, Olivier does not shrink from the rather different proposition that selfhood is frequently a matter of performance. His 1948 film both insists on Hamlet's authenticity and paradoxically allows for his histrionic self-making (see Chapter VII). This interest in performing the self has more recently moved to centre stage and offers a further example of *Hamlet*'s cultural linkages. Before the 1960s, hardly anyone paid attention to the fact that *Hamlet* is full of references to theatres and acting. In literary criticism and especially in the theatre, interest had focused most intently on the hero and his dilemmas, his inner quest for truth and authenticity, his psychological conflicts; Hamlet had become almost a real person whose individuality had impressed itself on generations of readers and playgoers. As Shakespeare came more to dominate university curricula and hence came under the scrutiny of sharp-eyed professors, new interests developed, in tandem with post-war cultural developments (existentialism, absurdist drama, and the like). Of these, the most prominent during the 1960s and 1970s was a fascination with Shakespearean 'meta-theatricality', i.e., its obsession with the art and effect of the theatre. Hamlet's fictionality, rather than his authenticity, became primary; he and his readers (and it was mostly through reading that this move took shape) became increasingly aware of his performance of selfhood, and his   use of theatricality to test and re-make his world. In 1980, the RSC under John Barton produced a version of the play that emphasized just these aspects, highlighting the idea of performance; the action took place on a makeshift platform set on the larger stage, with the characters donning costumes in full view of the audience, and taking props from a large basket at the edge before 'entering' on to the platform (see Chapter VI). In retrospect, we can see this shift in intellectual perspective, and the production it spawned, as the beginning of a post-modernist unravelling of stability, a privileging of the performed and self-consciously fashioned over the real and actual. The ground of the actual was being eroded as authentic behaviour melted into image and improvisation.

The various political and youth movements of the 1960s provided a curious counterpoint to the intellectual and cultural shifts just described. At the very time that youth were insisting on *more* authentic modes of behaviour and deriding the false consciousness of their elders, many of them, or their contemporaries, were in graduate school formulating theories about meta-theatricality and the inescapability of performance that committed them to an idea of selfhood which bypassed any possibility of authenticity; indeed the term itself was becoming increasingly irrelevant. Some of the contradictions at work here emerged in the famous RSC production of 1965, with David Warner as Hamlet (Chapter V). Warner was both utterly apathetic and galvanizing; in the name of contemporary youth, he registered a sense of lost selfhood, and he was deeply aware of himself as an actor in a play not of his own making. Once again, in the cultural move to a deracinated and fabricated subjectivity, Hamlet was in the vanguard – or at least was recognized as paradigmatic.

The same process of cultural reception is of course going on in the present. A very recent production of the play, directed by Adrian Noble for the RSC at the Barbican theatre in 1992-93 (it moved to Stratford in the spring for a short run), with Kenneth Branagh in the title role, makes this apparent. To round out this introduction, I want to take a look at this version as a prelude to my excursion into history. Then, at the end of the book, I will return to Noble and Branagh, in the hope of building a kind of frame for the whole project. Their production is useful since it provides a vivid example of many of the questions I have raised about the relation of text to performance, the place of theatrical tradition, the cultural position of the actor, the role of the theatrical in the definition of selfhood, and the construction of meaning in the face of indeterminacy, not to mention a crucial issue that I have not yet confronted – the role of *stage design* in the delineation of meaning.

First of all, as to text, Noble decided to do an 'uncut' version of the play. This was, so far as I know, a first for the RSC – when Michael Pennington broached the idea with director John Barton in 1980, the latter dismissed it as a 'Wagnerian folly' (Pennington 118). 'Full-text' versions are not unheard of – the Old Vic used to intersperse a few during its runs of a regular, cut version, such as the one in which John Gielgud starred in 1930, and the Guthrie/Olivier revival in 1937 (both discussed in Chapter IV). But these are the exception, not the rule, mainly because *Hamlet* is a very long play and audiences are likely to feel restless after four and a half hours in even the most comfy of seats. The text that Noble used was the New Cambridge edition, a conflated version with, therefore, no precise basis in any one early text, despite the flavour of authenticity that publicity for the production sought to evoke by advertising it as complete. One effect of his choice was to suggest that 'Shakespeare's' intentions were to be more fully served in this production than they ordinarily are, and this, along with the presence of Branagh as Hamlet, promoted the impression that here was a definitive version of this chameleon play. But this was to court contradiction: the full text, far from being definitive, is, as we have seen, an editorial construction, not a representation of Shakespeare's intentions, whatever they may have been.[3] At a time when the grounds of textual stability are in dispute, for the RSC to use a complete, conflated text, supplied to them by Cambridge University Press, seemed to make a statement. Consider the added fact that the New Cambridge texts are in direct competition with the Oxford editions, not only for a share of a crowded market but, more important, in a contest over textual *authority*. The editors of the Oxford Shakespeare have led the way in the battle against conflation, so perhaps it is no accident to see Cambridge taking an opposite line. Texts are no longer neutral, as they were thirty years ago when conflation was the uncontested norm.

The staging was at once thoroughly 'post-modern' and

nostalgically traditional, thereby seeming to reproduce the contradiction suggested by the textual choices. It displayed a double commitment to, on the one hand, psychological and representational realism and, on the other, a counter-naturalistic deployment of arresting images and symbolic scenic effects. In some ways, the production seemed to allude to the uncertainties and debates in contemporary theatre about representation and illusion. For instance, it made aggressive use of the proscenium stage and an array of proscenium curtains, breaking up the flow of scenes in the first half of the play with laborious opening and closing of curtains, recalling nineteenth-century techniques. This strategy seemed a deliberate step away from the fast-moving and flexible mode of running scenes together that has been the mark of most Shakespearean production since the time of Harley Granville-Barker, a playwright, director and critic who, in the early years of the twentieth century, helped to revolutionize Shakespearean performance by bringing it back to its roots in the Elizabethan stage and combining that with a keen sense of characterization, fast-paced speaking, and modern staging techniques (see Kennedy, *Granville-Barker*, and Styan). But these allusions to earlier modes of staging were not done exactly straight. The performance flagrantly broke through the frame in a whole variety of ways.

The huge Barbican stage was fitted up with a decorated false proscenium, lending an Edwardian air to the scene that was echoed in the costumes, but there was also a shallow apron representing a rather abstract, counterfeit graveyard, strewn haphazardly with dry floral wreaths and miniature crosses (one critic was reminded of a pet cemetery – C. Spencer, *Daily Telegraph*, 21 Dec. 1992). As the lights dimmed for the opening, there ascended into this 'graveyard' (via a trap) a spectral-looking but all too physical ghost, clad in a pure white Danish military outfit complete with white, World War I helmet; his back to the audience, he picked his way carefully through the leaves and walked to the rear of the empty stage in a mist of whirling light. Only then did the soldiers enter down front. The main stage space was defined by an enormous white scrim on a semi-circular frame, which was conveniently raised for the Ghost to pass beneath and then lowered. Later, the frame again rose to knee-height to mark the Ghost's appearance to the soldiers. The scene ended with a full curtain across the proscenium, which was then pulled part way back to reveal yet another curtain, slightly upstage, gauzy and white this time, and draped upwards to frame, on the stage left side, the ensuing court scene. Hamlet stood stage right in front of the still partly closed black curtain, facing away from the audience, staring into the dark. At the end of I.ii, the big curtain closed again and re-opened to reveal, huddled on the right side, Ophelia's beautifully evocative bedroom with whimsically painted furniture à la Peter Pan (M. Billington, *Guardian*, 19 Dec. 1992), including a wardrobe, bedstead, washstand and piano. One practical reason for the curtains became clear: in order to put together the lovely image of Ophelia's room, which was re-configured in a variety of powerful ways as the production continued, the producers had to rely on what used to be known in the nineteenth century as a 'front scene', played before a curtain or painted backdrop while the next full scene was assembled behind. Edwin Booth, for example, staged the first part of V.ii (Hamlet's colloquy with Horatio, usually cut) that way in order to cover the scene change from elaborately naturalistic graveyard to court hall. Of course, the practical purpose in Noble's version was not paramount; it arose from the decision, in keeping with the post-modern fondness for allusion and pastiche, to 'quote' Victorian/Edwardian staging techniques; the idea was not simply to allude to them, but to conjure them in order to resist them. This strategy allowed the production to place itself in relation to tradition and simultaneously to stage a subversion of that tradition.

The design in general carried the weight of meaning. Progressive decay was the theme. The first court scene was charming and well managed: the smiling King (John Shrapnel) and slightly apprehensive Queen (Jane Lapotaire), both dressed in white, drank champagne and controlled the court with, in Claudius's case, an oily ease (the feeling was that they had just come from celebrating their 'o'erhasty marriage'); next came the well-ordered domesticity of Ophelia's bedchamber. But before long, the scenic and spiritual integrity began to come unknit, so that, by the end, mere anarchy was loosed upon the world; all the various structures had disintegrated. For the whole last sequence, from Ophelia's mad scenes to the conclusion, the setting was a jumble of fragments, visual allusions to a lost wholeness matching those in Ophelia's poignant and mysterious songs. The piano, which had figured first in its proper spot in Ophelia's room – she played it quietly during Polonius's dialogue with Laertes and after her brother's departure – moved centre stage, both literally and figuratively. The mad scene began with the shattered young woman shuffling along in her father's clothes, the shirt blood-stained and the shoes, clownlike, much too large. She moved to a giant white tarp that lay centre stage, covering a mass of amorphous hillocks and lumps. A sudden yank and the cloth came billowing forward like a parachute, revealing a desolate landscape with the painted piano as centre piece, overturned table and grey chairs, and broken wreaths and clumps of dried leaves and flowers on the floor. This arresting image, so eloquently reflecting Ophelia's mental state (she reprised her earlier tunes as an accompaniment to her mad songs), remained on view for the rest of the performance. Here was a shattered society, all its images of harmony and significance blasted, the graveyard on the apron now linked to this cultural junkyard composed only of fragments.

The middle part of the play, starting with the play scene (III.ii) and continuing to Hamlet's departure for England (IV.iv), featured the boldest design choice of all, one that focused directly on the question of theatre. The effect was to turn the audience's gaze back on itself and force a meta-theatrical awareness on both characters and spectators. In a sense, then, the scenography moved from Victorian/Edwardian effects to 1960s and 1970s meta-theatricality and then into post-modernism, recapitulating design elements associated with the different periods. When the front curtain drew back for the start of III.ii, we were backstage with the professional actors as they prepared to go on for their royal performance. Some ran lines, others donned costumes or applied make-up at dressing tables with mirrors framed by rows of light bulbs; two men were fencing at the centre. The clothing was bright, loose and filmy, in marked contrast to the heavy blacks and greys, or the pallid whites, of the palace. A vivid red curtain was closed behind them, through which Hamlet entered to check out the proceedings and deliver his timely advice. Clearly this was the actors' 'front' curtain, which would open for the performance itself, with the on-stage audience on the far side, facing the 'real' audience. As the play was about to begin and Hamlet and

Horatio exited into the 'house', a sudden shift in lighting rendered the curtain redly transparent, revealing beyond an extraordinary theatre: a rising auditorium with red plush chairs on stepped levels, curving gradually upward until the whole thing became, astonishingly, concave, creating a bizarre perspective in which what could be identified as the back of the stalls was curved high over the lower range of seats, with the chairs fixed upside-down, the ceiling eerily mirroring the floor. The royal family and the other assembled dignitaries sat toward the front (right side up), their sharp responses and suspicious glances emerging from a space that was simultaneously stage and auditorium. We got to eavesdrop on them from backstage as it were, watching the actors perform towards the court and away from us, our position as spectators doubled and redoubled by the enclosed and enclosing space of viewing. The dumb-show and then the play itself, performed on and around a green couch at centre, had an Isadora Duncan look, all large expressive gestures and 'moderne' steps, the filmy costumes being used to balletic effect. All of this highlighted the theatrical, as did the moment Claudius calls for lights at the end of the interlude, often in recent productions played down, but not here. Instead, an overtly symbolic and very bright spotlight was trained on him from the side, and he stumbled off in terror.

The theatre within the theatre remained as the centrepiece of the design through the sequence of scenes that dramatize the hectic events of that momentous night at Elsinore. This turned the King's attempt at repentance, Hamlet's decision to postpone his revenge, his killing of Polonius, his subsequent hysterical confrontation with his mother and his pained response to his father's ghost, plus his capture and departure for England, all into *staged* events. For most of these, the theatre behind was fully visible, and even when it wasn't, as in the closet scene, the closed red curtain and leftover props (the couch, a make-up table, a wardrobe frame) remained as signs of the theatrical, reminders of the porous boundaries between playing and reality.

The seductions of the meta-theatrical came to a literal high point and were at the same time histrionically undermined, if that seems possible, near the end of this middle section. Claudius, alone in the 'theatre' after calling upon England to 'Do it' to Hamlet, brought his exit lines up to a very big, 'theatrical' climax ('Till I know 'tis done, / How e'er my haps, my joys were ne'er begun' (IV.iii.67-8)), at which point there began a loud clanking and shunting accompanied by a lighting change. And before our astonished eyes, the whole curved red auditorium with its plush chairs was lifted up into the flies above the stage, replaced by a cavernous, night-lit space for the start of the Fortinbras scene. This was a spectacular technical accomplishment that drew attention to the capabilities of the Barbican stage, introducing a further, and theoretically distinct, kind of meta-theatricality. Most of the concentration on the theatrical metaphor was enclosed within the fiction, the world of Hamlet, its ultimate interest being in producing 'reality-effects' as well as 'alienation-effects', the two in fact being linked to each other. But here we were brought outside the fictional world and made aware of the technical potential of the Barbican itself. As the great contraption disappeared into space, there was a slide back from one level of constructed reality to another, as the continued sounds of shunting and hissing from offstage turned out *not* to be related to the movement of scenery but were re-cast as part of the narrative; augmented now by large puffs of smoke, they identified the new locale as a vast European railway station (perhaps the same one that had figured earlier for the arrival of the players), where Fortinbras's modern army were clearly taking advantage of industrial technology to ease 'the conveyance of [their] promis'd march' (IV.iv.3) across Denmark.

The 'post-modern' air of this production was established not so much by its dedication to images of fragmentation and decay, which are the basic stuff of 'modernist' alienation, as by the self-conscious framing of such themes and the eclectic allusiveness of the staging. All we can do, it seemed to proclaim, was echo past achievements with witty but futile self-consciousness. But, as I mentioned, the production also displayed some commitment to naturalistic modes of representation and thus courted contradiction. On the question of character, the production was much less radical than it was from the point of view of staging. Kenneth Branagh played the main part conservatively, inserting himself into a long, but by no means untroubled, tradition of seeing the Prince in a richly positive, relatively unambiguous way (his rendering of the change in Hamlet at the end recalled Gielgud and Irving). His performance was highly praised, but to assess his impact fully we have to consider both his unique position in the British theatre at the present moment and his personal characteristics. He is that rare thing – a likeable phenomenon. Movie star, classical actor, theatre and film director, he has shown an enviable entrepreneurial talent. Something of a genius too at self-promotion, he published an autobiography at twenty-nine and at about the same time directed and starred in the film of *Henry V*, a move that seemed deliberately designed to challenge Laurence Olivier's celebrated hold on the public imagination's sense of the role and the play. It was as if Branagh were presenting himself as Olivier's replacement at the centre of British theatrical life – all before he was thirty. Interestingly, his portrait of Henry V, which began as a challenge to jingoistic readings of that patriotic hymn of a play ('the national anthem in five acts' as Trevor Nunn called it (quoted in Berry, *Directing Shakespeare* 57)), in the end came to be read as itself militaristic and politically conservative, a perception enhanced by the fact that Branagh sought out Prince Charles as his adviser on the loneliness of princes. Since then, perceptions of his place in British culture have evolved. Regarded only a few years ago as perhaps a bit presumptuous, a talented upstart, he has since established himself more firmly, and, judging by the reception of his recent *Hamlet*, has won the hearts of most of the critics. This may be because, like the character on whom he built his reputation, Henry Plantagenet, he can get what he wants and remain boyishly charming. If, like that same Henry, and like the character he played in his film *Peter's Friends*, which was released shortly before *Hamlet* opened, he seems as an actor to lack depth, that may not turn out to be a serious liability.

All this may help to account for the reception of his and Noble's *Hamlet*, which was, in a word, ecstatic.[4] Since my own response was more temperate (for me the production was provocative, even at times fascinating, and the main actor charming, but neither was great), I am led to wonder about the rave reviews, standing ovations, and extravagant comparisons: what do they all mean? And how do Branagh's position and reputation sit with the portrait of a fragmented and debilitated culture that the production as a whole offers? One possible answer is that Branagh's *presence* redeems the cultural emptiness, proclaiming the possiblity of continuity, significance, and success in the face of fragmentation and loss. The image circulated on the poster, programme cover, and various RSC publicity brochures catches something of these oppositions. It shows a blurred and grainy photo of Branagh, in black tights and singlet, his bare arms down and slightly spread in a gesture of atonement. He stands dwarfed in a featureless dark space, while dangling from his hands are two white straps that coil on the grey floor. The straps are hard to identify, though once one has seen the production, one can gauge their significance – they are the straps of a straitjacket used to ironic advantage at various points in the performance. Interestingly, this image, used for all the publicity, is never reproduced in the actual show. Its depiction of a passive, supplicating victim is in fact belied by much of what Branagh does on stage.[5] It is as though the public image of a defeated and melancholic Hamlet is transformed in the production itself into a vision of a depleted *world*, while Hamlet himself, like Antaeus, takes strength from seeming defeat and proclaims values such as personal integrity and, especially, friendship (here the temporal coincidence with *Peter's Friends* is telling) in the face of cultural collapse. This is further borne out by his most recent film, *Much Ado about Nothing*, which rescues the worst manifestations of patriarchy and turns them to laughter and fun; Branagh, in highlighting the theme of male bonding and camaraderie already in the text, and deliberately crossing racial and national boundaries in the casting (a black American Don Pedro, American actors for Claudio and Don John as well), manages to suggest the optimistic possiblity of negotiating the bitter conflicts that divide us, along the way obscuring the male characters' misogyny and giving us a fresh image of a wry, renewed masculinity. So, I would argue, the image of Branagh on the *Hamlet* poster and programme can be read as a kind of cultural projection which he himself, both in his 'real' life as actor and film maker, and as Hamlet, contradicts. In himself he offers a kind of redemption from meaninglessness and defeat.

This was suggested by Michael Coveney's review of the production in *The Observer*, Britain's most progressive Sunday paper (20 Dec. 1992). In a move that can be viewed as representative of the importance of Branagh, Shakespeare and Hamlet in contemporary British culture, it gave the production top of the front page coverage, with inset photos of Branagh on one side and Prince Charles on the other. And a catchy head-line: 'Alas, poor Charles. I know him ...' Above, there was a smaller heading that promised a review of 'a Hamlet for our times by Kenneth Branagh that makes Elsinore look like Kensington Palace [the London residence of the Prince of Wales]'. The inaccuracy of this claim can perhaps be explained by seeing it as a misreading driven by obscure cultural imperatives. If it were true that Kensington Palace looked like the Elsinore of this production, especially in the last phase with refuse scattered everywhere, the Palace might very well have been closed down by the health authorities. Beyond that, this *Hamlet* was only for our times if that meant some kind of reprieve from cultural longing – indeed, in the review itself Coveney describes Branagh as 'a great Hamlet *against* our time'. Arguing that the production could be 'read as a defence of the Prince of Wales, an unofficial but carefully planned promotion of the dilemma of modern monarchy', Michael Coveney went on to stress that, 'though Kenny's friends [like Peter's presumably] ... were out ... to cheer him on', his Hamlet, 'like Prince Charles, is an incorrigible loner and can only trust his chums like "adder's fangs"'. Now this is in fact untrue to the production, since this Hamlet, more than most, was delighted and sustained by his friendship with Horatio, who was sharply distinguished from sycophantic courtier (Osric) and false friends (Rosencrantz and Guildenstern) through his manner and costume, both of which were loose, warm and relaxed – his baggy corduroy matching his familiar and touching loyalty. What is interesting about Coveney's analysis, however, is the apparent need, even on the part of a left-leaning periodical, to recuperate the image of the Prince at the end of 1992, the 'annus horribilis' of the British royal family, with its series of scandals capped by a fire at Windsor and a final split between Prince and Princess (though before the damning revelations of the Prince's cellular misdemeanours). Even more intriguing is the fact that Coveney uses a player-king to effect this bit of cultural reconstruction. He describes Branagh as 'reclaiming his rightful place at the head of the RSC', thus constructing an analogy between Branagh as rightful heir to Shakespearean royalty and Charles as heir to England's throne. The politics of the theatre as an institution are interwoven, as they often were in Shakespeare's own day, with royal politics.

(In this setting, it almost seems as though the former player-king, Sir Laurence Olivier, had been cast in absentia as the ghost of Hamlet's father!) And the job of making the British feel better about the difficulties they face, not only with the royals, but with the economy, their relations to Europe and a host of other matters, falls 'upon the [player] king'. The message could hardly be clearer: 'Hamlet' is a fiction, a poor player whose meaning is constructed (in this case very conservatively constructed) according to personal and cultural needs. Coveney's 'misreading' thus seems symptomatic, not merely quirky, although of course his is only one of a wide array of responses; and it is obvious that no one really expects Prince Charles or Kenneth Branagh to affect the conduct of British politics. Still, Coveney's review suggests a cultural symbology, though I grant it speculative. Like 'The Murder of Gonzago', the drama on the stage talks back to the audience, engaging them in a mutually endorsed process of negotiating meanings. So what we see Hamlet doing in the course of the play – moulding the meaning of a performance/text to meet immediate and pressing needs – we can also observe in the world outside that larger performance/text called *Hamlet* (here being produced by that estimable institution, the Royal Shakespeare Company). It is an inescapable cultural operation. No wonder 'he who plays the [Prince] shall be welcome'.

Overall, it was the scenery that spoke most eloquently about meaning; seizing on the play's celebrated indeterminacy, it delivered a meaning both aesthetic and political – a politics of the self that was post-modern in its instability, self-reflexivity, fragmentation and allusiveness. Alongside, there were remnants of other, more traditional and even nostalgic forms of representation, visible chiefly in the acting of the main parts and in the presence of Kenneth Branagh, so that the whole experience became, in my reading, a response to crisis, a recuperative move in which the agony or folly of the 'post-modern condition' was acknowledged but put to the side by a vision of possible wholeness and integrity.

Whether we are talking about Garrick, Irving, Olivier or Branagh, about the eighteenth-century thrust stage with painted backdrops, the Victorian stage with its resources of gas-light and elaborate scenic verisimilitude, or the late twentieth-century stage with its awesome technical potential and eclectic mélange of styles, we need to remember that the theatre as a cultural practice is linked to other discourses and other kinds of meaning within a particular society. Visual style, actorly presence, Shakespearean cultural authority, all play a role. One thing I try to do in this book is to suggest, however tentatively, some of the links that may exist between how the theatre gives *Hamlet* meaning and produces Hamlet's subjectivity and how the culture generally approaches problems of meaning, value, and selfhood. There is a reciprocity at work in such exchanges, a circulation analogous in some ways to the circulation of goods or money within a culture. So too there is a reciprocity in the writing and reading of such a book as the present one, activities that not only play out some of the conditions of living in a *Hamlet*-affected world, in the 1990s, but which seek somehow to look beyond the cultural blinds of our own age to take a look, however framed, at other performances in other times.

CHAPTER II

Hamlet on stage 1600–1900

Performing the early texts

Even a brief consideration of the long and detailed history of
Hamlet in the theatre raises the fundamental problem of the
relations between text and performance. From the very beginning, as I outlined in Chapter I, there have been gaps between
the *'Hamlet'* that Shakespeare presumably wrote, and the Hamlets that actors have performed. Q1 is an early instance and
provides clues to the emphases of at least some of the 'original'
productions. The relations between F and Q2, the former partly
a result of theatrical cuts made for performance (or so it has
often been argued), point also to 'performance' having its way
with text. By the 1660s, when the theatres were reopened after
their long darkness during the Commonwealth, there was already
a stage tradition in evidence, based on a heavily cut version of
Q2. This version, which formed the basis of almost all late
seventeenth- and eighteenth-century performances, was eventually published in 1676 by Sir William Davenant, a theatrical
manager and entrepreneur, who had first produced the play in
1661. Full of small alterations and 'improvements', the Players'
Quarto, as it came to be called, printed the cut passages (over
800 of the 3800 lines) but enclosed them in quotation marks to
indicate that, in the words of Davenant's Preface, 'they are left
out upon the Stage'. Even before the closing of the theatres in
1642, it seems likely that the acting version of the play in
general use was punchier and less discursive than the one we
are used to – perhaps more akin to Q1 than most modern
scholars have been willing to admit.

What was omitted is instructive: the Danish ambassadors and
their mission, much of Laertes' advice to Ophelia and Polonius's
advice to Laertes, the whole of the Fortinbras scene (IV.iv,
including Hamlet's final soliloquy), the little scene between

Polonius and Reynaldo (II.i), parts of the other soliloquies with the exception of 'To be or not to be' (already, it seems, a 'classic' – see Hibbard 19), Hamlet's advice to the Players, the end of the closet scene (the counterplot against Rosencrantz and Guildenstern), Hamlet and Horatio's dialogue in V.ii, part of the dialogue with Osric, and most of the last section after Hamlet's death. The emphasis was on action. Interestingly, virtually all of these cuts are to be found in Olivier's 1948 film, a testament to the remarkable staying power of theatrical tradition or perhaps to film's coincident stress on action. Thus in the midst of the differences among the early texts – the instability of Shakespeare's *Hamlet* as a unitary object – the theatre developed a strongly conservative counter-force, a tradition of sameness based on text but extending to production values as well, most especially those associated with plot and central character. The plot in the cut text was tighter and more focused: built around the revenge action, it proceeded sharply and briskly to its appointed end. Most of the political dimension of the play, and certainly its international context (England, Norway, Poland), disappeared. Concomitantly, the main character constructed by this performance-text tended to be active, direct, and princely: more circumscribed than the one we are used to (himself a product of nineteenth-century literary criticism), less meditative and digressive, less 'mad' and tormented. Choice of text and conceptions of character are intimately related, and if today we tend to stress the indeterminacy of both, that is a new, even a 'post-modern' phenomenon. For most of their history, *Hamlet* and Hamlet, even while still holding their own as kings of infinite space, have been bound in the nutshell of tradition, every theatrical innovation scrutinized by a knowing and critical public.

It is worth emphasizing that not only do text and performance have a history, but their history is part of a broader social history that is bound up with *reception* as well as production. The theatre is shaped by, and helps to shape, the cultural needs and meanings of a particular historical moment. Hence, though tradition generally plays a conservative role, participating in the reproduction of cultural orders, there is always some kind of negotiation between tradition and innovation, ways that what is known is re-shaped into new forms that speak to new imperatives. The same struggle goes on today. Even scenically radical productions are often textually conservative, especially in Britain – witness the textual choice of Adrian Noble in the production discussed in Chapter I. The very fact that Shakespeare wrote in English seems to confer a burden of responsibility and authenticity: one should not monkey with sacred texts (though iconoclasm, predictable in such a context, also has its role to play). Critic Robert Cushman writes about an Italian production of *Henry IV*:

> Shakespeare in English and Shakespeare in foreign are different animals. Nobody cares if a translation is mucked about with. A British production seeking this degree of license would either have to play against the text ... or paraphrase, which is an abomination. There are those rhythms, prose or verse, and we are stuck with them. (quoted by Hodgdon 43)

This view may be naive, but it is very common. The assumption is that Shakespeare's texts are ahistorical, that they do not exist in, or have a, history. Their very rhythms are unchanging. This in turn assumes a kind of 'Englishman's burden' – Shakespeare is 'ours', and we have the responsibility of keeping his texts stable and whole, not 'mucking about' with them. The way performances are received and judged thus tends to produce a contradiction that can be hard to negotiate: performers must produce Shakespeare's texts but speak to their own culture.

Hamlet, because of the extraordinary range of his subjectivity and his seemingly endless variety, has, more than any other Shakespearean character, been constructed and reconstructed in the image not only of particular actors, but of whole generations. In what follows in this chapter, I want to look at the work of four actors of the eighteenth and nineteenth centuries who offered a version of selfhood, mirrored in the character they played, that spoke in salient ways to the cultures from which they emerged and which they helped to shape. In so doing, I am aware of the danger of perpetuating the discredited tradition of equating performance history with detailed accounts of how one or another famous actor played a single role. But one explanation is that the available source materials make such an emphasis almost unavoidable; moreover, leading actors express in heightened ways features of cultural style, and when they take on Hamlet they help to reveal an era's understanding of subjectivity.

Since, however, I have been discussing the relation between text and performance, I want first to scan the earliest texts for clues to that elusive creature, the 'original' performance on the open Elizabethan stage, something for which we lack the extensive documentation available for the other productions. *Hamlet* was probably first performed in 1600 with Richard Burbage, the most brilliant and famous actor of his time, in the leading role. Although we know little about the early performances, scattered hints survive. Among them is an elegy on the death of Burbage (in 1619), which tells of him playing, among other parts, 'Young Hamlet, Old Hieronimo ... [and] the grievèd Moor'.

The anonymous author goes on to describe what we assume, though even this is uncertain, is a moment in Act V of *Hamlet* :

> Oft have I seen him leap into the grave,
> Suiting the person which he seemed to have
> Of a sad lover with so true an eye
> That there, I would have sworn, he meant to die.
> (Chambers, *Elizabethan Stage*, vol. 2, 309)

This would seem to confirm that theatrical practice from the beginning tended towards a melodramatic rendition of the moment when Hamlet confronts Laertes in the graveyard. It also suggests that the choice to play Hamlet at least partly as a lover (leading perhaps to a soft rather than bitter approach to the nunnery scene) has been an option ever since Shakespeare's own day. Both these matters have provoked endless controversy throughout the long history of *Hamlet* performance. When, for example, Edmund Kean returned to the stricken Ophelia to kiss her hand before his exit in III.i, he elicited ecstatic praise from William Hazlitt and condemnation from G. J. Bell; and when John Barrymore refused to leap into Ophelia's grave he was attacked by a number of critics.

The Burbage elegy is helpful in another way, since it drives us back to the early texts for clues in our attempt to reconstruct what happened on Shakespeare's own stage. Since we do not know what version Burbage and company actually spoke, the printed texts offer at best tantalizing hints. As I outlined in Chapter I, there is no single narrative that can account for the differences among these early texts, and there are competing theories about their provenance and relative authority.

Hamlet's impulsive behaviour in the graveyard, as reported in the Burbage elegy, provides a case in point. Neither of the two 'good' texts, Q2 and F, mention anything about Hamlet leaping into the grave, though one of them, F, has a stage direction for Laertes to do so. And in both there are lines that can be interpreted to suggest Laertes comes out of the grave to outface Hamlet, and other lines that suggest that Hamlet may indeed leap in. In Q1, however, there is an unambiguous stage direction: *Hamlet leapes in after Leartes* [*sic*]'. This would seem to represent stage practice before 1603, when Q1 was printed, and since *Hamlet* was probably composed in 1600, we are fairly close to the original staging, at least in this one detail. Hamlet's leap also gives us a hint about the overall conception of the character – consistent, I think, with Q1's general emphasis on action and drive. Even though we can deduce from these bits of evidence that Hamlet, quite indecorously, leapt into his beloved's grave to challenge her brother, fastidious critics have often refused to accept this action as warranted, seeing it rather as theatrical debasement of Shakespeare's more lofty intention. For Philip Edwards (the editor of the New Cambridge edition used by Noble and Branagh), it is simply 'unthinkable' to 'couple Hamlet's defiant confrontation of Laertes and Claudius with a jump into the grave and a scuffle' (223n), though he does not say why.

Perhaps Edwards, like many critics and actors, finds the leap unthinkable because it does not square with his idea of Hamlet's princeliness. His view may also be tied to a long-standing and widely held idea (though it has not gone uncontested) that Hamlet returns from his sea-voyage and encounter with the pirates a spiritually renewed man, marked by a peaceful self-understanding and acceptance of the 'divinity that shapes our ends'. This Hamlet, wiser, steadier, more resigned, has put his rancorous, potentially violent side behind him and is ready to face his fate. Would such a man leap on to his beloved's bier to challenge her brother? It is noteworthy that the two 'good' texts, Q2 and F, though both silent about Hamlet's graveside decorum, present rather different pictures of the prince in what follows, when he comes to describe his actions to Horatio and apologize to Laertes (V.ii.1-80, and 225-44; see Werstine; Taylor). Q2, for example, omits the lines: 'But I am very sorry, good Horatio, / That to Laertes I forgot myself, / For by the image of my cause, I see / The portraiture of his' (75-8), which appear in F and in a garbled version in Q1. Here, then, Hamlet admits the rashness of his behaviour and draws a conscious parallel between Laertes's cause and his own. Without external prompting, he then in F takes the first opportunity to apologize to Laertes, who, we should note, is portrayed as more admirable than he is in Q2, where the parallels between himself and Hamlet are not stressed (Werstine). In Q2, he makes no such admission and even mocks Laertes's self-importance during his bantering with Osric. He is then, in another passage unique to Q2, reminded of his courtly duty by his mother's timely message ('The Queen desires you to use some gentle entertainment to Laertes before you fall to play' (206-7)), and so apologizes to his opponent in a way that could certainly be construed as strictly 'pro forma' (though the speech of apology is substantially the same in both). There are, then, distinct performance possibilities offered by the early texts. When Edwards writes of the stage failing to 'meet the challenge of the personality that Shakespeare created', he himself fails to see that Shakespeare seems to have 'created' more than one personality and it is in the nature of stage performance to embody differing visions of such a multiple figure.

An idealized vision of Hamlet is often linked to an idealized vision of Shakespeare as an author. Again Philip Edwards provides a clear example, since he combines brilliant scholarship with the propensity to create explanatory narratives that in themselves are revealing of the whole process of interpretation so typical of the history of *Hamlet*. Shakespeare *writes*, bookkeepers and actors then distort what he has written. 'It is sadly true,' says Edwards, 'that the nearer we get to the stage, the further we are getting from Shakespeare' (32). Thus is raised the bogey of 'theatrical corruption', a telling metaphor frequently invoked by scholars to explain textual variation. That Shakespeare wrote explicitly for the theatre, that he was an actor as well as a writer (tradition has it that he played the Ghost in *Hamlet*), is acknowledged but then somehow erased. In such a scenario, the ideal Shakespeare is a unique creative artist, single not multiple, solitary not collaborative; he is the origin of that 'ideal' text which is, as Edwards argues, not identical with *any* of the early texts but still somehow there and supremely authoritative. Edwards is caught between an awareness of the indeterminacy of the text and a desire to fix and stabilize what appears to be protean and unstable. He is committed on the one side to the logic of revision itself as a way of explaining some textual variation and hence to some notion of a multiple text and authorial second thoughts, and on the other to an idea of a composing and perfectly composed Shakespeare who writes once and for all and then parts company with his text, forced to abandon it to a cruel fate of contamination and mutilation. Only a text free of such contamination can protect the true and original meaning. To allow the text to sink into uncertainty and indeterminacy is to forgo control over its meanings – it is to open up the dangerous potential that it might mean anything, even things the author (who is now, under the onslaught of Foucault and post-modernism, in recession) never intended.

This view of the personal and cultural authority of Shakespeare is very widespread, and it is connected both with the authority associated with *reading*, as distinct from performing, and with particular notions of character and subjectivity. Edwards is not alone in including in his idea of Hamlet a distrust of theatrical representation. When he suggests that Shakespeare's fellow actors may have 'ironed out' the play's complexities and simplified the 'personality that Shakespeare created' (27), he implies first that Hamlet, though complex, is stable, unitary and knowable, and further that this personality can be known more fully through reading than through stage representation. There is thus an implied hierarchy: reading generates deeper, truer meanings than performance. Reading is an individual, subjective practice, different from the collaboration demanded by the collective act of performance. Since the 'modern subject' is an individual, and our modern values are individualistic, the preference for reading over performance as a register of meaning can be seen as part of a wider cultural process. The construction of a modern text, such as the prestigious New Cambridge editions, is thus not an isolated cultural event, but reproduces an ideologically weighted notion of character and subjectivity, whether that notion be applied to an historical author such as Shakespeare or a fictional person such as Hamlet.

Let me return now to Burbage and company. And here of course I have to frame my own narrative, since editors, critics, and actors must in the end produce particular fictions of *Hamlet* in order to fill in the gaps in the various texts. Although we cannot say for certain, the theatrically derived text in F, together with its frequent consonance with Q1, seems to indicate not only that Burbage did leap into the grave to grapple with Laertes, but also that the spontaneous sympathy with Laertes discernible in the F text marked his interpretation of the final scene, rather than the cooler, more calculated character of Q2. Both brutal *and* sympathetic then, more oscillating and less consistent perhaps than some modern actors, but for all that no less 'real'. Burbage's generous charisma may even have contributed to Shakespeare's refining of Hamlet's character in the direction of more sympathy. That Burbage might have influenced Shakespeare to make certain changes, either in discussion or by his manner of playing the part at rehearsal or even after the 'opening', in no way undermines the integrity of Shakespeare's achievement. It does, however, mean that both text and character, even at their very inception, were in some sense plural – and that therefore the most salient characteristics of the stage history of *Hamlet*, multiplicity of texts and diversity of characterization, were present from the outset.

Garrick and the eighteenth century

There are scattered references to performances of *Hamlet* in the years that followed its first publication, the most surprising being the news that the play was twice acted on board Captain William Keeling's ship, the *Dragon*, while it stood off the coast of Sierra Leone in 1607-08, as 'entertainment for Portuguese and English guests and as beneficial occupation for the crew'; Keeling 'envited,' he says, 'Captain Hawkins to a ffishe dinner, and had *Hamlet* acted abord mee: which I permitt to keepe my people from idlenes and unlawfull games, or sleepe' (Child lxxi, and Chambers, *Shakespeare*, vol. 1, 334). Troupes of English actors also brought a version of the play, perhaps something like the text of Q1, to Germany in the early seventeenth century where it was eventually translated and undoubtedly much changed. Meanwhile, in England, a performance tradition was establishing itself (see Child; Hibbard; Sprague, *Actors*). The only recorded performances before the Restoration were at court in 1619-20, and again in 1637, probably with Joseph

Taylor, Burbage's successor, in the leading role. After the Restoration and the reopening of the theatres, which had been closed in 1642, the play was reserved to Sir William Davenant, who introduced Thomas Betterton to the role he was to play on and off for over forty years. The bookkeeper for the company, John Downes, wrote in 1708 that Davenant, '(having seen Mr Taylor of the Black-Friars Company act it, who being instructed by the author Mr. Shakespeare) taught Mr. Betterton in every particle of it; which by his exact performance of it, gained him esteem and reputation, superlative to all other plays' (quoted in Hibbard 17). One problem with this pleasant story is that Taylor joined the King's Company three years after Shakespeare's death and so could hardly have been 'instructed' by the immortal author! But that he both saw and imitated Burbage seems likely. Nevertheless, the theatre is always changing, in concert with cultural styles, and there is little doubt that Betterton was as different from Burbage as the reign of William and Mary was from that of Elizabeth.

Betterton's style of acting the part was formal and stately, in keeping with Restoration standards of decorum and aristocratic ease. In the scene with the Ghost, for example, rather than the vociferous rage and fury of lesser actors, Betterton excelled in portraying 'an almost breathless Astonishment', coupled with 'an Impatience, limited by filial Reverence' (Colley Cibber, quoted in Sprague, *Shakespearian Players* 12) to discover why the Ghost has come. Cibber goes on: 'he made the Ghost equally terrible to the Spectator as to himself', but in doing so, 'the boldness of his Expostulation was still govern'd by Decency, manly, but not braving'. In keeping with Hamlet's advice to the players, restraint was a hallmark of his acting, as was a careful attention to detail and a vocal variation that made his words sound like 'his own natural self-deliver'd Sentiment' (Sprague, *Shakespearian Players* 19). He seems to have avoided the monotonous 'chanting' that marked many of his successors in the early eighteenth century. Formal without being operatic, Betterton managed to convince his audience of the reality of his feelings and impersonations, even against the odds engendered by encroaching old age and decided physical bulk. Richard Steele, in the *Tatler*, describes him in 1709, at a time when he had been playing Hamlet for almost fifty years:

Had you been to-night at the play-house, you had seen the force of Action in perfection: your admired Mr Betterton behaved himself so well, that, though now about seventy, he acted youth, and ... appeared through the whole drama a young man of great expectation, vivacity, and enterprize. (quoted in Child lxxiii)

Though all that remains is a faint echo, we can recognize in Betterton, as we can with all great actors, that outstanding presence which produces awe. Barton Booth, complaining that as the Ghost he had been 'bullied' by a later actor, remembered Betterton: 'When I acted the Ghost with Betterton, instead of my aweing him, he terrified me. But divinity hung round that man' (quoted in Sprague, *Shakespearian Players* 12).

The divinity that hung around David Garrick (1717-79) was of a different kind, but just as palpable. If Betterton was a Jupiter, Garrick was more like Mercury, constantly on the move, shifting and changing even his physical shape (or so it seemed), bringing messages to an enthralled, if also at times somewhat sceptical, public. Garrick's acting was characterized by bustling vividness, rapidity of movement, emotional variety, and visual appeal. His eyes were his greatest asset, his 'turns' (quick shifts from one emotional state to another) his most famous strategy, and his attentiveness to psychological detail his most important contribution to the art of acting. Garrick brought the actor's body back to centre stage, giving it a prominence it likely also had when Burbage dominated the scene, but which it had gradually lost in the later seventeenth and early eighteenth centuries, with their neo-classical emphasis on intellection and measured speaking.

Garrick was very much a man of his age, and nowhere so clearly as in the stress he put upon individual subjectivity and upon feeling that was firmly grounded in the body. The hero for him was a creature of emotion and physical impulse (Woods 42) and the actor's inculcation and representation of feeling was designed specifically to induce sympathy in the audience, even for villainous figures like Macbeth or Richard III, or cantankerous ones like King Lear. 'Sentiment' was a key word in the second half of the eighteenth century, and, even though it became debased in reference to both drama and social life, it remained a crucial cultural value. Viewed in tandem with the rising hegemony of the middle class and the growth of entrepreneurial capitalism, the prominence of feeling can be seen as a genteel softening of the values of upward mobility and socio-economic competitiveness as these latter came to dominate certain features of cultural life. The ideal middle-class man, a figure in many ways embodied by Garrick, cultivated feeling partly because of an optimistic belief in human perfectibility, and partly perhaps because sentiment rendered invisible some of the less ingratiating sides of human behaviour that manifested themselves in economic life. Garrick actually helped to further this cultivation of feeling in his public; his work in the theatre not only reflected cultural values but helped to create them. His acting was 'a mechanism by which new ways of moving, of speaking, and of thinking about the self were brought into prominence' (Woods 23).

Garrick idolized Shakespeare. In that way too he was a man of his age and contributed to its cultural development. It could indeed be said without too much exaggeration that the eighteenth century 'created' Shakespeare as we know him. For the first time, the texts were being edited with some care, with an eye to authenticity and exactness. Simultaneously, performance was working to construct an image of the great national author as quintessentially British as well as universal. In fact, in an age devoted to the expansion of British hegemony around the globe, the two characteristics, universality and Britishness, came to be recognized as virtually synonymous rather than contradictory. Textual study, the work of a legion of editors, culminated in 1790 in the great ten-volume work of Edmund Malone. When Malone's edition came out, no less a figure than Edmund Burke, the great statesman and fervent opponent of the French Revolution, wrote to congratulate the scholar, expressing his admiration and his conviction of the value of Shakespeare as an exponent of British values (De Grazia 6-7).

Garrick's contribution to the general move to construct Shakespeare as the central pillar of British culture was paradoxical. Like everyone in the theatre, he was cavalier about Shakespeare's texts. The editions that were being produced for readers had little effect on theatrical performance, although it is noteworthy that Garrick frequently went back to the early texts to restore certain lines and to insert original readings which had been 'improved'. But at the same time he was quick to re-write Shakespeare as it pleased him – something he did not only with *Hamlet*, as we shall see, but with *Romeo and*

Juliet, Much Ado about Nothing, and *The Winter's Tale*, among others. Nevertheless it was in the theatre that Garrick made Shakespeare the man of sentiment and good sense that he popularly became for the eighteenth century and that to some extent he still is for the British public. That is to say, Shakespeare is still widely regarded as being gentlemanly, good-natured, and on the sensitively liberal side of important issues. Until quite recently, for example, feminist readings of Shakespeare have tended to see him as aware of patriarchal oppression and somehow subverting, combating, or at least exposing it (though the image of Shakespeare as a benign liberal has now come under fire from leftish academics). This desire to see Shakespeare in a humane and positive light, accurate or no, seems to me an eighteenth-century invention, and certainly Garrick helped to popularize it.

With *Hamlet*, Garrick directed his extraordinary powers towards the depiction of a complex sensibility. Interest in individual psychology was a hallmark of his acting and a feature of his mind that drew him to Shakespeare, whose unsurpassed knowledge of 'human nature' was in the eighteenth century becoming a keynote of his pre-eminence as a dramatist. Shakespeare's interest in the details of character, his insight as a practical psychologist and the wide-ranging sympathy he displays in his portrayals helped to define his peculiarly British genius (a view still prevalent today). Thus Garrick's acting became both a reflection of, and a contribution to, his culture's construction of Shakespeare. So too the growing interest through the eighteenth century in the complex and shifting inner life, the slipping of one passion almost imperceptibly into another, was made manifest in Garrick's portrayals and embodied in acting theory that stressed the importance of moment-to-moment reaction (Donohue 22-3).

Hamlet had always of course been multi-faceted. But how to make him a man of feeling, most likely to appeal to contemporary sensibilities? Garrick's choice is revealing: he stressed love for his father. Hannah More, a friend of Garrick in later years, wrote in a letter to her family:

> Hamlet experiences the conflict of many passions and affections, but filial love ever takes the lead; *that* is the great point from which he [Garrick] sets out and to which he returns: the others are all contingent and subordinate to it, and are cherished or renounced,

as they promote or obstruct the operation of this leading principle. (More 47; see also Mills 34-5)

To make Hamlet first and foremost a devoted son entails a number of consequences: the revenge motif is given a softer source, one grounded in genuine and sympathetic feeling – even the bursts of anger develop from grief; any sense of delay, significantly reduced anyway because of the cut text, can be seen as an expression of sorrow; and the decision finally to act, strongly emphasized by changes Garrick made to the script of Acts IV and V (discussed below), could be seen as a clear rising above such grief. So too the castigation of his mother was softened, and the scenes with his father's ghost were heightened, becoming for many spectators the dramatic centre of the whole performance.

At the same time, it is not to be supposed that Garrick was unmanly; angst-ridden torment in the modern vein was nowhere visible. His madness was distinctly play-acted and, again according to More, he 'never once forgot he was a prince; and … [manifested] the highest polish of fine breeding and courtly manners' (46). Georg Lichtenberg, a young German traveller and intellectual who saw Garrick often in the 1770s, describes his first soliloquy:

> Garrick is completely overcome by tears of grief … tears which flow all the more restrainedly, perhaps, because they are the sole relief of an upright heart in such a conflict of warring duties. The last of the words: 'So excellent a King' [in the first soliloquy], is utterly lost; one catches it only from the movement of the mouth, which quivers and shuts tight immediately afterwards, so as to restrain the all too distinct expression of grief on the lips, which could easily tremble with unmanly emotion. This manner of shedding tears … betrays both the heavy burden of grief in his heart and the manly spirit which suffers under it. [At the end of the speech], I and my neighbour, to whom I had not as yet uttered a word, looked at each other and spoke. It was quite irresistible. (Lichtenberg 15-16)

Here we have Garrick's characteristic mix of strong emotion and restraint, producing, at this highly pitched juncture, a 'manly spirit' in the protagonist and a powerfully communal feeling among at least the male members of the audience, a moment of bonding in the presence of a new representation of masculinity. Some audience members, especially early in his career, regarded Garrick's excessive physical movement as unbefitting a gentleman, much less a prince, whose mark ought to be dignified and self-possessed repose rather than vigorous activity (Woods 21-2). But what can perhaps be traced through his whole career is the process by which Garrick helped to bring middle-class values such as vigour, sensibility and exertion into social dominance.

The high point of Garrick's Hamlet's relationship with his father came on the battlements, a scene made famous by Lichtenberg's precisely detailed account and by a hundred references throughout the period, including Johnson's sardonic reply to Boswell's inquiry whether he would not, were he to be confronted with such an apparition, 'start' as Garrick did: 'I hope not,' said Johnson. 'If I did I should frighten the ghost.' Lichtenberg was more impressed: Hamlet, dressed in a black French suit of modern cut, appears on the walls with his cloak wrapped around him and his hat pulled down over his eyes. There is a sharp sense of expectation in the air: 'the whole audience of some thousands are as quiet, and their faces as motionless as though they were painted on the walls of the theatre.' The Ghost appears before anyone is aware of his presence, partly because Garrick has moved to one side and drawn all eyes toward him. At Horatio's 'Look, my lord, it comes', Garrick

> turns sharply and at the same moment staggers back two or three paces with his knees giving way under him; his hat falls to the ground and both his arms ... are stretched out almost to their full length ... his mouth is open: thus he stands rooted to the spot, with legs apart, but no loss of dignity, supported by his friends ... His whole demeanour is so expressive of terror that it made my flesh creep even before he began to speak. The almost terror-struck silence of the audience, which preceded this appearance and filled one with a sense of insecurity, probably did much to enhance this effect. At last he speaks, not at the beginning, but at the end of a breath, with a trembling voice: 'Angels and ministers of grace defend us!' (10)

To us, this hardly sounds like naturalistic acting, though it is precisely for making his characters so 'natural' that Garrick was almost universally celebrated. There are several reasons for this, centring on different understandings of the term 'natural'. In contrast to the more overtly artificial style of the preceding generation, Garrick's acting certainly seemed more like ordinary life; but the natural did not necessarily mean the absence of technique, or of a technical awareness among the audience (Lichtenberg is both moved and observant of Garrick's strategies). In fact, the natural and the mechanical were to some extent allied during this period, in the wake of Newton; the body was viewed as a kind of animate machine (Roach, 'Garrick' 432-3). A further question surrounding Garrick's 'naturalness' touched on the issue of the actor's own subjectivity. Was it necessary for him actually to *feel* the emotions he was representing? Eighteenth-century interest in the relation between the passions and their bodily manifestations spilled over into the age-old debate (still very much around today) about the relation of feeling and technique in the representation of emotion (see Roach, *Player's Passion*). As applied to Garrick, the term 'natural' indicated that he convinced the spectators that he (the actor as well as the character) really was experiencing the emotions he was representing, and implied too that the spectator was able to *share* that experience. This achievement depended primarily on bodily sensations, physical motions transferred from stage to auditorium. Garrick's body is what attracts Lichtenberg's attention; as A. C. Sprague notes, Lichtenberg's description focuses on the visual, while Cibber's description of Betterton's handling of the same scene, quoted above, concentrates on speech and voice (*Shakespearian Players*, 24); but what Garrick is doing affects more than the eyes – Lichtenberg's 'flesh creeps', the whole audience is 'terror-struck' into silence, with motionless faces 'as though they were painted on the walls of the theatre'. Even the comically naive Partridge in Fielding's *Tom Jones*, at first sceptical of the Ghost, 'fell into such a violent fit of trembling that his knees knocked against each other' (Bk. 16, Ch. 5). The bodies of the audience are drawn in and together. Note too the skill with which Garrick marshals even the minutest detail: he speaks 'Angels and ministers ...' at the *end* of a breath, not at the beginning. Later, his eyes remain 'fixed on the ghost' as he moves to extricate himself from his fellows, until at length he

> turns his face toward them, tears himself ... from their grasp, and draws his sword on them with a swiftness that makes one shudder ... Then he stands with his sword upon guard against the spectre ... [as] the ghost goes off the stage.

He remains motionless until the Ghost disappears from view, making sure the Ghost 'keep[s] his distance', then begins to follow, 'now standing still and then going on, with sword upon guard, eyes fixed on the ghost, hair disordered, and out of breath, until he too is lost to sight' (Lichtenberg 9-11).

Such details illustrate how the naturalistic is constructed through an art that demands immense physical control – abetted sometimes by clever contrivance. Garrick's 'disordered hair' has attracted a lot of scholarly interest because a certain hair stylist named Perkins once claimed to have contrived a mechanical wig for Garrick's use in this scene, causing his hair to rise ominously and mysteriously off the back of his scalp. This may not have been as outlandish as it seems to us, since it was in keeping with contemporary mechanistic theory about the relation of passions to bodily motion. Such a theory also helps to explain the peculiar detail of Garrick's exit, 'now standing still and then going on', suggesting a 'visible effort' to get his 'thunder-struck machine creak[ing] back into action' (Roach, 'Garrick' 438). Furthermore, the whole scene is designed to represent visually a process by which Hamlet, at first terror-struck himself, overcomes his fear, masters himself and goes forward to seize his destiny. This 'intrepid self-mastery born of filial loyalty', according to one critic, 'is the sign of a universally virtuous motive which demonstrates Hamlet's worthiness to rule' (Wilson 382), and hence plays a part in the inculcation of moral values which Garrick, along with so many others of his time, felt to be the very basis of his art.

Whatever Garrick actually felt is therefore not only unrecoverable but finally irrelevant. His acting is 'natural' because of what he makes his audience feel on their pulses; and what they feel depends on their predispositions, themselves conditioned by things like current physiological theory. Once again, the hilariously literal-minded Partridge is a telling witness. Chided by Tom at being afraid of 'the warrior upon the stage' (the Ghost), Partridge justifies himself by retorting, 'if that little man there [Garrick was exceptionally small] ... is not frightened, I never saw any man frightened in my life'; and yet upon being asked, after the play is over, which actor he preferred, Partridge unhesitatingly names the King. The others protest that 'Hamlet is acted by the best player who was ever on the stage', but Partridge is unconvinced:

'He the best player!' cries Partridge, with a contemptuous sneer; 'why, I could act as well as he myself. I am sure if I had seen a ghost, I should have looked in the very same manner and done just as he did ... [but] the King ... speaks all his words distinctly, half as loud again as the other. Anybody may see he is an actor.'

Fielding's irony deftly points to the distinction between artifice and nature as Garrick's audience understood it.

Garrick himself, while committed to technique, frequently maintained that, for him, feeling the inner motions of the part was crucial. In a letter, he declares his almost Stanislavskian sentiments: 'I pronounce that the greatest strokes of genius have been unknown to the actor himself, till ... the warmth of the scene has sprung the mine ... the [great actor] will always realize the feelings of his character and be transported beyond himself' (quoted in Donohue 220). At another time, he provides a small instance of how feeling and technique may combine; describing the brief pause he habitually made in the line, 'I think it was to see – my mother's wedding' (Hamlet's response to Horatio's 'My lord, I came to see your father's funeral'), Garrick explains: 'I certainly never stop ... (that is close the *sense*,) but I as certainly *suspend* my voice, by which your ear must know that the sense is suspended' (quoted in Sprague, *Players* 26-7). The insistence on feeling, the belief that the movement of the words derives from an inner motivation that the audience may be made to share, the commitment to detail of character, are all present. But so, unmistakably, is the carefully prepared artifice of representation. As Johnson reputedly remarked, 'No, Sir, Garrick left nothing to chance.' How far he was willing to go can be illustrated not only by the possibly apocryphal story of Perkins the hairdresser but by the better authenticated fact that he had the chair used in the closet scene especially contrived so that it would fall clattering to the floor when he sprang to his feet upon, once again, the timely entrance of his father's spirit.

These strategies to increase dramatic effect served the larger overall purpose of convincing the audience of Hamlet's sentiments and ultimate self-mastery and thereby engaging their sympathies with him in his central pursuit. We must not forget that the sharply cut text that Garrick shared with Betterton and indeed with actors generally from 1670 to 1800 produced an active and robust Hamlet, relatively unreflective and bent on revenge – not the melancholy and hyper-sensitive poet invented by various Romantic critics (Coleridge's indecisive intellectual for example, or Goethe's 'costly vase' designed for 'lovely flowers' but incongruously made to hold an oak tree that shivers it to pieces (Furness ed., *Variorum* 273)). Thus Garrick portrayed a Hamlet whose madness was unambiguously feigned, and part of a clear plan. Adopting the dress described by Ophelia, though with a modern cut to make it the more accessible to his audience, he entered for 'To be or not to be ...' with arms folded in the traditional 'melancholy' posture, dishevelled hair and a 'lock hanging over one shoulder'; one of his black stockings had slipped to reveal white under-socks and a loop of red garter (Lichtenberg 16). He thus signalled his playacting to the audience, but at the same time he frequently managed to convey other, more authentic feelings. At the beginning of the nunnery scene with Ophelia, he was momentarily carried away by gentle and delicate feelings, but then recollected himself and assumed the frenzied tone of madness; even then, he would allow a 'real tenderness' to shine through Hamlet's 'ineffectual endeavours to hide it' (Thomas Wilkes, quoted in Mills 40).

Garrick's interest in streamlining the plot of the play without losing the intricacies of psychological exploration led him finally to alter it radically, eliminating what he called the 'rubbish of the fifth Act' – Hamlet's journey to England, his encounter with the pirates and dispatch of Rosencrantz and Guildenstern (described to Horatio in IV.vi and V.ii), the gravediggers, and the climactic duel. For most of his career, Garrick had played in an acting version similar to Davenant's, though with many original lines restored; but in 1772, just four years before his retirement, he allowed himself to enact a 'bold deed', the 'most impudent thing' he had ever done: 'I have play'd the devil this winter, I have dar'd to alter *Hamlet*, I have thrown away the gravediggers, and all the fifth act, and notwithstanding the galleries were so fond of them, I have met with more applause than I did at five and twenty – this is a great revolution in our theatrical history' (quoted in G. W. Stone 893).[1] The text as altered ends abruptly after Laertes returns in IV.v to confront Claudius, is shocked by his sister's madness and, under the King's tutelage, turns to revenge against Hamlet. Skilful interpolation of some of Laertes' lines from the graveyard scene and from IV.vii sets the stage for Hamlet's surprising and unmotivated appearance. (He has apparently acted on his resolution, interpolated by Garrick at the end of the 'How all occasions' soliloquy, to 'sweep to [his] revenge'.) The Prince challenges Laertes, as he normally does in the graveyard, and Laertes responds with a drawn sword. As the two prepare to joust, the Queen cries out, and the King intervenes:

> We will not bear this Insult to our Presence,
> Hamlet, I did command you hence to England,
> Affection hitherto has curb'd my Pow'r,
> But you have trampled on Allegiance,
> And now shall feel my Wrath – Guards!

But Hamlet is quick in his response:

> First feel mine – (Stabs him)
> Here thou Incestuous, Murd'rous, damned Dane
> There's for thy treachery, Lust and Usurpation!

At this point, Garrick seems to have introduced the business of the King actually fighting back, instead of being 'stuck like a pig on the stage'. In so doing, he took the advice of Shakespearean editor George Steevens who wrote to him in 1771: 'A stab given to an unarmed or defenceless man has seldom a very happy effect. An Englishman loves a spirited, but abhors a phlegmatic exit' (quoted in Sprague, *Actors* 181). Laertes then revenges 'My Father, Sister, and my King' by running Hamlet through. There is an odd ambiguity in the stage direction here since it implies Hamlet kills himself or at least allows Laertes to stab him: 'Hamlet runs upon Laertes' sword and falls.' One effect of this is to reduce Laertes' moral responsibility, thus rendering him less guilty; and the other, even more important, is to maintain Hamlet's complete mastery of the situation – very different from the original, where, as Dr Johnson complains, the hero's death is 'effected by an incident which Hamlet had no part in producing' (Furness ed., *Variorum*, ii, 146). Horatio prepares to revenge his 'Prince and Friend' but is restrained by the dying Hamlet who links his hand with that of Laertes, enjoining them to 'unite your Virtues / To calm this troubled Land' (G. W. Stone 920). The wretched Queen has meanwhile rushed offstage and fallen in a trance outside her chamber door. Her fate, and that of the unhappy and mad

Ophelia, are thus left uncertain, though the kingdom itself is safe in the hands of Horatio and Laertes – neither of whom, we recall, is of royal blood. Shakespeare's careful restoration of hierarchy in the person of Prince Fortinbras is pointedly omitted in the interests of two upwardly mobile gentlemen.

All this may seem like madness, but there was method in it. That the innocent (Ophelia especially, but Gertrude perhaps as well, and even Laertes) should suffer with the guilty offended contemporary notions of poetic justice and propriety. Dr Johnson wrote that the 'gratification which would arise from the destruction of an usurper and a murderer is abated by the untimely death of Ophelia, the young, the beautiful, the harmless and the pious'. So too the looseness of the fifth act is avoided: the seeming digressiveness of the gravediggers (whose slapstick comedy frequently threatened to obscure 'some necessary question[s] of the play'), the improbability of Hamlet's escape from Rosencrantz and Guildenstern and his encounter with the pirates, the witty but superfluous exchange with Osric, the theatrics of the duel – all are abandoned and replaced by a lightning quick and startling denouement.

Much more important in this version is not what Garrick so boldly removed, but what he equally boldly, but much less notoriously, put back in. For if the ending of the play is truncated, the first four acts are much more complete than they had been at any time since Burbage. Most of the standard cuts have been reversed – including Claudius's long speech to Hamlet in I.ii, the Danish ambassadors in both I.ii and II.i, much of Polonius's advice to Laertes in I.iii and his scene with Reynaldo (II.i), the Ghost's speeches to Hamlet in I.v, Hamlet's advice to the Players (III.ii), the lines normally excised from the play-within, many of those cut from the closet scene, and most of IV.iv, including the 'How all occasions ...' soliloquy (though Fortinbras, consistent with his absence from the finale, remains offstage, only his 'trumpets and drums' audible). Garrick also restored Hamlet's morally ambiguous speech over the praying King, 'Now might I do it pat', a scene which he had cut in earlier performances, probably because it puts Hamlet in a less than flattering light (Mills 41). Taken together, these restorations mean that material originally cut from the F text and present only in Q2 here appears on stage for what may have been the very first time. The cumulative effect was to change the traditional focus. The subsidiary characters acquired greater stature, so that Claudius, for example, was allowed his moral scruples and became less of a cardboard villain, while Polonius, traditionally clownish, was shrewd and calculating as well as sententiously wise ('dotage encroaching upon wisdom' as Garrick had put it years before (Burnim, *Garrick* 163)); Horatio and Laertes were given more range, and even the Queen was allowed more emotional scope.

As for Hamlet himself, without losing the vital and active qualities that marked the performance, he became somewhat more introspective, the restored passages tending to evoke 'the conflicts within Hamlet's being' (G. W. Stone 900). The handling of the final soliloquy (IV.iv) provides an example of the complex mix: Hamlet's self-doubt, his ambivalence towards the military heroics of Fortinbras, which he both honours and deflates, his wide-ranging awareness of his own power and weakness are all invoked – but then, departing from Shakespeare, they are all resolved in the change that Garrick made to the last two lines. The quarto's final couplet is tantalizingly uncertain: 'O from this time forth, / My *thoughts* be bloody, or be nothing worth' (emphasis added), following which Hamlet is marched off to England. Garrick, in keeping with his general insistence on rational and virtuous control, makes the speech a prologue to determined action, all doubt dissolved: 'O from this time forth, / My thoughts be bloody all! the hour is come – / I'll fly my keepers – sweep to my revenge', a resolve that he then, as we have seen, unhesitatingly acts upon.

Thus did Garrick transform *Hamlet* in the last years of his career. His 152nd and last performance was on 30 May 1776, part of a series of farewell productions of all his most famous roles, which made Hannah More feel as though she were 'assisting at the funeral obsequies of these individual characters' (More 49). The tickets sold out in two hours, and many of those who saw it considered that Garrick had never been greater (Burnim, *Garrick* 173). News of his retirement eclipsed even the disturbing reports from overseas; Londoners would, for the moment at least, rather have kept Garrick than America. After his very last appearance, on 10 June, he came forward and 'addressed the Audience in so pathetic a Manner as drew Tears from the Audience and himself & took his leave of them for Ever' (quoted in Burnim, *Garrick* 193). As More wrote about his final *Hamlet*, 'I would not wrong him or myself so much as to tell you what I think of it; it is sufficient that you have seen him; I pity those who have not' (48).

Three years later he was dead. No actor had ever been so successful or become so rich and so well-placed. His death set off 'a flood of public grief without parallel in English literature, the arts, or the stage' (Burnim, 'Looking upon His Like' 182-3). His funeral procession was the grandest that had ever been witnessed for anyone short of a monarch. It stretched past thousands of mourners for over a mile down the Strand and Whitehall to Westminster Abbey, where hundreds more jammed the entrances seeking admission. Dukes and earls served as pallbearers, and though many were no doubt on hand for reasons more social than personal, as many more felt a deep grief. Hannah More recalls how 'The bells of St. Martin's and the Abbey gave a sound that smote upon my very soul' (65). She describes the choir advancing to the grave, singing a Handel anthem, 'then Sheridan, as chief-mourner; then the body (alas! whose body!), with ten noblemen and gentlemen, pallbearers; then the rest of the friends and mourners; hardly a dry eye – the very players, bred to the trade of counterfeiting, shed genuine tears ... Such an awful stillness reigned, that every word was audible. How I felt it!' (67). It is remarkable how similar this description is to those which chronicle the effects of Garrick's acting itself. It is as if, even in death, Garrick's power over his audience and his fellow actors is undiminished. His body is still centre stage, and its remarkably expressive character, its extraordinarily malleable adaptability, is still present; he could still drown the stage with tears. Like Lichtenberg's assertion of community with his theatrical neighbour, Hannah More's multi-levelled exclamation expresses the binding power of Garrick's physical presence: 'alas! whose body!'

Edmund Kean (1787–1833)

During the nineteenth century, Hamlet became a Romantic. Edmund Kean was strong and active in Garrick's mode, but infused a bitter energy and Romantic fire into the role as well; his was an unsettled and mercurial brand of Romanticism. Gradually, however, Hamlet became more the wan thinker than the spirited swordsman. Under the influence of writers like Goethe, Coleridge, and Hazlitt, he was transformed into an image of the Romantic writer himself, thoughtful, contemplative, so weighed down by his superbly sensitive consciousness as to be incapable of decisive action. At the same time, developments in playhouse construction, stage lighting and design, along with an increasing interest in pictorial realism, produced a striving for scenic authenticity, sometimes brought to the most minutely elaborate extremes. With actor-managers such as Booth and Irving, who exerted control over every aspect of their productions, detailed scenery matched detailed acting, defining a naturalistic atmosphere and uniquely individualistic characters. Scenery became more and more an adjunct of character.

Coleridge once remarked of Kean that 'seeing him act was like reading Shakespeare by flashes of lightning'. The phrase catches precisely Kean's extraordinary ability to *electrify* his audiences. Metaphors of fire, of electricity, of lightning flashes, recur over and over in descriptions of his acting, indicating a vain effort to convey the power he wielded from the stage. One commentator wrote that an 'animating soul' gave 'fire' and 'energy' to his performances, so that one could almost say 'his body thought' (*Examiner*, quoted in Hillebrand 114). The image of brilliant flashes suggests more than just his effect; Fanny Kemble describes Kean as captivating but inconsistent:

> I do not know that I ever saw him in any character which impressed me as a *whole work of art*; ... in every one of his characters there is an intense personality of his *own* that, while one is under its influence, defies all criticism – moments of such overpowering passion ... looks and gestures of such thrilling, piercing meaning, that the excellence of those *parts* of his performances more than atones for the want of greater unity in conception and smoothness in the entire execution. (430, italics in original)

In *Hamlet*, for example, moments of calm reflection and philosophical meditation were much less effective than the passionate tenderness of the nunnery scene, the biting ironic wit of the scenes with Rosencrantz and Guildenstern, or the brilliant and graceful athleticism of the duel.

Kean has frequently been compared to Garrick. Both were uncommonly small (less than 5ft 4in) and Kean especially was quite unprepossessing; both laid great stress on physical acting, on strong passions, on changing facial expression. 'Nature' was the key word applied repeatedly to both of them. As with Garrick, what counted as 'natural' was passion, a certain waywardness and oscillation, an extreme expressiveness. But the overall aim to which they directed their bodily energies was crucially different. Garrick sought ultimately a consistency and coherence – a psychological wholeness of characterization. Kean's power was rougher, more tempestuous, more in keeping with the wild mountain scenery that so appealed to his contemporaries. His mission seemed to be to break up the sense of cohesion embodied in his classical predecessor John Philip Kemble and expressed generally by the conservatism of the English theatre – to bring discord and multiplicity instead of harmony and unity (S. Williams 105-6). His very inconsistency of portrayal contributes to this disjunctive sense. Thus the kind of selfhood Kean projected was different from that of Garrick and the culture he epitomized; it was fragmented, uneven, divided, very 'modern' in one sense of that ambiguous term, and very much in keeping with Romantic sensibility. Advanced thinkers in Kean's time, absorbed by uniqueness, by the deranged, the anti-social and the outlandish, found in the actor and the personality he projected both on and off stage a sign of their own alienation.

For all his power, Kean was extremely limited in his range – much more so than Garrick. He had no gift for comedy, because he 'had no gaiety; he could not laugh; he had no playfulness that was not as the playfulness of the panther showing her claws every moment' (Lewes 20). He was brilliant as Iago for that very reason. But as Hamlet, he was less successful; since the quieter, more intellectual features of the character escaped him, his portrayal became known for its 'points', the innovations he brought to the part at a time when 'new readings' and departures from tradition were instantly noticed by audiences and either hissed or cheered. Even more than the other great actors of the eighteenth and nineteenth centuries, Kean's career manifests a constant negotiation between the heavy conservatism of theatrical tradition and the cultural demand for striking departures and novelty. His most famous innovations tell us much about how he sought to make a role like Hamlet electric.

Of these, the one that raised the most comment was his handling of the nunnery scene, especially its final moment. Opinions differ as to how wild Kean's approach to Ophelia was.

He certainly avoided much of the noisy stamping and raving that had become part of stage tradition (some of it originating with Garrick), treating her with 'mournful gravity' (*Examiner*, quoted in Mills 81), and downplaying the pretended madness. Garrick had managed to convey tenderness for Ophelia showing through the pretence, an achievement probably beyond Kean's range; instead Kean seems to have oscillated. He screamed the final 'To a nunnery, go' and rushed off, only to stop at the very 'extremity of the stage', pause, and then return slowly with an 'almost gliding step'. A 'pang of parting tenderness' wrenched his vehemence from him, and he bent softly, with a 'deep-drawn sigh' to 'press his lips to Ophelia's hand' (Ludwig Tieck, quoted in Mills 81-2). This had 'an electrical effect upon the house' according to Hazlitt, who judged it 'the finest commentary that was ever made on Shakespeare. It explained the character at once ... as one of disappointed hope, of bitter regret, of affection suspended, not obliterated, by the distractions of the scene around him' (14). Although Kean's behaviour seemed to give the lie to Claudius's remark a few lines later, 'Love? his affections do not that way tend' (III.i.162; Mills 82), the inconsistency did not seem to bother him, nor did it bother the many nineteenth-century actors who imitated him, culminating with Beerbohm-Tree in 1892, who stretched the sentiment to its limit: stealing back unseen to a stricken Ophelia who had collapsed on a couch, Tree bent and kissed 'one of the tresses of her hair' – one of those Viking braids which by that time had become *de rigueur* (Sprague, *Actors* 155). Barrymore's long tortured pauses, in which his love for Ophelia struggled against what he felt he had to do, were in the same vein. But since the 1920s Hamlets have tended to be harsher with Ophelias, and in many recent productions (Noble/ Branagh for example), paroxysms of sexual desire compete with tenderness and erupt into violence, a madness of conflicting impulse and inchoate feeling having replaced pretence altogether. Even so, the *conflict* displayed by Kean can be seen as the wellspring of even these developments, with their overt representation of sexual feelings.

Kean, like Garrick, was able to create a Hamlet of rapid changes, one whose 'sensibility is so keenly alive, that every trifle administers fresh pangs to his distress' (*Examiner*, quoted in Hillebrand 124). Like his great predecessor, he also detected at the basis of Hamlet's character a strong strain of filial affection which gave to the Ghost scenes a memorable pathos. Face to face with his spectral father, he maintained his composure, and, even after the Ghost's departure, his behaviour was far from mad; he 'gazed for some time at the spot where the Ghost had disappeared, and then "came forward with an eye of supplication, as if he implored the Sacred Deity to aid him in his purpose"' (Mills 79, quoting Frances Phippen). Such moments reveal that passion need not be conveyed only in outbursts – there can be a powerful charge in subdued emotion as well.

So there was clearly variety in Kean's rendering – it was not all high-pitched. But most of the time there seems to have hovered a *potential* for lightning flashes, even if it was not always realized. He even succeeded in giving the most famous meditation in the play some of his characteristic savagery. Rather than 'philosophic reflection', Kean made 'To be or not to be' part of his characterization, seeing it as an emanation of Hamlet's 'desire for death', itself the result of his 'loathing of those about him'. Its 'impassioned and heart-breaking reflections' were thus made to arise from personal circumstance rather than from a detached observation of a universal predicament (see Mills 80, who quotes the *Examiner*, 20 March 1814).

Kean's career after his tumultuous early successes traced a slow but relentless downward trajectory. He never stopped acting; but he also never stopped drinking, and his personal affairs became more and more messy. Many a time he was hissed off the stage for being drunk, but just as often he was able to recall the amazing power to electrify that had been his mark since the beginning. He died, like Macbeth, 'with harness on his back', collapsing in the middle of a performance of *Othello*, the part that more than any other epitomized his whole career. Just a few months before, in December 1832, Lewes saw his Othello for the last time and left a moving record of it:

> How puny he looked beside Macready [the new leading actor of the period, a much larger man, who played Iago], until in the third act, when roused by Iago's taunts and insinuations, he moved towards him with a gouty hobble, seized him by the throat, and, in a well-known explosion, 'Villain! be sure you prove,' etc. seemed to swell into a stature which made Macready appear small. On that very evening, when gout made it difficult for him to display his accustomed grace, when a drunken hoarseness had ruined the once

matchless voice, such was the irresistible pathos ... which vibrated in his tones and expressed itself in look and gestures, that old men leaned their heads upon their arms and fairly sobbed. (15-16)

Lewes recognized that the performance was 'patchy', with some parts misconceived and others 'tricky' or 'gabbled', but, he adds, 'it was irradiated with such flashes that I would again risk broken ribs for the chance of a good place in the pit to see anything like it'. Aside from affording a telling glimpse of playhouse manners, this sets the stage for Kean's final act. For it was during this scene, at the very moment when Othello rouses himself to threaten Iago (played by his son Charles), that, just three months later, Kean fell into Charles's arms, and whispered, 'I am dying – speak to them for me' (Hillebrand 326-7). His end was in its way as spectacular as his initial triumph, living up to the Romantic legend that he himself had fostered.

Edwin Booth (1833–93)

The great American actor Edwin Booth, scion of a theatrical family and brother of the notorious John Wilkes Booth, brought a deeply sensitive Hamlet to an admiring public. Though solidly within the British tradition, his portrayal can nevertheless be seen as responding to distinctively American needs. In Booth, Kean's 'flashes of lightning' found no answering vibrations; Booth's was a calmer, more ethereal glow. His acting of Hamlet produced a 'steady light which illumines the beauties of [Shakespeare's] magnificent poetry, and reveals the intricacies of his teeming imagination with an equable and instructive ray' (*New York Times* 7 Jan. 1870, quoted in Shattuck 91). 'Equable' suggests the quiet, restrained manner, the melancholy delicacy with which Booth approached the role. Of all the adjectives lavished upon him, one of the most common was 'spiritual', and the metaphor most often adopted to convey that quality was a ray of inward light. His spiritual brightness flowed outwardly to the actor's eyes and countenance at certain intense moments, while at others it was marked by a responsive glow from the theatrical gas-lighting that had by Booth's time been rendered capable of subtle and intricate effects. Mary Isabella Stone's description of 'There's a special providence in the fall of a sparrow ...' provides some sense of the interior illumination: 'A rare, *spiritual* expression comes over his countenance, which glows with the "light that never was on land or sea" [quoting Wordsworth's "Elegiac Stanzas"]' (137). In order to manifest this spiritualized light in scenic terms, Booth was partial to moonlight – so much so that he even staged the graveyard scene at night to take advantage of its effects. Booth's moon had a tendency to emerge dramatically from behind tossed clouds. When the ghost first appears to Hamlet in I.iv, 'Moonlight breaks out and shines directly on his deathly white, awe-struck, yet eager and excited face'; later, on the more 'removed ground' where the ghost has led him (Booth made this an evocative grove of mighty oaks), once again the moonlight falls on his face as the ghost stands 'almost hidden in [the] shadow of [the] trees' (M. I. Stone 31, 34). So too the moon shines magically through the casement during Hamlet's excited confrontation with his mother in her closet and the ghost's unexpected appearance there. In the graveyard, it registers Hamlet's abstracted melancholy: on 'Alas, poor Yorick!', for Stone '*the* most exquisitely beautiful thing *said* by Booth', moonlight is 'again upon his face striking it sidewise'; a little later, eavesdropping on Ophelia's mourners, he 'lifts a ghastly face of agony – on which the moonlight strikes – then he buries it again in Horatio's friendly bosom'. Thus did Booth seek some correspondence between the depth of soul he wanted most to project in his characterization and the theatrical means, both actorly and scenic, by which he chose to represent it.[2]

From the 1864-65 season when he played Hamlet in New York for one hundred nights, an American record to be broken only in 1923 by John Barrymore (who quite deliberately closed his *Hamlet* after 101 performances), Booth became more and more identified with the role, inspiring critic after critic to echo the judgment of George Curtis, editor of *Harper's*, that Booth 'is Hamlet as he lived in Shakespeare's world' (April 1865, Shattuck 60). The identification worked both ways – not only was Booth Hamlet, Hamlet was Booth; as an appreciation in *The Atlantic Monthly* remarked, a 'spiritual constitution' and 'rare delicacy and sensibility' characterized them both. Like Hamlet, Booth was 'nobly human to the core' and afflicted too with a fine melancholy; like the prince, he had to 'hold his peace when his heart was breaking' (perhaps a reference to his brother's assassination of Lincoln in 1865).[3] The American thirst for heroes, so familiar to us today, was already well established in the mid nineteenth century.

From such comments, and from the eyewitness accounts, we form a picture of an intensely thoughtful Hamlet, reflective and sad, 'bold in action' in minor matters, as Clarke says, but failing when the stakes are high, a 'man of first-class intellect and second-class will' (Clarke, see also Shattuck xiv, 221). In his Notebook, Booth stresses Hamlet's intelligence and purposefulness, always anticipating his enemies' moves, losing control only when he murders Polonius. Not for a minute is this Hamlet mad, though he occasionally bursts out in extreme excitement (notably, after the Ghost's departure and again after the 'Mousetrap'). Booth marked clearly the distinction between the play-acted madness and Hamlet's 'true' sanity. Even when he assumed the antic disposition, he maintained a princely courtesy and gentlemanly demeanour. His was an idealized reading, very much in Goethe's mould, whose famous metaphor of the vase riven by an oak tree when it 'should have borne only pleasant flowers in its bosom' encapsulates the Romantic Hamlet's exquisite, but tragically inadequate, sensibility. Booth epitomized what the Romantic writers had been talking about (though we may also discern in his Hamlet a trace of that elegiac pessimism characteristic of Victorians like Matthew Arnold). As Shattuck points out, Hazlitt's memorable description of Hamlet, in which he outlines those aspects of the hero that Kean failed to depict, found its exemplar half a century later on a different continent: Hamlet 'is not a character marked by strength of passion or will, but by refinement of thought and feeling … He seems incapable of deliberate action'. A 'gentleman and a scholar', he is 'wrapped up in the cloud of his reflections, and only *thinks aloud*' (Hazlitt 10-12; Shattuck 22-3).

Booth's rendition was clearly more complete, more of a piece, than Kean's vividly uneven portrayal. But in some important respects, their interpretations converged, a sign perhaps of their Romantic instincts, despite the differences in their versions of Romanticism, Kean's tending to the Byronic, Booth's to that of Keats in his great odes or Arnold in 'Dover Beach'. They played the Ghost scenes with a similar mix of tenderness and filial awe, rather than the fear made famous by

Garrick (Shattuck 142; see also Mills 135). And each gave a special emphasis to the word 'Father' in Hamlet's address to the spectre. Booth knelt and spoke it 'in a tone of yearning fondness' (M. I. Stone 32). His collapse at first seeing the Ghost was less violent and more pathetic than either Kean's or Garrick's. Again Stone's description is striking: 'sinking down, down, his limbs giving way ... his arms are outstretched against the two others, while his hands grope about on their breasts and arms in an aimless, failing way' (31-2). In following the Ghost off, Booth neither held his sword in front, as Garrick had, nor brandished it back toward his companions in Kean's manner; he merely shook his right hand gently out behind to hinder them, and then raised the hilt of the sword in both hands like a cross to ward off any evil intention (a bit of business he had invented by accident years before). As he went off stage right, moonlight streamed in from the same side, throwing a long cruciform shadow behind him (Shattuck 146; M. I. Stone 33).

Booth treated Ophelia with careful and loving tenderness, as Kean had, but was in general less volatile and more restrained. In what was then a relatively new move, Booth caught sight of the eavesdroppers, thus motivating and to some extent palliating his harsh behaviour toward Ophelia. He did so very early in the scene, after 'I humbly thank you, well, well, well' whereas most actors who have adopted this stagy but unnecessary expedient wait until just before 'Where's your father', in order to motivate the unexpected question. Booth placed it early so as to turn almost the whole scene into an 'act' for the King's benefit (Shattuck 190). This did not mean he stamped or raved as Garrick had, nor that he oscillated from fury to melting softness like Kean. He behaved throughout with studied courtesy and restraint, and, though he always insisted that Hamlet harbours no love whatsoever for Ophelia, his audiences came away with a completely different sense. Having received from her the packet of remembrances she had been instructed to re-deliver, he retreated and, 'unseen by anyone', kissed the packet – 'I *did* love you *once*' was spoken in a tone of 'earnest tenderness' that carried 'conviction of his love and truth to every hearer'. Thus Stone (p. 73); but Clarke records that Booth never took the packet, so that she left with it still in her hand, a move that revealed a 'continuing bond' between them. Regardless of any variations in specific details over the years, it is clear that, despite Booth's disclaimers, his love for Ophelia did not come across as play-acting. His pretence was more obvious on a line like 'It hath made me mad', which Clarke understood as multi-levelled, including both regret and reproof, though, with its 'singular artificial air', it was mainly a formula to mislead the eavesdroppers. Occasional sarcasm and harshness served to convey Hamlet's conflicting feelings: love warring against distrust, a desire to speak frankly and take her into his confidence contending with the need to protect himself by covering up his true sentiments. The little exchange, 'Where's your father? / At home, my lord', was clearly a test, since Booth had already known for some minutes where her father was. His censure of her duplicity was sharp but courteous: 'No accusation, no reproach, could be so terrible as the sudden plucking away of his hand, and the pain of his face as he turn[ed] from her' (Calhoun).

The last part of the scene was Romantic in Kean's vein. His departure was marked by a long, lingering look, ambivalent in its mix of warmth and watchfulness, but the tug of affection yielded finally to a commitment to his larger purpose. He embraced her with *'infinite tenderness'* and kissed her forehead, his back to the audience so that the 'fine shape of his head' and his 'wavy black locks' created a strong visual contrast with her 'golden tresses' (M. I. Stone 75-6). Stone's account of it, with its slightly archaic, Pre-Raphaelite ring, says much about Booth's appeal. He offered a vision of the beautiful that was, perhaps, especially appealing in the context of late nineteenth-century America. It was an era of runaway capitalist enterprise and materialist frenzy, a period of rapid growth and brash national confidence. To that not insignificant segment of the population that valued art as an antidote to the amoral pursuit of coin, Booth's gentle and genteel devotion to the Ideal offered an alternative. It was true, of course, that the very pursuit that many found impossibly vulgar was gradually turning America into a world power and, incidentally, making possible the accumulation of vast collections of old world culture by wealthy new world industrialists. To turn away from Mammon was itself a cultural luxury, and Shakespeare offered a kind of capital that made such a move possible. We can therefore surmise that an enterprise such as Booth's was generated by, and implicated in, the very capitalist processes to which it seemed to stand in opposition. It is as though the culture of rampant acquisitiveness and vulgar hucksterism produced its own opposite – a benign spirituality to balance the crass materialism.

With his mother, as with Ophelia, Booth was various and complex. Entering with 'latent combativeness', he swung between reproach and reverence till the fateful interruption of Polonius. His quick mind impulsively seized on this opportunity 'to punish the Queen by slaying the King before her eyes' and he ran him through (Shattuck 225-6). After this, 'a desperate air as if the events of the time were too great to leave him leisure for regret' (Clarke) propelled him to accusation and a lofty, sensitive awareness of his mother's degradation. This Hamlet certainly did not enter into the darkness with her, as some modern ones have done. The famous puzzle of the pictures ('Look here upon this picture, and on this') was resolved in 1870 by the use of miniatures. In 1881, however, in a compromise with the opposing tradition of full-length wall portraits, the Queen wore a Claudius locket (which Booth tore from her neck and dashed to the floor) while Hamlet stood beside and pointed to his father's portrait (M. I. Stone 102-3), gaining a symbolic victory based on the sheer size of the different representations. A neat move with the Ghost added variety and a momentary shiver: when Booth told his mother, 'look you there', he pointed outward but kept his eyes on her. The Ghost meanwhile had slipped around behind him, and when he followed her glance he was appalled to find nothing there – could he have been deceived after all? A frantic search located the ghost again, the emotional fright leading to a new calm when he refused her attempted blessing, remaining earnest and firm. The scene closed, as tradition dictated, after 'I must be cruel only to be kind', leaving out the final thirty-seven lines with the counterplot against Rosencrantz and Guildenstern. The end was marked, in 'exquisite contrast to the stormy parts of the interview', by a deeply tender good night, featuring the same embrace and forehead kiss that he had used with Ophelia (M. I. Stone 106-7).

The last act produced its share of novelties. As befitted his gentlemanly demeanour, Booth's jesting with the gravediggers was abstracted, more habit than merriment, and he did not leap into Ophelia's grave (as Kean had). With Horatio, his friendship was strong and true – that was one of the chief characteristics of his portrayal. To show the friendship in a quiet but genuine light may have been one of the reasons Booth retained the first seventy-four lines of V.ii, which had since Betterton's time always been cut. But as Clarke shrewdly noted, the main reason was to make time for the set change from the elaborately realistic graveyard (complete with grass, foliage, a heap of dirt, slanting gravestones, part of an ancient church, and a cemetery wall backed by a vista of trees and a far-off spire) to the court setting for the duel. Accordingly, Hamlet and Horatio whiled away the bright morning in an arched gallery of the castle, with a shimmering landscape of river and fields in the distance. The ultra-modern capabilities of Booth's new theatre (built in 1869) made such a quick shift possible through the use of 'rise-and-sink' machinery; the portico screen would have been mounted on 'first grooves', not far behind the proscenium, leaving lots of room behind for the major change.

Into this gallery tripped the fop, Osric, whom Hamlet treated with genuine courtesy – with some weariness perhaps, but no mockery. Stone, surprisingly, calls this the scene she would 'most mourn to miss seeing, or have "cut out"'; she is moved by his serenity and by the smile 'which two or three times lights up his fine features as he turns toward Horatio'. At the same time, there

> still lingers that ineffable melancholy, so deep that no ordinary matter can touch more than the [surface] of his mind … Yet somehow we feel that the terrible pressure of his destiny has slightly lifted … and we catch a glimpse of what Hamlet might have been before his mother's second marriage, or father's death. (132)

It is a fitting prelude to the spiritual resignation of the speech about providence already mentioned, and to the final catastrophe, with its strong feeling of what might have been.

In accordance with tradition, Booth omitted the lines about madness in the apology to Laertes. Hamlet's equivocation here ('Was't Hamlet wronged Laertes? Never Hamlet … Hamlet denies it. / Who does it then? His madness' – V.ii.233-7) had never pleased actors, who had usually sought to idealize the Prince's moral uprightness. In Booth's case, the lines would have seemed doubly deceitful, given the unwavering sanity of his interpretation. The duel followed quickly, and moved forward with zest and ardour. In the first bout, Hamlet spun on his heel and nipped Laertes by thrusting under his own left arm. After much skilful parrying, Laertes finally wounded Hamlet in the breast and, infuriated, Booth rose to the challenge by moving in close, grasping his adversary's sword and driving it home. His anger mounted on hearing of the plot against him, and he rushed to trap Claudius by the throne; having caught hold of him, he stabbed the King twice through the neck. Immediately afterwards, he seemed dazed; his manic energy had drained away and, like David Warner a century later, he 'staggered from the deed ... all his vigor departed'. There was little dignity nor a sense that he would stand by his act – it was simply over. Thus 'thrown back upon his intellect and spirituality', the present having for the most part receded (Clarke), he attends only to Horatio, whom he desires to live for his sake. Hamlet's love for his friend is marked by a 'caress' of Horatio's arm which changes quickly into a 'clutch of bodily support' (M. I. Stone 146). Horatio, of course, cradles the dying Prince and, in a bit of new business introduced in 1883, lifts the miniature of Hamlet's father from his own breast (where Hamlet had fastened it as a token before the duel) and 'holds it before the eyes fast glazing in death' (M. I. Stone, 147, 139). The play ended, as was typical, at Hamlet's 'The rest is silence' and Horatio's two lines of benediction. Drums and a march were heard offstage, there was a brief tableau with Hamlet lying dead at centre stage and all those left alive looking off expectantly, and then the curtain fell.

The restrained nobility of it all is what most strikes Stone, while Clarke remarks on 'the homelessness in such a death'. In his general assessment that follows the detailed description, Clarke comments that Booth fails to kill the king more through 'lack of will power' than from any 'excess of conscientious scruples'. There is no 'moral shrinking' but rather a 'dearth of force'. While unfailingly courteous and gentle, he was never hopeful – 'he sees the appalling side of facts'. Booth's was a 'poetical' Hamlet, full of art and rhetoric, 'essentially life-like, but life elaborated and thrown into rhythmical shape'. Booth's devotion to an ideal art seems to have been conceived, consciously or not, in opposition to the social and cultural changes of his day. He wanted no part of the realism that was then invading the novel, with its depiction of actual social conditions, nor of the debased notions of beauty that were infiltrating the visual arts. His was essentially a conservative worship of an Ideal that provided a haven for many who were themselves uneasy in the vulgar and dynamic society of late nineteenth-century America. It may be no coincidence that his most famous portrayal, the one with which he became closely identified, should be characterized by a 'dearth' of that very 'force' which was the most conspicuous cultural feature of his time. His Hamlet was an implicit critique of his culture's materialist drive, but a critique contained within a larger system of tolerance that not only allowed but also subtly disarmed it.

Henry Irving (1838–1905)

Henry Irving, it was often said, could neither walk nor talk. He lacked the basic technical equipment of even a competent actor. For Shaw, his voice was 'a well cultivated neigh' and his walk, in the words of Shaw's friend, William Archer, seemed less a result of 'volition' than of 'an involuntary spasm' (Archer 63). Even a sympathetic critic such as Edward R. Russell could liken Irving's walk to that of a 'fretful man trying to get very quickly over a ploughed field' (Russell 58). The American critic, Henry Austin Clapp, in a judicious and well-balanced appraisal, points to the 'amazing paradox' that this 'most successful and cultivated of English actors' has 'not learned how to sit, stand, or move with the ease, repose, vigor, and grace … appropriate to attitude or action; and, worse even than this, he does not know how to speak his own language' (199-200). There are countless parodies of his bizarre pronunciation and unnecessary interjections. Ellen Terry, his leading lady for more than twenty years and a firm supporter, nevertheless seems to draw a secret satisfaction (a bit of revenge perhaps for Irving's continual domination?) from quoting an anonymous critic's satiric transcription of Irving's Shylock: the line 'Why then, it now appears you need my help – Go to then' comes out as 'Wa thane, ett no eperes / Ah! um! yo ned m'elp / Ough! Ough! Gaw too thane! Ha! um!' (Terry 297).

Nevertheless Irving was extraordinarily successful. Almost single-handedly he gave to the late Victorian theatre a respectability and artistic status that it conspicuously lacked in the 1860s when he began, and in the process he turned his Lyceum Theatre into a temple of worship and an ethical beacon. Such religious and moral metaphors are ubiquitous in accounts of his career. Even his critics acknowledged his power: 'Mr. Irving's theatre has become one of the established wayside shrines on the paths of culture, at which the devout dilettante never fails to make his orisons', wrote Archer (95), who, despite his ironic tone, used the received metaphor to make his point. Irving appealed to virtually every level of society, bringing the various and often conflicting classes together in temporary social harmony: 'There is probably no artistic institution in England which unites all classes as [the Lyceum] does' (Archer 29). His was a popular art, uncongenial to advanced intellectuals like Archer and Shaw, not because they despised him but because they saw him as a potential ally in their struggle to transform and modernize the British theatre (and indeed all of contemporary society) – but an ally who continually let them down. His popularity and what it meant for the cultural role of the theatre was officially recognized in 1895 when Irving was knighted, the first actor ever to be so honoured. Two days later Oscar Wilde was sentenced and sent to prison (Rowell 169), while in that same year Shaw's fruitless efforts to get Irving involved in producing one of his plays, *The Man of Destiny*, led only to public quarrels and journalistic sallies (Holroyd 348ff.). Irving's art was a backward-looking one; he rarely produced new plays and certainly avoided any with the critical edge of Wilde's or Shaw's. And his conservatism was, of course, rewarded, while their radicalism was deeply suspect.

Irving's art was founded on two pillars, Shakespeare and melodrama; his Shakespeare was itself melodramatic, full of lurid lights and shadows, with a decided slant towards the sentimental. In this tendency can be found part of the reason for his success despite his strange mannerisms. For it was the romantic glare of the sensational, combined with an attentiveness to the particularities of character and scene, that gave Irving his special power. His magnetism is summed up in the term 'intensity', of which attribute, says Archer, 'Mr. Irving might stand as an allegorical embodiment': 'The law of supply and demand holds ... in the world of art. We wanted intensity and we have got it, making the fortune of the lucky man who brought it into the market just at the right moment' (53-4). Archer introduces an economic turn of phrase, not simply as a metaphor, but as a precise description of the relations between culture and cash. Re-working the famous law of the free market together with Matthew Arnold's dictum about the historical concatenation of the man and the moment, Archer introduces the notion of cultural capital – what the time 'invests' in Irving and vice versa. I would add an element that Archer does not mention: Irving's own contribution to the making of that 'demand' which he then is able to supply. He does not just mirror the time's interest in 'intensity'; his art helps to create and disseminate that cultural ingredient.[4] *Why* the Victorians might have come to value intensity so highly is not readily apparent – but we can speculate that it had something to do with subjectivity and the cultivation of the private self, removed from the gritty pursuit of industrial growth, imperialist expansion and political conflict. Irving, moreover, sought to combine intensity with the ideology of the domestic – the Englishman's castle-like home where the father's benevolent rule made possible the private cultivation of every member of the bourgeois family.

Of Irving's other strengths, Henry Clapp identifies two that help account for his success and that are, as well, relevant to his approach to *Hamlet*. These are 'artistic propriety' and 'intellectuality' (208ff.). By the former, Clapp means a sense of pictorial exactness and appropriateness which combined with Irving's intensity to make him a brilliant stage manager as well as 'the most entirely picturesque actor of our time' (211).[5] His unwavering attention to detail in matters of scenery, lighting, movement, and costume as well as the physical look and feel of his characters, marked his whole career; he was a complete devotee, a martyr to the cause of his art. As for his intellect, it was this that most impressed his critics and was undoubtedly a leading reason why Shaw spotted him as an ally and then felt betrayed when Irving refused to join Shaw's cause. Irving applied his careful intelligence to all aspects of production, starting with the text. With *Hamlet*, he went back to the early texts, thought through the various possible readings, and made his many changes, cuts, and restorations on the basis of a full consideration of character and meaning. According to Clapp, his learning, intelligence, and acumen made him especially suited for Shakespeare's most celebrated role: 'with Hamlet's habits of introspection and metaphysical speculation the actor's sympathy is most intimate and profound' (220). His restless intelligence seeks to etch a unique character. For it is subjectivity, shaded and nuanced, that is the end towards which Irving's art moves; his aim is to bring the interior life into view through precise pictorial and physical representation.

Irving's Hamlet was in the tradition of Booth's, though more emotional than spiritual, more mercurial and tormented, subject to real rather than feigned hysteria. He in fact combined some of the characteristics of Kean and Booth. Like the latter in basic gentleness, in his love for Ophelia and his mother, in his reverence for the ghost and deep friendship with Horatio, he differed in being more casual in his manner and attitudes, more individualized and less 'Ideal'. His mannerisms, mocked as they often were, served to give the character an edgy particularity; his was a staccato physicality, his body unsuited to the unified classicism of Kemble or Booth. Instead he was disjointed, angular, fragmented – like Kean only more so, a disunified, but for that very reason unique, self. This of course drew criticism similar to that levelled at Kean, and subsequently at a parade of twentieth-century Hamlets, namely that this dislocated figure was no prince. Irving was more susceptible to this charge than any of his predecessors because his style was more impressionistic, 'calculated to focus attention upon hands or face' rather than on the whole body, classically composed (Hughes 12). He hardly fit Ophelia's flattering description after the nunnery scene ('The glass of fashion and the mould of form ...', III.i.150-61), but as his supporters were quick to ask, how much weight should be given to what a young woman says about her lover? And furthermore, was it not reasonable to believe that there have been actual princes who neither moved nor spoke in conventional 'princely' ways? Have they all been perfectly composed? Irving's task, in such a view, was to represent a particular prince in a 'real' and desperate situation, not to convey some abstract notion of princeliness.

The Ghost scene reveals the continuities and some of the differences between Irving and those who went before him. His reaction to the Ghost, like Kean's and Booth's, was reverent and filial, but his handling of the aftermath was his own. Kean had remained vibrantly subdued; Booth had collapsed rather spectacularly (and too realistically for some, whose voices prevailed to make him soften the business to bring it more in line with proper decorum – Shattuck 152). As for the 'tables' in which Hamlet writes the commonplace notion that a man may smile and yet be a villain, both Kean and Booth cut them altogether, thus skirting an obvious difficulty (is Hamlet really so naive as to treat such an idea as a revelation?). Irving, in contrast, did not omit the tables, nor did he, like many a minor Hamlet of his day, inscribe his banal thought 'with grand deliberation and careful pose'; rather,

> his snatching them from his pocket, and writing on them, is the climax of an outburst hardly distinguishable from hysteria. Hamlet is evidently one of those who ... find in solitude a licence and a cue for excitement, and who, when alone and under the influence of strong feelings, will abandon themselves to their fancies. (Russell 82)

Thus did small individualized incidents serve the construction of character. Russell observes a further refinement of this propensity to extravagant sensitivity: Irving's Hamlet 'has a trick – not at all uncommon in persons whose most real life is an inner one – of fostering and aggravating his own excitements' (66). Like a man with a toothache, he could not stay away from his own pain; for such a character, the choice to feign madness came naturally – it was merely an extension of an inner tendency. Unlike that of Garrick, Booth, or Kean, his hysteria was real and hence proved an appropriate cover for his later behaviour. Bursts of 'almost unhinged and yet consistently ordered excitement' (Russell 87) punctuated his performance. For example, the end of the long second act soliloquy brought a telling bit of business. Traditionally actors had leapt on the couplet ('The play's the thing ...') to make a point; Irving, in contrast, made it 'the natural culmination of a train of thought rather than a sudden idea' (Hughes 14). But then, in a reprise of his tablet-writing, he suddenly rushed to a pillar, propped his notebook against it, and began, as the curtain fell, 'to scribble hints for the speech he mean[t] to write' (Russell 87).

In the moment after 'The Mousetrap', we can discern the same interplay of delirium and order. The early parts of the play scene were acted with suppressed feelings and an enforced calm. As always, the bawdy interplay with Ophelia was cut, and her manner, in the wake of the nunnery scene, was sad and reproachful. Ellen Terry actually wept and dropped her fan, which Irving picked up and put to its traditional use as a screen. Oddly it was of peacock feathers – soon it would be clear why. Hamlet seemed spirited and insouciant, but all the while watchful and 'feverishly impatient' (Hughes 60, Russell 96). In conflict over his love for Ophelia and the need he perceives to treat her callously, and torn too by the desire to burst out against the King and the need to restrain himself, he held on till the climactic moment, avoiding the crawl across the stage (a much imitated move initiated by Kean) but taking an unconscious bite or two from Ophelia's fan. Then, on the rising and startlingly quick disappearance of King and court, he suddenly let go:

> spring[ing] from the ground, [he] darts with a shrill scream to the seat from which they vanished like ghosts, flings himself ... into the chair which the King has vacated, his body swaying the while from side to side in irrepressible excitement ... A still greater, because wild and bizarre, effect follows as Hamlet leaves the chair, and in a sort of jaunty nonsense rhythm chants the seldom-used lines:
>
> > For thou dost know, O Damon dear,
> > This realm dismantled was
> > Of Jove himself; and now reigns here
> > A very, very – peacock. [III.ii.281-84]
>
> At the last word, said suddenly after a pause, he looks at Ophelia's fan, which he has kept until now, and throws it away. (Russell 97)

Such an apparently inconsequential move anchored Irving's conception; here was Hamlet at the peak of hysteria, but it was a madness contained and pointed – most tellingly of course by his takeover of the throne itself. Concentration on such small physical details gave the performance its nervous idiosyncrasy, and hence its 'reality' for his cheering audience.

Character, for Irving, was defined by just such details. His approach to individuality forms an instructive contrast with Garrick who, more than a century before, relied on a quite different notion. Irving's version of subjectivity stressed the unique and inalienable, whereas Garrick stressed the typical; both were committed to precision and psychological exactness, but Garrick tended to seek the representative gesture, the move that made him *like* other men, while Irving found ways that distinguished him from others. Irving's way, of course, has become the mark of twentieth-century subjectivity, with its stress on the uniqueness of individual experience. The shifts from Garrick to Kean to Irving can hence be used to trace the fitful trajectory of the human subject, at least in its European manifestations, over almost two centuries.

Irving's special skill at conveying mixed feelings came out especially in the scenes with Ophelia and Gertrude. Each of them, he felt, had betrayed a bond of love and trust, as in lesser ways Polonius and Rosencrantz and Guildenstern also had. This was the source of his bitterness and derangement (Hughes 52-3). Like other nineteenth-century actors, Irving could not resist the idea that Hamlet loves Ophelia and suffers at her rejection. But worse than that is the thought that she is in league with his enemies. The very beauty that attracts him he regards as a weapon. In a classic Victorian move, Irving wrote that 'Hamlet's mother's beauty had been her snare, had tempted her adulterous lover' (quoted in Hughes 55), thus laying responsibility for the man's crimes, or at least his sexual crimes, upon the woman. So Ophelia's 'snare' produced a struggle between love and duty, those great abstractions weighed in a hundred Victorian novels, but here physicalized in hands 'that hovered over Ophelia' with 'passionate longing' (Terry 140). In the nunnery scene, he came to her 'as a lover whose hitherto untamable passion had wilted before the fiercer tumult which overwhelmed his soul' (L. Irving 246). His sharpest words, 'I loved you not', are uttered, according to Irving, not 'in judgement [but] in an agony of pain' brought on by the 'conviction that he must break with Ophelia, cost what it may' (quoted in Mills 164). The only pretended madness was at the beginning of the scene. Later, he was carried along in a frenzy until, glimpsing the watching Claudius and Polonius, he shifted momentarily to quiet grief at 'Where's your father?' and Ophelia's equivocal answer. This led not to the traditional play-acting for the eavesdroppers' benefit, but to his closest brush with escalating madness, though in some later performances he pulled back the ending of the scene, delivering the final 'To a nunnery, go!' with an 'ironical and mournful expression' (Mills 165) and returning in 1885 (his last assault on the part), to lay a kiss on Ellen Terry's trembling hand.

Terry tells an anecdote that reveals much about Irving's attitude to detail and to control. Irving's leading lady for over twenty years, she consistently subordinated her charm to his intensity. Preparing for Ophelia in 1878, she had in the manner of the time assembled her own costumes; when he asked her about them, she explained that she intended to wear black for the mad scene. 'They generally wear *white*, don't they?' Irving asked quietly, to which she replied that she found black more interesting. The subject was dropped, but the next day, Walter Lacy, Irving's Shakespearean adviser, approached her to ask if she really meant 'to wear black in the mad scene'. 'Why not?' she responded. Lacy's reply has gone down in theatrical history: '*Why not*! My God! Madam, there must be only one black figure in this play, and that's Hamlet!' (Terry 170-1). The incident reveals Irving's need for control over every detail. In relation to his theatre company, he was the classic Victorian father, patriarchal, authoritarian, relentlessly attentive to the details that shape lives.

He accordingly extended the rather cosy domesticity that productions throughout the century had exhibited. If for the Victorian *paterfamilias* a man's home was his castle, Claudius's castle took on all the characteristics of home. Saxon pillars notwithstanding, the atmosphere was firmly domestic – all references to foreign affairs were of course excised, Claudius's role was cut and shaped so that he resembled the typical melodramatic villain more than a head of state, the women were given a sharper emotional role so as to define Hamlet's personal conflicts in purely subjective terms (without any political dimension), and the décor was designed to make the palace seem lived in. The rooms looked 'usable and used', the characters moving through them 'as if they were at home'. Altogether, 'an air of castle domesticity' produced a 'conception of a house blighted by' carnal, bloody, and unnatural acts (Russell 65). No wonder that Max Beerbohm, after years of *Hamlet*s placed in such cosy surroundings, waxed ironical: 'I am too much at home in Elsinore,' he wrote in 1901. 'I seem to have stayed there so often, to have written so many letters on its notepaper' (quoted in Jackson 111).

Terry's lovely, pathetic, and plaintive Ophelia, clad in white in the mad scene, the very picture of a 'pre-Raphaelite saint' (Hughes 68), fit smoothly into this homey patriarchal atmosphere. In preparing for Ophelia, she went to an asylum to observe the inmates, but found most of them 'too theatrical'. One girl, however, sat vacantly, 'waiting, waiting', till suddenly she 'threw up her hands and sped across the room like a swallow' (Terry 169). Struck by the pathos and poignancy of the sudden move, Terry made startling transitions a mark of madness. What she did not realize was that in some ways even this nameless girl was 'theatrical', the forms of her madness dependent on images of feminine prettiness, passivity, and repressed sexuality associated with Ophelia throughout the nineteenth century. In other words, versions of Ophelia both on stage and in a multitude of pictorial images played a key role in determining how 'madness' was itself conceived and in shaping the representation of specifically female forms of derangement – not just in art but in medical literature and in the cultural imagination generally. The sexual element was always just below the surface. The risqué verses of her mad songs, like the bawdy innuendo before the play, and even the lines in Gertrude's elegy about the 'long purples' to which 'liberal shepherds' give a suggestive name, were universally cut. Nevertheless a suppressed eroticism crept into representations of madness both on stage and off; and in the medical literature a link between madness and female sexuality, especially during the troubling period between the onset of adolescence and marriage, became well established, culminating in Freud's studies in hysteria in the 1890s (see Showalter 80-9).

Viewing Gertrude within the same domestic framework tended to turn her into a weak and thoughtless betrayer of family values, a woman lacking the force to be truly evil (her amazement on 'As kill a king?' cleared her of implication in her husband's murder). Still, her betrayal 'was the source of her son's misery' (Hughes 64, 62) and an emotional narrative was invented that made reconciliation with her in the closet scene pivotal to the action and to Hamlet's state of being. The domestic reunion of father, mother, and son was given extra power by two innovations. First, Irving dispensed with both portraits and miniatures for 'the counterfeit presentment of two brothers', instead staring and pointing into the emptiness downstage, imprinting the *imagined* presence of his father in his mother's soul; second, the ghost entered, as in Q1, in 'his night gowne', again adding a domestic touch and, most daringly, Gertrude caught a glimpse of the apparition and screamed (Hughes 65). This brought the original family together and led to the much praised moment when Hamlet laid his head on her lap. Russell's description gives us the full-blown picture of sentimental domesticity: 'A son kneeling where he said his first prayers, to implore the mother who taught him to lisp them to forsake her sin, is an incident worthy of the greatest poet, and only to be fitly enacted by the greatest of tragic actors' (100). That this incident was invented by the tragic actor and not the great poet seems to have gone unnoticed.

The reconciliation produced a new force and direction in Hamlet, marked first by his cool dragging away of Polonius's body, which some observers objected to but which helped to counter the sentimentality of the previous moment. This new determination, no longer troubled by hysteria, led rapidly through a deeply cut Act IV (the first four scenes entirely eliminated) to the dignified stoicism of the graveyard scene and the briskness of the finale. At the grave-side, Irving was melancholy and philosophical in Booth's mode; no leap into the grave marred his new dignity. Later, he moved to the duel with calm belief in 'the divinity that shapes our ends' – a line, usually cut, transposed from early in V.ii to the end of the speech on the special providence that tracks even the fall of a sparrow.

The same mood held through the duel, played sportively, with 'ease and brilliancy' (Russell 102). The exchange of rapiers happened without Hamlet being aware that he had been fatally scratched, and it was not till Laertes's dying confession that rage took over and he rushed to seize the King 'by the collar of his royal robe', ran him through and flung him 'backwards to the earth like carrion' (Russell 102). The aftermath was brief. Hamlet collapsed on the throne, replaying in a tragic key the moment of triumph after the play. His death was private, all the courtiers crowding around the King and Queen, and only the faithful Horatio attending on Hamlet (Hughes 76). The curtain fell on 'The rest is silence', a hush broken only by the mournful sound of a solo oboe. Thus was the final tragedy turned inward, made singular and rare – the unique subjectivity of prince, son, lover, delivered as the very mirror of nineteenth-century personhood.

CHAPTER III

The 1920s: old ways meet the new stagecraft

The matinée idol as Prince: John Barrymore, New York and London, 1922–25

What the audience saw when the curtain rose at the Sam Harris Theatre in New York in 1922 for Arthur Hopkins's production of *Hamlet*, with John Barrymore in the title role, was vastly different from what audiences would have seen twenty years before at the Lyceum. Robert Edmond Jones's startling set, with its dominant central staircase and architectural solidity, its sculptural sense of space, defined the simplicity of the whole production and itself depended on crucial scenic and conceptual changes that had occurred under the aegis of the early twentieth-century *avant garde*. Instead of the multiple sets typical of the nineteenth century, Jones contributed a single, versatile design consisting of a very large archway at upstage centre with six wide and imposing steps leading up to it. Below the steps was a platform about five feet deep which followed the line of the side walls angling outward from the staircase toward the wings, and two steps below the platform was a large central playing area on the stage floor itself. Colourful draperies were stretched across the central platform to create a front playing space for a number of the interior scenes. Through the upper archway could be seen a distant skyscape, and going up and off from just behind the archway were flights of steps on either side. Clearly influenced by the 'new stagecraft' recently set in motion by designers like Gordon Craig and Adolphe Appia, this set announced itself as very much *au courant*. Appia had championed the idea of 'sculptured light' on stage (greatly aided of course by the advent of electricity) and had sought scenic means to render character rather than produce a pictorial backdrop. It was he who discovered the value of actual steps onstage, rather than painted ones on flats, and who realized that the stage floor 'was the key to a new vocabulary of space' (Kennedy, *Looking* 44). Craig, the son of Ellen Terry and an important designer, director, and theorist, regarded *Hamlet* as a 'monodrama' and stressed spiritual simplicity; his designs for an unlikely and much bedevilled production of the play in 1911 at the Moscow Art Theatre (in collaboration with Stanislavsky) were extremely influential, despite the 'brilliant failure' of the production itself (see Senelick). Jones, says Kennedy, 'conducted the New Stagecraft to the new world', his set for *Richard III* in 1920, also for Hopkins and Barrymore, being a decisive step in the process (Kennedy, *Looking* 140-1).

What such sets as Jones's made possible was fast, flexible staging, dispensing with curtains and long breaks between scenes – a return, that is, to something of the Elizabethan manner, though the approach was anything but archaeological. Reformers like William Poel at the beginning of the new century had sought a return to the original stage conditions; but Harley Granville-Barker, who followed Poel, knew that antiquarianism could kill a living theatre. He spoke of the need to 'invent a new hieroglyphic language of scenery' (quoted in Trewin, *English Stage* 56), one that would 'astonish the twentieth century' (Kennedy, *Looking* 75). Along with designer Norman Wilkinson, he had sought to realize that aim with three epoch-making Shakespearean productions at the Savoy Theatre in 1914 (see Kennedy, *Granville-Barker*, and Mazer). World War I brought to a halt some of the feverish artistic experimentation that characterized the period between 1900 and 1914, but, after it was over, survivors throughout Europe began to pick up the pieces and introduced a new, more politicized element into the aesthetic mix. Less ravaged by the war than the continent, England and America were slower to renew the experimental fervour than places like Germany and Poland (by the late 1920s, Berlin had become the *avant garde* capital of Europe), and the major theatres remained strongly pictorial. This may be one reason why the Hopkins/Barrymore production, despite the innovative design, owed as much to the Victorians as it did to the new stagecraft. The production is an index of the kinds of changes that were in the wind; it displayed a double allegiance, to tradition and to a more up-to-date approach. As will be clear from the accounts of the Birmingham Repertory and Old Vic productions in this and the following chapter, the new was only gradually displacing the old.

The use to which the set was put, for example, conflicted in certain ways with the design itself. The scenic scheme should have allowed for a well-paced performance of a much fuller text than was used (Shaw complained of 'the breath-bereaving extremity of cutting out the recorders'), but instead the set, 'with its blend of solid architectural structure and flowing draperies, expressly devised to simplify and expedite the action, did nothing of the sort, but ... tended to delay and confuse it' (J. Ranken Towse, *New York Post*, 17 Nov. 1922). There were curtains between scenes, and rather static tableaux were 'discovered' by the rising curtain. The costumes too contained a hint of contradiction. Barrymore's was 'timeless' (Mills 192): black tights, a long, loose, black doublet open at the neck with a white shirt showing under it, an opulent necklace and belt. Though not the dress of a man of the 1920s, it was not entirely out of line with the times either, given the loose, relaxed, almost casual air it conveyed. But the rest of the costumes tended towards the traditional, with more than a suggestion of the Viking look that had plagued the play for generations.

Barrymore's Hamlet betrayed something of the same kind of caution evident in the direction. Like the thane of Cawdor, nothing in his life became him like the leaving of it: he died splendidly. Such well-arranged deaths take time, but Barrymore was in no hurry. Just before his final line, 'The rest is silence', he 'reach[ed] up with [his] entire body – look[ed] out – taking a long time – say ten seconds' before collapsing, as Horatio, holding him by the waist, laid him gently on the stage floor, head towards the audience. Ten seconds is a very long pause in the theatre. But it wasn't, apparently, enough: the following season, Barrymore stretched the pause to twice its original length.[1] Such pauses, and they were typical of his approach to the part, are no longer in vogue. They slow the play down to a dead march; today's audiences would be twitching in their seats if they had to sit through two or three successive scenes of a production such as Barrymore's. Some spectators then felt the same way.

Barrymore's pauses were not simply an indulgence left over

from nineteenth-century performance practices. They were exceptional even by those outmoded standards. Taking on Hamlet was for him a serious undertaking; he wanted to prove he was more than simply a matinée idol. So he puzzled over every word of the text (truncated as it was despite its four-hour playing time). Critics on both sides of the Atlantic praised his intelligent, even intellectual, line of attack. His concern with, and for, meaning was one factor in his decision to give full weight to every moment. But there were, of course, drawbacks; inveterate playgoer Gordon Crosse remarked in his diary (vol. 9, March 1925) that Barrymore's 'attitude of graceful melancholy' was appealing at first, but all too soon 'the cloud of dullness settled thicker and thicker'. Bernard Shaw thought Barrymore was writing his own non-verbal play within Shakespeare's text, and found it presumptuous. And several London theatre critics, even when they liked the show, noted that, despite the many cuts, the witching hour had struck before they were out on the West End streets.

Barrymore's cerebral approach to the language stemmed from his desire to understand the text *in detail* and to convey that understanding fully. James Agate praised him for manifesting 'the finest possible sense of values in the case of single words'. A line like 'How weary, stale, flat, and unprofitable ...' seemed to emerge from a succession of images 'which come into the mind before the word is coined to represent them'. But this virtue also had a 'corresponding defect': not just 'want of pace ... but of power' as well as an unfortunate tendency to choose a single word (e.g. 'fit and seasoned for his *passage*') for an 'explosion' (*Sunday Times*, 22 Feb. 1925). Hubert Griffiths found this kind of delivery too 'studied', and noted Barrymore's relative lack of 'feeling for a phrase', or a whole poetic line (*Observer*, 22 Feb. 1925). Here then the desire to be naturalistic, to think through the meaning in an almost Stanislavskian vein, came into conflict with the perceived need to give a poetic ring to the line.

As for the pauses, some detracted from the main line of development and seemed inconsistent, a contradictory effect of thinking too precisely on the event. In his mother's closet, pausing before he lunged at Polonius behind the arras made what should be a desperate, impulsive move seem deliberate. ('If Hamlet did not kill Polonius instantly,' asked *The Bookman*, 'would he kill him at all?' – April 1925.) So too in the plot Hamlet develops to devise a play to trap his uncle, a long pause during the soliloquy ('Fie upon 't, foh! / About, my brains!' (II.ii.587-8)), accompanied by a pensive rocking back and forth in his armchair, his head in his hand, made it seem a brand new idea. But Barrymore had taken long pauses earlier when he first beckoned the Player to him and requested 'The Murder of Gonzago', suggesting that he was working out his plan then; this tended to exaggerate what is already an inconsistency in the text. Later in this same sequence, Barrymore used pauses to give the famous curtain lines all the emphasis they could take: 'The play's [extended in soft tremolo] the thing [pause] / Wherein I'll catch the conscience of the King' (II.ii.604-5). This was followed by another five count, Hamlet thinking intensely all the while; then, as Taylor's promptbook describes it, he 'takes "tablet" from [his] bosom, writes in it – thinks – mutters lines – writes – goes out R'. Curtain. End Act I. This was to extend and exaggerate a bit of business made famous by Irving. As Desmond McCarthy remarked, it made 'a splendid curtain, but damn curtains'. He objected to a misplaced 'climax of emotion' which should, he argued, come after the play scene, not here (*New Statesman*, 7 March 1925).

One can sense from these details the kind of studied and self-conscious dramaturgy that typified Barrymore's approach to the role. And the cultural milieu in which he played generally appreciated the, to us, mannered style. When the curtains opened to discover a tableau of the court group already on stage in I.ii, with Hamlet sitting 'thoughtful and melancholy' in an armchair down stage right, there was prolonged applause from the London audience – an indication of the relative con-servatism of that audience, despite the depredations of Granville-Barker and his kind; and Barrymore sat brooding through it (*Daily Express*, 21 Feb. 1925). Sitting and brooding can in fact be seen as key markers of Barrymore's performance, in sombre opposition to the dashing figure he cut in actual life. Never bitter, mad or dangerous, his was a Romantic Hamlet, inspired by Goethe's description of a 'lovely, pure noble and profoundly moral' young man who 'sinks beneath the burden he cannot bear and must not cast away' (quoted by Frederic Dean, *NYT*, 17 Dec. 1922).

At the same time, Barrymore was informal, relaxed, gentlemanly, in the mode of the early 1920s; his manner of speaking could be casual as well as mannered, and much of his behaviour was low-key and gentle. Many reviewers praised him for his naturalism, though if we were to see him today we would find his performance formal and artificial.[2] He adopted the interpersonal style of a man of his generation (born in 1882, he was forty when he first played Hamlet); and he appropriated too some of the democratic spirit of his American upbringing, setting Hamlet more in line with an attainable ideal rather than portraying him as an inaccessible aristocrat. The company he formed around himself was not designed to show off the master's talents at others', and the audience's, expense – many of the critics commented on the strength of the whole company, and several remarks in Lark Taylor's promptbooks indicate a camaraderie and ease of fellowship in the company that was breezy and democratic rather than rigid and hierarchical. Proud of but at the same time self-conscious about his Americanism, he was very nervous about appearing in London, Shakespeare's own city, in *Hamlet*. He worked hard to eliminate all traces of an American accent, but his wild impetuosity, fuelled by Dom Perignon, sometimes caught his fellow actors off guard.[3]

In movement, Barrymore was relaxed, athletic, casual. He sat through several of the soliloquies, keeping his gestures simple. He put his arm around the Player when instructing him and his troupe on the art of acting; he broke away from his effusive praise to Horatio (III.ii) with a 'half-reluctant shyness' that established both his sensitivity to his friend and his masculine embarrassment at showing it; he sat quietly beside Ophelia's grave, 'with Yorick's skull between his hands, speaking perfectly ... the great prose passage' with a kind of 'measured and quaint melancholy' (McCarthy). In fact, though he moved throughout 'with graceful agility', McCarthy thought him at his best 'when seated', during the soliloquies, or 'fingering his inky cloak while the King and Queen endeavour to persuade him to put off that all-too-pointed mourning'. But this simple grace was punctuated at times with a violent, convulsive movement, such as his famous ten-foot leap to the King at the end, which reminded several critics of Douglas Fairbanks and other swashbucklers of the silent screen. Fairbanks had in fact coached Barrymore during the New York rehearsals of the duel scene.

1 John Barrymore as Hamlet and Fay Compton as Ophelia (1925) in a romantic moment, showing his famous profile and loose 'timeless' costume, and her traditional Viking look.

The treatment of the women in the production marked something of an advance over the rather insipid Gertrudes and aggressively wistful Ophelias that had been the tradition for so long. It is difficult at this distance to get a sense of how these roles were played – the records (reviews, promptbooks etc.) tend to favour the lead actor and concentrate on the main character. The conventional praise of Constance Collier's Gertrude in almost all the British reviews tells us little about what she actually did or how she understood the part. *The Times* commented that she 'accounted at sight for the uxoriousness of Claudius' (20 Feb. 1925), but this emphasis on her decorativeness ignores her character. Barrymore's own praise for her, 'You have invested this character with sensuous beauty, enhanced by a certain full-blown provocativeness which I feel certain is exactly what Shakespeare meant' (*Confessions*, n.p.), gives us a hint, but we lack details. From the New York promptbook, we note Gertrude occasionally restraining or tempering her husband's tendency to bully – as when, in the midst of his hectoring Hamlet ("'tis unmanly grief, / It shows a will most incorrect to heaven ...' (I.ii.94-5)), she put her hand on his arm and in response he again became quiet and smiling. Apparently her provocativeness gave her a certain power, but, as Stark Young wrote of Blanche Yurka, who played the part in New York, she conveyed 'the loose quality in this woman that subjected her to the King' (*New Republic*, 6 Dec., 1922), a comment that reveals a classic male bias. Later, when Polonius began to speak of Hamlet's lunacy, she again laid her hand on Claudius's arm, very solicitous and perhaps a bit guilty in her admission that the source must be 'his father's death and our o'erhasty marriage'. Such little moments hint at an interior life – her awareness that her love for her husband causes her son grief, her dilemma about how to fulfil the double and contradictory demand to please both of them. Later in the play, when the text offers the actor interesting opportunities for a more deeply rendered characterization, her role suffered the traditional, cruel cuts. The whole of IV.i, for example, the aftermath of the closet scene, disappeared. In it, the actor has the chance to convey a growing alienation from her husband, an uncertainty about how to assess the wild behaviour of her son that she has just witnessed, or a glimpse of her own guilty complicity in the death of her first husband (even though, presumably, she has not known all the 'facts'). Is she protecting Hamlet or does she truly think him 'mad as the sea and wind'? There are a number of ways to approach the scene, but with it gone the character is robbed of depth. So also, just at the onset of Ophelia's mad scene, Gertrude has a short soliloquy (IV.v,17-20) that gives us another glimpse of her guilty conscience, a feature of her character that producers and lead players, in their concentration on Hamlet, regarded as obtrusive. Gertrude does not want to see or speak to Ophelia – she feels implicated somehow, and Ophelia's presence seems to thrust the Queen's glance back at herself as in a mirror. And so, the speech disappeared; traditional Gertrudes were not to be too complicated. Blanche Yurka was worried that it was 'hardly worth her capabilities' and that playing it might 'hurt her as a leading woman' (Taylor, 'My Season' 3). Although 'regal [and] beautiful' in her flowing red gowns, she could, thought Taylor, 'have done it better if she had had a finer appreciation of the part' (83), a comment that suggests a superficiality to some extent forced upon her by the diminution of the role. Barrymore's unkindest cut of all was the excision of Gertrude's long and tender description of Ophelia's death – something of an aria, to be sure, but important in that it cements the sympathetic connection between the only two women in this oppressively male-dominant court.

The closet scene, which provides the Queen with plenty to go on even with the many traditional cuts, was controversial. Several critics detected Freudian overtones in the excessive tenderness with which Barrymore's Hamlet approached his mother, and in the several passionate embraces that punctuated the scene. His harshest words to her were spoken in a kind of trance, just before the Ghost's entry, when he was enveloped in the eerie light that had accompanied the Ghost's earlier appearances, so that he was, presumably, possessed by the angry spirit of his jealous father. He went rigid, body trembling, voice hoarse, gave a loud gasp and fell to his knees.[4] The Ghost here, as he was throughout the original production, was audible only, unseen except for the greenish light (Furness, 'The Hamlet' 230); but he seemed to take up a station off right where Hamlet's eyes came to fix upon him, allowing Barrymore to play the sequence with his famous profile etched against the black and gold screen on the platform behind. After the Ghost's departure, Gertrude's 'what shall I do?' was isolated by cuts so that it became an unanswered quandary, and she seemed lost. Hamlet had recovered some of his hard intellectual edge, facilitated by the surprising decision to retain his cynical lines about the dead Polonius (traditionally cut): 'I'll lug the guts into the neighbour room ... This counsellor / Is now most still, most secret, and most grave, / Who was in life a foolish, prating knave' (III.iv.212-15). He even threw in a final 'Bah!' as he bent over the body. But the pause between 'Good night' and 'mother', his final line in the scene, suggested to some that he was in the end asking for forgiveness and showing himself the 'gentle Prince' (*Spectator*, 28 Feb. 1925). Gertrude, meanwhile, was left alone, broken by a long stabbing sigh as she started out the other way.

There was then to be some sympathy for this woman of 'sensuous beauty', clad in brilliant red throughout, caught in a trap not of her own making, a simple woman really, plagued by grief but not by guilt. Her death, praised by some as seeming inevitable rather than arbitrary, was handled naturalistically: she drank from the bitter cup centre stage, gave it back to the hovering Osric, wiped her son's brow as he knelt in front of her and returned to her bench to watch the next bout. When the furious fight between Laertes and Hamlet ensued, she started up as if to prevent it, as she had done by Ophelia's graveside, but sat down again rather abruptly, struggled to keep from falling, rose briefly for 'The drink, the drink ...' and then fell to the stage, to be almost forgotten in the frantic action that followed. So, all in all, there was sympathy, pathos even, but something less than the full humanity or interiority that can be gleaned from a fuller text and that most recent actors have sought to give her. In that sense, the representation of her as a woman lagged behind the changes in the cultural role of women evident, for example, in the pre-war suffragette movement and its continuation into the 1920s.

Ophelia, as played at least by Fay Compton in London, 'combine[d] virginal charm and wistfulness to a degree which I am sure has never been approximated', as Barrymore said after the closing. He thought her the 'most adorable Ophelia since ... Ellen Terry' (*Confessions*), and most of the reviews confirm this sense. The London *Star* called her a 'Burne-Jones picture of girlish beauty and innocence' (20 Feb. 1925). Others pronounced her especially fine in the earlier scenes, but less effective when mad; 'sweetness', said Ivor Brown, 'is not an ordinary attribute of lunacy' (*Manchester Guardian*, 20 Feb.). Herbert Farjeon, however, thought her 'imaginary flowers [she wore a wreath of flowers in her hair but passed out none] much more moving than the so-obviously-real or artificial' ones normally used

(*Sphere*, 7 March). Whatever the reaction, it was clear (and the photographs confirm it) that her playing was traditionally soft and wistful – she had a 'child's importunacy' (Agate, *Sunday Times*, 22 Feb.). The critics' male appreciation makes it clear that she was no 'new woman', though a few scattered critical notes do suggest possibilities of depth. One writer speaks of her 'fine intellect' (A.E.M. in *Evening News*, 20 Feb.) and the *Sunday Express* (22 Feb.) mentions that she was 'obviously in love with the Prince', which added colour to her broken-hearted reactions to his rejection of her ('I loved you not') or his cynical comment on the briefness of 'woman's love'. But her story remained firmly in the background, and her characterization unchallenging.

The promptbook reveals a certain edge in the mad scene as played by Rosalind Fuller in New York. Coquettishness, a misplaced provocative sexiness, seems to have been a key ingredient in her interpretation; she played up to the men on stage. She sang her St Valentine's song 'very gaily', approached the King boldly when he reached out to her, and directed her next verse to him: 'Young men will do 't if they come to 't, / By Cock, they are to blame' (IV.v.60-1). She spoke pointedly to the Queen on 'You promis'd me to wed', and moved steadily toward Laertes as he expressed his pain at seeing her so distraught, 'ogling' him, coming up uncomfortably close and offering him the rosemary. Alternately coquettish and vacant, glaring at the King when she spoke of her father, she seemed volatile and sexually charged as well as innocent. Lark Taylor remarks on 'a certain lewd quality in the mad scene' which he finds offensive but which Barrymore and director Arthur Hopkins very much liked ('My Season' 3). Stark Young noted 'a hint of that last betrayal that insanity brings, indecency', which he thought 'sharpened the effect of madness' (*New Republic*, 6 Dec. 1922). The vague priggishness and male protectiveness implicit in comments like Young's or Taylor's, set beside the clear approval of Barrymore and Hopkins, perhaps registers some of the ambivalence felt towards the emergent shifts in the perception of women's freedom and sexuality, shortly to be reflected in the flapper skirts and provocative dances that typify for us 'the twenties'. In any case, innocent sexiness, whether in nineteenth-century depictions of mad Ophelias or young girls such as Dodgson's Alice, or in the newer guise glamorized by Hollywood, was of course an image designed for male consumption.

During the preparations for the intrigue against Hamlet (III.i), Ophelia stood still and quiet on the platform centre, while Rosencrantz and Guildenstern bowed and scraped and the Queen moved solicitously to her. As king and courtiers left the stage, Ophelia lingered slightly before following the others out. The stage was empty for several seconds before Barrymore entered through the curtain that was draped across the upper arch for the various interior scenes (a scenic choice that to some degree undid the radical thrust of Jones's single set). He came pensively down the stairs and sat in his armchair downstage for the 'To be or not to be' soliloquy, which he delivered quietly, in the sharply intellectual vein that marked much of his performance. After 'And lose the name of action' (III.i.87), he permitted himself a long pause and a sigh, glancing casually off right where he espied Ophelia advancing tentatively towards him: 'Nymph, in thy orisons / Be all my sins rememb'red.' Her 'redelivery' of the string of beads from around her neck prompted him more to sadness than to anger. Throughout the scene, he was quiet, sensitive, and intense – more the lover than the outraged or bitter Prince. As such, he was in the tradition of Kean and Booth. Several critics felt that this Romantic approach repressed a crucial dimension of the character. Desmond McCarthy, for example, argued that Barrymore generally missed Hamlet's dark, acerbic ambivalence: 'Where Mr. Barrymore's interpretation failed throughout was in conveying Hamlet's bitter-gay, intellectual exhilaration, which is the desperate reaction of a thinking, sensitive nature against life's humiliations' (*New Statesman*, 7 March 1925).

Shaw complained that Barrymore had turned Hamlet and Ophelia into Romeo and Juliet, a tendency noticeable not only in the restraint of the nunnery scene and his clutching of Ophelia's beloved hand before he turned to go, but in the aftermath as well. Ophelia spoke her soliloquy after Hamlet's exit as a record of blasted love, and her entrance in the play scene disturbed Hamlet's attempt at a well-orchestrated antic disposition. She came in alone, a minute or two after the rest of the court, interrupting Hamlet's 'Be the players ready?' He started, took a three-second pause and began again. She crossed the stage and sat on a bench below the wide staircase, where

Hamlet immediately joined her ('Here's metal more attractive'), reclining on a purple rug at her feet in the traditional pose. Hamlet's teasing, perhaps bitter, obscenities following this were, as they always had been, cut, and the show began.

The play was staged in a unique way, the Player-king and Player-queen miming their parts on the top platform in the centre of the archway, using exaggerated gestures, very formal and ritualistic, while the first and second Players, stationed on the stairs at the side, declaimed the lines 'in a sort of chant' (promptbook). The separation of the words from the action may have given the sequence an *avant garde* flavour, a bit like the Ballet Russe (the actor who played Lucianus, Vadim Uraneff, was a Russian mime), while its obvious stylization marked it off clearly from the (by comparison) naturalistic casualness of most of the performance. Slightly oriental flute music accompanied the interlude, becoming fast and wild for the poisoner (mimed by Uraneff as the First Player spoke his portentous lines), who was made up as a caricature of Claudius, with white face, red circles under the eyes, and black lips, reminiscent, according to Taylor, of a Chinese mask.

Hamlet's interruptions of this ornately pictorial scene were sharp and sarcastic. Lounging slightly right of centre on his rug, he launched a provocative assault on Claudius, who was regally enthroned on the other side. This position meant that the court faced upstage to watch the play, but it allowed a three quarter profile of Barrymore as he turned to attack the King; and he wisely refrained from the traditional business of slithering across the stage in an ecstasy of recrimination. The King's apprehensive question, 'What do you call the play?' produced a long silence – the music had stopped, the Player-king was lying across the arch, his head supported in his hand, and the whole court was waiting. Barrymore stretched the pause from ten to twenty seconds, staring at Claudius all the while, before suddenly sitting up and barking, 'The Mouse-trap'. Then, as Lucianus poured the poison into Gonzago's ear, Hamlet, in a swashbuckling display of athletic power, suddenly leapt up and across the stage to whisper *his* poison in his uncle's ear: 'You shall see anon [very long pause] how the murtherer gets the love of Gonzago's wife' (III.ii.263-4). The King, utterly undone, shrieked in terror and Hamlet leapt again to stage centre as pandemonium broke out, with everyone speaking at once and moving quickly to the exits. With such proof, there was no doubt about Claudius's guilt; and Hamlet's elation, expressed physically ('See him gyrate like a top in the play scene!' (*The Times*, 20 Feb. 1925)), was clearly justified.

After this, the recorder scene with Rosencrantz and Guildenstern was cut (although the promptbooks reveal some reluctance about this, the scene being reinstated at one point and then cut again), so that the action moved swiftly to an interpolated, and sentimental, farewell to Horatio just before Hamlet departs for his mother's closet. Then there was another jump to the King's soliloquy ('O, my offence is rank …'). So here was Hamlet's chance for revenge, coming hot on the heels of the proof he had sought and, in this production, very clearly gained. But, as we know, he hesitates. His speech, 'Now might I do it pat', has been variously interpreted – as an excuse for inaction or as a genuine expression of a bitter desire to send his enemy to hell. Barrymore took the latter course (he was not uniformly gentle), as was probably inevitable given the considerable paring down of the whole sequence together with the emphasis on the King's obvious guilt and Hamlet's physical elation. The scene was staged very simply, a tab curtain with images of saints on it through which the King, and then Hamlet, entered: 'Here are the uplifted hands, there the sword drawn. Here, sick conscience, power, and tormented ambition; there, the torture of conflicting thoughts, the irony, the resolution. Two bodies and their relation to each other … the essential drama … No tricks, no plausible business, no palace chapel. And no tradition' (Stark Young, *New Republic*, 6 Dec. 1922). In his reading, Barrymore made it clear that he was serious about wanting to send his uncle's soul to hell but managed at the same time to hold on to audience sympathy. A delicious leer on 'incestuous pleasure' and a taunting and gleeful tone at the end – 'that his soul may be as damn'd and black / As hell [pause] whereto it goes' (with a raised eyebrow and almost child-like delight in imagining such an appropriate end for the wickedest of men) – sealed the reading, significantly reducing the threat of moral taint by bringing us to share his glee (III.iii.94-5).[5]

The same inclination to avoid a potentially ugly side of Hamlet produced in the next scene that 'possession' by his father's spirit already described, in which his lurid attack on his mother ('Nay, but to live / In the rank sweat of an enseamed bed, / ... honeying and making love / Over the nasty sty!' (III.iv.92-3)) was translated into the voice of her understandably jealous husband. Here perhaps was one reason for the Ghost's invisibility throughout the production in its first season, i.e., to suggest an occult power to penetrate Hamlet's soul and to throw the emphasis on Hamlet's psychological state.[6] The Ghost's injunctions thus became potentially more ambiguous and unsettling than they traditionally had been, more implicated in the puzzle of contradictory interpretations that are the mark of a modern understanding of the play. The Ghost was represented by a vague greenish light on the backdrop, visible through the large central arch. During the initial colloquy with Hamlet, it flickered and faded, then formed into a brief, spectral image of an armoured king, the whole vision being accompanied by the 'moaning and whissing of the wind' (promptbook), while the voice came from off stage. The effect on Hamlet was devastating. Kneeling through the Ghost's revelations, he fell on his face on 'Remember me', as the last light faded away. Despite his efforts to rise, his sinews were so unstrung that they refused to 'bear [him] stiffly up', and he collapsed again. Only near the end of his speech ('O villain, villain ...') did he regain his physical powers and leap energetically to his feet. His behaviour with the guards as they rushed in was the closest he came in the whole production to losing his grip, as he darted around in great agitation, recovering occasionally to make light of his hysteria.

Traditionally, the final scene (V.ii) had begun at line 75: 'But I am very sorry, good Horatio, / That to Laertes I forgot myself', leaving out the tough-minded and unsympathetic lines about Hamlet's dispatch of Rosencrantz and Guildenstern. This of course served to enhance Hamlet's gentlemanly and gracious princeliness, but suppressed his more dangerous and aggressive side. Barrymore began the scene twenty lines earlier, at 'So Guildenstern and Rosencrantz go to it', retaining some of Hamlet's hard remorselessness, and also cut the lines referring to his genuine contrition about 'forgetting himself' with Laertes. As well, much more of the sarcastic interchange with Osric was kept than usual; the end result of these adjustments was a rather harsher picture of Hamlet than usual, one consistent with his attitude in the 'prayer scene', but somewhat at odds with the pains Barrymore had elsewhere taken to soften the character. The finale, in emphasizing the athletic and naturalistic, did not follow up on these darker suggestions, though it strove to augment the portrait of the sweet and tender prince of tradition with physical grace and vigour.

An interweaving of formality and naturalism characterized the duel and its aftermath. The preliminaries were ceremonial and symmetrical, but cutting across this mode was Barrymore's relaxed testing of the foils, which he whipped about in a showy way, bending the point of one on the stage to try its resilience. The fight itself was often quite violent and unpredictable, Barrymore's famous stage spontaneity sometimes causing unforeseen damage to a series of unfortunate actors playing Laertes. At the moment when Laertes 'hits' Hamlet, Barrymore exclaimed loudly, then laughed – but feeling his breast with his hand and seeing blood on it, the realization that he had been betrayed suddenly dawned. Staring hard at Laertes, who avoided his eye, Barrymore moved to furious attack, gained possession of the unbated sword and then ostentatiously felt the point, letting out another triumphant exclamation and rounding on his guilty opponent. The ritualized formality had by now disappeared, and the climax was marked by Hamlet's great leap to the King, his violent stabbing and thrusting of the poison to his adversary's lips, while all around the court scattered to the exits, crying out 'Treason'.

The formal entry of Fortinbras, so often cut in the past, restored order. At first Fortinbras entered from the side, but after the opening performance this was changed to a much grander entrance through the central archway, announced by a trumpet blast and preceded by several captains who stationed themselves on the stairs. Most of the final forty-five lines were cut (the English ambassadors, Horatio's lines about 'carnal, bloody and unnatural acts', and Fortinbras's own claiming of the Danish throne), leaving only a few words of explanation and the eulogy over Hamlet's dead body. Hoisted aloft by the four captains, Hamlet was carried up the stairs in the classic pose, his head downstage and flung back toward the audience. A signal from Fortinbras led to a long flourish of trumpets, three loud solemn drumbeats and a gradual fading of the lights, as Hamlet was borne off through the archway, leaving an uncertain Osric kneeling by the dead Queen and a grieving

Horatio bent over a table with his back to the audience and head on his arms.

This moving tableau with its strategic blend of the ceremonial and the personal registers the oppositions dramatized and negotiated by this powerfully influential production. Both 'traditional' and 'modern', it helped to pave the way for some of the less obviously sweet, sane and gracious Hamlets, such as those of the young Gielgud and Olivier. But there were more daring experiments in the wings, even as Barrymore's production was charming the West End. And some audience members were clearly looking forward to the change. The critic for *The Spectator*, reviewing Barrymore, argued that there is a strong case for quite a different conception of the hero, a dark and violent Hamlet who attacks Ophelia and Laertes with bitterness (Barrymore, like Booth, had refused to leap into the grave to fight Laertes), tells lies, dispatches Rosencrantz and Guildenstern without compunction, and plunges at times into madness. He predicted that this 'immoral' Hamlet, a prey to 'excitements of the blood', would soon make an appearance: 'Some day an up-to-date actor will give us the psychoanalyst's Hamlet' (28 Feb. 1925). He would not have to wait long. In November of that very year, the first modern-dress Hamlet walked on to a London stage and displayed just that rebellious, bawdy-minded and rasping quality that many had found wanting in Barrymore's celebrated reading.

Hamlet in plus-fours: Birmingham Repertory Theatre, 1925

No production of *Hamlet* seems to have received as much advance publicity as that staged by Barry Jackson and H. K. Ayliff at the Kingsway Theatre in London in 1925.[7] Some measure of the cultural importance of the play and the traditions of its performance can be gained from the newspaper articles announcing the shocking and rumour-laden details of this '*Hamlet* in plus-fours'. Reports from Ottawa and Toronto, New York and Boston, Cape Town and Bombay, as well as from nearly every city and town in the UK, outlined the horrifying, if also titillating, 'facts'. Hamlet was to appear in the dress of the day; morning coats, plus-fours, flapper dresses, bobbed hair, revolvers and motor cars were to make their painful Shakespearean debut on the stage of the Kingsway Theatre.

(The fact that the Birmingham Repertory Theatre under Jackson had already staged a modern-dress *Cymbeline* was hardly noticed.) Debate centred on the value and significance of theatrical tradition, the relation between old verse and new design, the question of the modernity of Shakespeare. Jackson himself entered the fray with an article in a Birmingham Repertory Theatre newsletter that was later reprinted (in reduced form) in the London *Daily Mail* (6 Aug.) and in the performance programme. He argued that traditional costumes put a 'veil' between audience and play, abetting the 'sublime unnaturalness' of the verse, and leading as often as not to bewilderment or boredom. He wanted to break away from the feeling of 'superstitious awe' that traditional production generates in the spectator and replace it with an 'understanding that he has been witnessing a real conflict of credible human beings'. Dedicated as Jackson had been for years to the new stagecraft (he was thoroughly familiar with the theories of Gordon Craig), and influenced as he was by the modern style of Shakespearean production and verse-speaking inaugurated by William Poel and Granville-Barker, this foray into naturalism was less a departure than it might have seemed. But the press seized on the shock of the clothing, even though some moderate voices reminded readers that in Garrick's day, as in Burbage's, it was normal for Shakespeare's characters to be garbed in contemporary finery.

In the event, most of those who came to scoff stayed to applaud. Even those who regretted a diminution in the poetic dimension of the text recognized that the play succeeded powerfully as drama. This was partly because the characters other than Hamlet tended to grow in stature and interest when thrust into a modern setting. They became recognizable and rounded, each with a separate life, like characters in a Shaw or Ibsen play. One critic went so far as to declare that 'Hamlet is not the principal figure in his own play' (Griffiths 61). So too the plot, hurried along by a series of cuts designed to reduce the philosophical, meditative aspects of the text and by a very quick pace, was given the dash and bite of a modern thriller (Cochrane 132).

The sheer speed provided the most telling contrast with Barrymore. Although Ayliff's text was considerably longer, the show itself was almost an hour shorter, lasting for just over

2 Polonius in winged collar and three-piece suit (A. Bromley-Davenport) counsels Ophelia (Muriel Hewitt), her hair in 'winkles' and
wearing a 'parchment coloured crêpe-de-Chine' dress with a 'box
pleated skirt' in the Birmingham Repertory's modern dress production that shook London in 1925.

three hours including a twelve-minute interval (Cochrane 129).
The set, while less obviously 'new' than Jones's spectacular
staircase and archway, was simple and uncluttered, enabling
rapid shifts and fluid movement. The main design feature was
a raised rostrum stretching across the middle of the stage with
two steps leading up to it, framed by a false proscenium. At the
back there was a painted drop representing a wall of the palace,

with two large windows, and in front was a wide playing area fitted with different items of furniture for different scenes. Curtains behind the false proscenium defined different spaces for various 'front' scenes (rather in the Victorian manner); the graveyard, for example, was represented by a curtain with tombs, a Danish cross, and an obelisk painted on it. The designer, Paul Shelving, was a gifted scene painter, less interested in architectural monumentality than in subtle coloration. But the hint of traditional style in the look of the set did not extend to its use; pace and continuity of action were the keynotes. And the costumes, also designed by Shelving, distracted attention from any remnants of tradition that may have remained in the rest of the visual scheme.

The chief effect of the modern costumes was not in the end to shock the audience, but rather to free the actors. Ordinary clothes made it difficult to attitudinize, to adopt false postures and stereotyped responses; above all they encouraged swift speech and naturalistic manners. And, given the importance of sign and gesture in the theatre, different manners tended to create different characters. Frank Vosper, who played Claudius, described this process in an article published during the London run. His first appearance each night was, he says, nerve-wracking: he knew that the audience, after a dark opening scene with a faintly luminescent ghost (the modern costumes only vaguely visible), was waiting for the jolt of the court scene. And it was a jolt, with the King and courtiers in tails, the Queen in a dazzling short dress with a 'fish-tail train' and Hamlet in a 'dark lounge suit and soft collar' hunched in the foreground (Anne Temple, *Glasgow Bulletin*, 26 Aug.). Vosper knew he had nothing to fall back on. He lacked 'the reassurance of robes', the 'decorative' if also 'pompous and theatrical' presence conferred by costume. But he recognized that his panic was actually liberating – that the decorativeness that he nostalgically hankered after is really a hindrance. He felt 'swamped' in traditional dress, while in dinner jacket or tails he can appear 'fairly soigné', attractive enough to account for Gertrude's 'o'erhasty marriage' and human enough to feel 'undisguised desire' for her (Vosper, *Theatre World*; J.T.G., *Sketch*, 2 Sept.). In another example, he remarks that the siphon bottle from which he added a squirt of soda to his tumbler of whisky after the trauma of the play scene gave him a naturalistic grip on the moment that the traditional paper maché goblet smelling of gold paint inhibited.

The reviews comment endlessly on the white spats, the monocles, the ubiquitous cigarettes, the gravedigger's bowler hat, the 'Oxford bags' (a much derided type of very loose trousers) worn by Osric and Laertes, Laertes' drawn revolver, Ophelia's short, flimsy black dress in the mad scene, the Queen's 'shingled' hair and her rich negligée in the closet scene, with its 'wide square sleeves' and its 'beautiful sunburn-tinted folds' (*Manchester Weekly Guardian*, 27 Aug.). There was a bridge game at the beginning of II.ii, dance music (the 'Charleston') behind Hamlet's first soliloquy, and occasional sounds of motor cars 'off'. Hamlet smoked through the 'How all occasions' soliloquy and confronted Claudius in the fourth act in his dress shirt with black tie undone, while a mad Ophelia fitted jazz dance steps to her traditional ballad tunes. The Players arrived resplendent in the latest fashion: the women in cloche hats and fur-trimmed coats, the first player in a suave golfing outfit. They performed the play scene as an obvious contrast to the world they inhabited in 'reality' – in traditional costume and in front of a highly Romantic painted backdrop.

Though all this may be seen as but the trappings and the suits of show, taken together such choices do represent both a challenge to tradition and a real change. Many of the ideas about the play's performance that are now commonplace can be traced back to this remarkable production: Claudius as 'well-groomed and foxily diplomatic' (Ivor Brown, *Saturday Review*, 29 Aug.) and even rather charming, Polonius as shrewd and politic, Ophelia as sexually explosive in her mad scene, and Hamlet in particular with an ugly, violent streak, the 'rebel against home-life' common in the drama of the period, a 'prose Hamlet of petulant snarl and unbridled jest' (Brown, *Manchester Guardian*, 26 Aug.). Equally, the emphasis on the close family unit when Polonius and Ophelia bid farewell to Laertes (I.iii), the establishment of a loving and physical relationship between Claudius and Gertrude that then gradually deteriorates, and the evocation of a domestic atmosphere in the smooth running of the court (rather than a hieratic and ceremonial one) have all been seen many times since, as have smaller touches such as the ubiquitous whisky bottle or the sharp, sexual aggression against Ophelia before the play-within.

Most of all it was the deliberate rejection of Romanticism that ultimately seemed the most modern. One of the keys to the anti-Romantic presentation was to reduce Hamlet's importance, both his stature and his appeal, turning him into one of a group of concerned participants. Of the several means by which this was effected, the chief one was the actor himself, Colin Keith-Johnston. He had acted mostly in contemporary plays, and his delivery was naturalistic, staccato, unpoetic. He had 'just that caddishness born of despair that the romantic Hamlets dare not present'. 'Loose-tongued' and 'bawdy-minded' (*Saturday Review*, 29 Aug.), he was young, disenchanted, angular; certainly not princely in the usual sense, but 'democratic' and intellectual (*Sketch* , J.T.G., 2 Sept.). Unlike Barrymore and practically every other actor before him, he simply did not dominate the scene. This marked a decisive break with the actor manager tradition that had controlled production of the play in Britain since Garrick's time. Here was a Hamlet who was neither famous nor old, not the one luminary in a company of nonentities, but simply an actor among many. Several reviewers praised his spontaneity – his gift for speaking complex speeches 'as though they had but instantly come into his head' (Edith Shakleton, *Evening Standard*, 26 Aug.). Though some complained that Hamlet had been turned into Horatio, making it impossible to plumb the depths of the play's mystery (John Shand, *New Statesman*, 5 Sept.), most felt that Keith-Johnston's anti-Romantic sharpness gave his portrayal a vitality and a lively ironic edge which compensated for the loss of grace. Even a characteristic 'little turn inward of his right foot' could produce an effect of moodiness and dejection (Temple, *Glasgow Bulletin*). All this helped to produce a main character with whom the largely young audience could readily identify, even if he was not always completely admirable.

This new Hamlet was announced immediately by the way Keith-Johnston handled his very first line. 'A little more than kin, and less than kind' (I.ii.65) had always been spoken as a pained aside. Here however Hamlet addressed the King directly and boldly. The contest of 'mighty opposites' was put unhesitatingly into motion. 'Youthful defiance' (*Spectator*, 5 Sept.) was the initial mark of the performance, and if this led to some inconsistency in the later capitulation to his mother's wishes and his uncle's plans, it was an inconsistency that many in the audience understood. With his mother, as with Ophelia, he was brutal; he pulled her about the stage in the 'closet' scene, and lunged violently at Polonius with a sword that he had drawn from a ceremonial suit of armour at the side. (The ingenuity of this was duly noted, lending support to the view that Gordon Crosse expressed in his notebooks, that there was at times a real danger of the audience attending more closely to the cleverness deployed to meet the challenge of modernization than to the play itself.) With Ophelia in the nunnery scene, Keith-Johnston was harsh and bitter one moment, erotically compelled the next. At one point, he dragged her down some steps, then suddenly pulled her into an embrace, his anger and desire all twined together.

Dressing Hamlet in both the clothes and the feelings of the day made him recognizably ordinary, and thus helped to move his dilemmas and crises into the arena of the audience's actual concerns, reducing his remoteness. The same process enhanced the portrayal of several other characters, notably Laertes. Instead of a mere unthinking foil to Hamlet as he often is, Laertes here (Robert Holmes) became someone to care about; he and Ophelia had an affectionate relationship which made his brotherly lecture about Hamlet's dangerous affections (I.iii) friendly rather than nasty, as it sometimes is; while he spoke he was busy addressing a luggage label to Paris, and she kissed him after he had finished. When in turn Polonius delivered his advice to Laertes, sister and brother stood close together, and all three laughed when Polonius allowed that the 'apparel oft proclaims the man' (and the audience no doubt joined in). The atmosphere was cosy, domestic, happy. When Laertes returned much later to revenge his father's death, his feelings were immediately understandable; and so his angry attack on Claudius was serious and strong, complete with lots of shouting (building offstage as Claudius spoke of sorrows), sounds of breaking glass, some shots, and then a crashing entrance. Judicious cutting made the scene brisk and exciting and set up a vivid contrast with Laertes' quiet and pained response to his sister's madness which follows directly. He watched her intently during the flower-giving episode, as she slipped the rosemary into his hand and the pansy into his buttonhole. She flitted away but returned to give him the daisy. 'Do you see this, O God?' was quiet but intense as he sat unmoving until Claudius, having led the Queen off and come back, touched him on the shoulder, making him jump. After the graveyard scene, Claudius snatched a moment to beckon Laertes to him for more whispered plotting, but the scene ended with Laertes left alone on stage, again quiet and thoughtful, before the black curtain came down that would form the backdrop for the succeeding sequence between Hamlet and Horatio. So the desire for revenge that motivated Laertes through this section was given a deep emotional source, linking it to Hamlet's, and his basic decency was emphasized at the end when he seemed reluctant to continue with the plot – speaking 'And yet it is almost against my conscience' directly to the King instead of as an aside. His own death thus became in itself a minor tragedy, throwing light on Hamlet's, and extending the range of interest in the play beyond the main character.

There was as well the treatment of the King and Queen to broaden audience interest and deflect it from concentration on Hamlet alone. As I noted earlier, their relationship had a markedly erotic element in it from the outset, certainly easier to play, and more meaningful to an audience, in Noel Coward duds than in Viking furs. There was, for example, a moment early on, just as the plotting to decipher Hamlet's 'madness' was getting into gear, that nicely combined the sexual with the genuine care and concern that characterized their relations early in the play. Gertrude, who had been playing bridge with a dowager and the court chaplain, went to her husband for a brief private colloquy. The ambassadors had been called in, footmen were clearing the bridge table and trays of coffee, readying the chamber for official business. With Polonius out of the room, the two conferred about Hamlet's distemper (II.ii.54-8), Claudius seemingly as concerned as his wife, and then they came together in an embrace and a kiss. As the official visitors entered, she walked slowly back upstage and sat by a window, her back to the proceedings, seemingly in a reverie, only returning downstage again after they left, eager to discuss her son's suffering.

A parallel, but contrasting, moment later on underlined the change in the relationship between King and Queen. After the 'closet' scene (a misnomer here since there was no 'closet'), the Queen collapsed sobbing on the couch at centre stage, and Claudius entered to her. (This is the beginning of IV.i in the text, a scene cut by both Barrymore and Irving but which, as I said above, offers scope to Gertrude, something Ayliff and Dorothy Massingham, who played the part, were quick to take advantage of.) Claudius reached out to touch her, but she shrank away from his hand, and afterwards, in an unscripted exit, she slowly followed Rosencrantz and Guildenstern out when they were sent to search for Hamlet, refusing to wait for her dejected husband. Claudius sat heavily on the couch and lit a cigarette, mulling over his new situation: 'How dangerous is it that this man goes loose ...' (lines from the beginning of IV.iii, his speech to Gertrude at the end of IV.i and the whole of IV.ii having been cut). This had the effect of isolating Claudius, of speeding up the conspiracy against Hamlet, and of screening Gertrude from any involvement in what was to happen to Hamlet. For a moment after Ophelia's death, and Gertrude's great speech describing it, the Queen seemed to yearn for the physical comfort of her husband's presence, and leaned her head on his shoulder. But in the final sequence she remained separate from him, entering later than he for the duel, drinking the poison and then supporting herself against a wall upstage well away from him, and finally being helped to a chair to die alone. Claudius, however, after being stabbed, staggered to her feet and fell, physical closeness ironically regained in death.

These kinds of moves dramatized what was really the central conception in the portrayal of the King and Queen. Rather than the static figures they had usually been, Claudius a 'bloat king' and Gertrude a weak, vain, and sensuous woman, they became more dynamic characters, changing as the play went on. Each developed a sense of guilt. In the scene with Hamlet, Gertrude suddenly realized with a shock that her desire had implicated her unknowingly. Her line, 'As kill a king?' in response to Hamlet's accusation marked an abrupt and emphatic eye-opening (Crosse). Claudius, for his part, suffered under a growing consciousness of the seriousness of his crime, his feelings in the prayer scene extending into other moments of brooding self-consciousness.

The complete sequence of scenes from the end of 'The Murder of Gonzago' through to Hamlet's departure for England (III.iii–IV.iii) was played in one setting, a sort of private chamber shared by King and Queen, thus providing a single resonant physical space in which to enact the psychological dynamics just described. This meant that Claudius's prayer and Hamlet's attack on his mother, Hamlet's soliloquy over the praying Claudius and his subsequent killing of Polonius, Claudius's private and unsuccessful attempt to comfort Gertrude and his public dispatch of Hamlet, were all played continuously and in the same room. Aside from being an excellent example of the speed and economy that the production typically sought, this move abetted the general concentration in the production on naturalistic characterization. The King especially benefited. After the play, for instance, as the curtain rose for the second part, he was discovered in anxious conference with Rosencrantz and Guildenstern, then plotting with Polonius, evidently dying for a drink, to which he helped himself from the whisky and soda on the table before turning to less worldly forms of consolation – i.e. his desperate attempt to pray. Despite his smart dressing gown and the other modern accoutrements, Vosper's acting here evidently became a little overwrought (Cochrane), so that the opportunity of revealing an inner conflict was lost; certainly underplaying the stress rather than waxing operatic would have been more in keeping with both the rest of Vosper's performance and the production as a whole. The moment when he sat smoking on the couch after Gertrude's departure achieved the desired tone more aptly, and at the end of that scene, after the interrogation of Hamlet, his ambivalent fascination with and aversion from violent death were nicely caught by a psychologically telling bit of business: as he turned to go, he suddenly recoiled sharply from the sight of Polonius's still fresh blood on the floor. Then, in a gesture fraught with implication, he bent to touch the congealing blot with his finger (promptbook).

In general then, Claudius was no longer played, as he always had been, 'entirely from the point of view of his nephew' (Palmer 681). Who before, wrote Palmer, 'had ever asked why … Gertrude liked Claudius better than his brother?' Who had dared present Claudius as 'superficially the more agreeable fellow'? The result was not just a gain in characterization for both Gertrude and Claudius, but an increase in dramatic interest as well. The audience, 'instead of merely waiting for Claudius to be killed', became involved in 'a real duel' between nephew and uncle (681-2).

Most critics agreed that the character who, along with

Claudius, benefited the most from the translation to modern dress was Polonius (played by A. Bromley-Davenport). Without the clothes it would have been difficult to break the old tradition, as stiffened with age as the Viking costumes, of making him the comic butt, the doddering, senile old busybody and long-winded fool. But with a dapper Whitehall look, he could suddenly become shrewd; he had the 'airs and graces of diplomacy' and uttered his platitudes with humour (*Sketch*, 2 Sept.), thereby giving him control over them instead of vice versa. He 'came to life perfectly in a morning coat' (*Evening Standard*, 26 Aug.), and part of his vitality was the sense he conveyed of being a recognizable politician, playing his public part with a kind of 'bright cynicism' (*Era*, 29 Aug.). Once again a character was released from being presented only from Hamlet's point of view. While, as I said, Polonius's family ties were affectionate, his commitment to political exigencies outweighed his domestic affiliations. Even during the initial scene with Ophelia, after Laertes' departure, he sat at his desk coolly writing a letter while he questioned his daughter, folding and sealing it as he rose to give her the heart-breaking order that ends the scene: 'I would not, in plain terms, from this time forth / Have you so slander any moment leisure / As to give words or talk with the Lord Hamlet' (I.iii.132-4). His priorities were equally evident in the moments surrounding the nunnery scene. Before, he stood with arm around Ophelia and, as he set her out as 'bait', he picked up the book that Hamlet had left behind from the previous scene, enjoining her to read. This made the idea of 'colouring her loneliness' with a book spontaneous rather than planned, reducing the sense of cold calculation at his daughter's expense. But afterwards he all but ignored her, escorting her out after his two cursory and unsympathetic lines, and quickly returning to the King and further plotting.

Ophelia, though compliant with her father and tossed around in the nunnery scene, was not a shrinking violet. Appropriately for this age of flapper skirts, roadsters and the Charleston, she had her own desires. Edith Shakleton noted a 'Freudian streak' in her, suggesting something of both the sexual feeling and its repression that another critic, J. K. Prothero, saw as the basis of Muriel Hewitt's performance. For Prothero, the 'suggestion of sex suppression' which is in the text but had always been eliminated on stage, was here enacted, so that the bawdy songs in the mad scene were given a new meaning (new, at least, to London, where Fay Compton, as we saw, played an excessively pure Ophelia to Barrymore's Hamlet, different from the rather more provocative figure created by Rosalind Fuller in New York). Ophelia, 'fettered by the brotherly love of Laertes [and] the parental restrictions of Polonius, had suffered the thwartings of her natural instincts to a dangerous degree' (*G.K.'s Weekly*, 5 Sept.). With inhibitions cast aside and clad only in a 'short flimsy black frock' (Cochrane 144), she gave an erotic explosiveness to the full text of her suggestive songs, accompanying them with a few modern dance steps to forge the links to contemporary youth. If this was not exactly a feminist reading, it at least showed a consciousness of the changing position of women in an era when suffragism, after a long struggle, was on the point of securing votes for all women (partial franchise had been granted in 1918, but full voting rights equivalent to those of men were still a few years away), and when sexual morality was loosening and the double standard under something of a strain. Ophelia's story, while subordinate to Hamlet's, was still recognizably a story, and one that a large proportion of the audience (male as well as female) could relate to.

Some aspects of a production like this one are necessarily more difficult to integrate into the conception, perhaps none more so than the Ghost – who is likely to be even less convincing than usual in evening dress. Ayliff's solution was to trick him out in an old-fashioned Danish military uniform, with peaked cap and short cape. A faintly luminous sheen was added to produce the needed aura of otherworldliness, and his scenes were shrouded in darkness, presumably to make his unreality, and the oddity of sentries on the battlements, a little less out of place than they might have seemed. For similar reasons, he remained invisible during the later scene in the Queen's chamber, truly a figment of Hamlet's imagination, his lines spoken from above. These tactics, while not eliminating the incongruity, at least made it unobtrusive. That Barrymore and Hopkins had adopted an almost identical strategy for dealing with the ghost suggests a general unwillingness to foist what was now regarded as an outmoded and melodramatic device on an up-to-date audience. Clearly there was no possibility of a perfect translation from the sixteenth to the twentieth century, especially when one wanted to stress the contemporary pertinence of the old text. Ayliff and Jackson wanted to bring out certain features of the play, and to do that they had to sacrifice others. In doing so, they were different neither from the actor managers who preceded them nor the interpretive directors who were to follow in their wake several decades later.

The play scene too posed some difficulty; troupes of wandering players driven from the city by 'little eyases' were not surprisingly an unknown commodity in 1925. As in most productions, the lines about the boy companies and the 'war of the theatres' were cut, and the play itself was presented, as Gordon Crosse described it, in the manner of a Victorian 'command performance' complete with satin programmes, the (Danish) national anthem, and a 'brightly painted curtain' decorated with a pretty canal scene enclosed in a *trompe l'oeil* gilt picture frame. The curtain was then 'rolled up to show a brilliantly lighted stage behind', with a backdrop depicting a hill-top castle and distant cloud-scape (Crosse vol. 9, and production photos). The performance itself parodied traditional Shakespearean production, the actors adopting extravagant poses to the accompaniment of melodramatic music and lighting, even a lurid 'flicker' upon the entry of Lucianus (Cochrane 143, and promptbook). The contrast with the modernism of the show in the Kingsway was highlighted by seating the King and Queen centre stage with their backs to the audience. The *Weekly Scotsman* commented on the vividness of their presence 'in sharp black silhouette against the brightly coloured scene … so that a tense movement of their hands dominates all' (quoted in Cochrane 143). But others found the scene less successful, the play incongruous or inappropriate for such a sophisticated court, and hence not likely to stir Claudius to guilty self-revelation or Hamlet to cavorting triumph.

The deaths of the two 'mighty opposites', though unceremonious in comparison to tradition, retained nevertheless a fair dose of Romanticism. A good sharp stab with the foil was enough to finish off Claudius, with the result that the highly melodramatic touch when Hamlet forces the poisoned wine down his greedy throat could be silently elided. But he still managed to stagger rather lengthily about the stage to collapse at Gertrude's feet, his head hanging backwards over a step. Hamlet, still dressed in his plus-fours, wrested the poisoned glass away from Horatio with a violent yank, a hint of his earlier savagery again in evidence; but stretched on the padded settee centre stage, he made a decorous rather than a brutal end (Horatio's lines about 'casual slaughters' were cut), and the final image of his being borne aloft up the steps to the sound of drum roll and trumpet was pure nineteenth-century Romanticism and almost identical to Barrymore's ending.

Clearly it was not either possible or desirable to dispense entirely with tradition. But this production nevertheless stands as a landmark. The redoubtable William Poel recognized this when he wrote to Jackson after the opening: 'Your achievement is another nail in the coffin of the rotten traditions ... which came into vogue in the time of Betterton' (quoted in Cochrane 146). We only have to look at the subsequent history of the play's production to see how far-reaching that achievement was. The use of costume and design to elicit character and highlight theme, the complex treatment of most of the major characters, the recognition of uncertainties and harsh interrogatives in the text, an insistence on the text's 'modernity' and immediacy in relation to its audience, all these were to become staples of *Hamlet* production, and, though many took time to reappear, they are all still to be encountered today.

CHAPTER IV

Gielgud and Olivier in the 1930s

Despite the changes heralded by such experiments as the Jackson/Ayliff production described in the previous chapter, the London theatre in the 1930s still depended largely on the star system and success was defined largely as success in the West End. The establishment of a 'National Theatre' of the sort long sought after by Granville-Barker and his colleagues was still far in the future. Commercial imperatives and a boulevard ethic ruled the day. The Old Vic, on the south bank, was then something of a fringe theatre, both culturally and geographically, dedicated largely to Shakespeare (almost the complete cycle of plays had been produced over several years in the early 1920s). Although John Gielgud's first *Hamlet* originated there, it 'arrived' only when it was transferred to the Queen's Theatre on Shaftesbury Avenue. The notion of *Hamlet* as an ensemble piece rather than as a vehicle for a star actor-manager, though evident at the Birmingham Rep, had not yet penetrated the theatrical establishment. Hence the old imbalance between lead actor and supporting players was still the norm. This was true even at the Old Vic, not so much because of the way the company was run or plays performed (the Barkerite stress on simplicity was the rule), but because of how the performances were regarded by mainstream critics. Few indeed of the reviewers had time, space, or inclination to dwell more than cursorily on features of production other than the performance of the main role. Critics, in fact, were reluctant to cross the river to visit the Old Vic, preferring to wait until productions were transferred to more familiar territory.

John Gielgud and *Hamlet*

When Gielgud first took on Hamlet, then, the character, under the weight of a long tradition of star actors and actor-managers, was still to a large extent the play. But since Gielgud was a young, not yet famous actor working with a company associated with a progressive approach to Shakespeare, he was free to break from tradition, as was director Harcourt Williams. Not surprisingly, therefore, the production did not shy away from harshness and disillusion. Gielgud was less committed to the wholeness and spiritual integration of the part than he would be in later years, more given to ugliness and wreckage. It was, after all, late 1929; times were tough, the great depression was beginning to stir, the optimism and dash of the 1920s were in steep decline. So too the 'modern' flair of a production like that of Jackson and Ayliff, with its frank recognition of sexual danger and psychological pain, had spoken to a new and receptive audience in a fresh way; and the quicker, more aggressive pleasures of the new stagecraft had found a welcome response. It was almost inevitable that the Old Vic would suit itself to the new ethos.

One element that was still missing, as it always had been in the British theatre (unlike, say, in Russia or eastern Europe), was politics. It is noteworthy that even during the 'dirty thirties', *Hamlet* remained a resolutely non-political play. This was true even as Polonius changed from clown to shrewd political insider, and Claudius, no longer a mere 'bloat king', became a smooth and ruthlessly efficient operator. Aspects of the text's political context gradually crept back in, but the emphasis remained domestic and psychological. Harcourt Williams describes the first court scene as 'domestic first and political afterwards' (*Saga* 90); accordingly, in 1929, he placed the Queen with some of her ladies on the upstage rostrum, 'embroidering a length of brocade', while other members of the court stood around in small groups as the curtain rose. Claudius (Donald Wolfit) strode in as if from hunting, handing gloves and hat to one attendant and taking a glass of wine from another; his opening speech was informal. But, as Gordon Crosse remarked, 'as the play went on we found that this smiling king was also a cunning schemer and a character of some power' (vol. 12). If some of the characters became more recognizably political, the text remained more or less what it had usually been; most of the traditional cuts were retained, with the result that both the international context and the wary surveillance typical of the Danish court were excluded or de-emphasized.[1]

Vocally and scenically, Williams inclined to the theories of Poel, Granville-Barker and Craig. He wanted rapid speaking in a natural voice, and in an actor like Gielgud he found the ideal exponent of classically tinged but authentic speech. The set was simple, with rostrum and apron, a wedge dividing the main acting area into two distinct spaces. Traverse curtains were used to cover scene changes, allowing for continuous playing right through to the end of Act II, with its tempting curtain line, 'The play's the thing / Wherein I'll catch the conscience of the King'. The costumes were Elizabethan, with ruffs and farthingales; Gielgud, perhaps under the visual influence of Barrymore, appeared some of the time at least in an open shirt and braided doublet. While Viking tresses and leggings had infected many of Barrymore's supporting cast, here the Renaissance style was consistent and refreshing, in keeping with the light naturalism that Williams was seeking.

Gielgud made a point of not skirting the unpalatable side of Hamlet. In this first wrestle with the role, he may have been reacting against the Romantic whitewashing of certain of his predecessors, such as the sweet-voiced Forbes-Robertson, and sought to 'find the violent and ugly colours in the part' (*Actor and his Time* 81). He was able, too, to take advantage of his youth (he was twenty-five, much younger than Hamlets normally were), giving an added poignancy to the 'tantrums and despair of the opening scene' (ibid.), and perhaps also accounting quite naturally for some of Hamlet's quick cruelty or thoughtlessness. Most of the reviews of the production admired the clarity of the narrative line, the intelligence of the central character, and the 'very human' modern young man, complete with a streak of cruelty. Ivor Brown, who had praised Keith-Johnston in similar terms five years before, mentions the need to balance 'beauty … and the ugly mockery of disillusion' and found the performance 'angry, violent, and tender as the sense demands' (*Manchester Guardian*, 29 May 1930). Richard Jennings was delighted by the young Gielgud's ability to manifest the 'conflict between the man of action frustrated in Hamlet and the meditative power that helps to account for that frustration' (*Spectator*, 14 June 1930, 971).

Over the next fifteen years, Gielgud played Hamlet hundreds of times in a variety of different productions.[2] More than any single actor of the twentieth century, he became identified with the part; and though there were many small differences between one version and another, as well as a recognizable development in the maturity with which he approached the character, there was also a strong continuity, one that derived from a consistent conception. Today, in the aftermath of the director's theatre, such continuity would be unlikely, precisely because differing conceptions of the play and its meaning would compete with, and necessarily colour, the playing of the main part. Indeed, few contemporary actors would come back to the same role over and over in different productions. As his popularity and fame grew, people flocked to the West End or Broadway to see Gielgud play Hamlet (not to see *Hamlet* with John Gielgud in the lead). It was perhaps inevitable that Gielgud would develop a vocal and physical style that persisted from one production to another.

We might try to characterize that style, and Gielgud's whole approach, by remarking on the restless intelligence, the lightning sensitivity of reaction, and the princely elegance and courtly assurance that persisted underneath the distraction, pain or anger. Near the end, in the graveyard, he evinced a 'crepuscular calm', which then led to strong and sharp action in the finale, though it was action underwritten by dignified renunciation and acceptance (Gilder 96, 10). One of the misconceptions that criticism has fostered concerning Gielgud's Hamlet, especially in contrast with Olivier's, is that Gielgud is classical where Olivier is Romantic, poetic where Olivier is athletic, musical where Olivier is impressionistic. Such an interpretation is far too restrictive and simple. Gielgud is not, was not, an elocutionist given to orotund and exquisitely phrased readings of famous verse – he was, is, an actor, able to characterize through the exact and realistic rendering of hundreds of details, with speed, verve, and wit, the person he encountered in the text. Michael Billington gives an example of how, in Gielgud's reading of the 'To be or not to be' soliloquy (and critics of every stripe have emphasized the skill and intelligence of Gielgud's soliloquies), he 'hinges everything on the way the dread of something after death "puzzles the will"', building the whole speech around those three revealing words (Harwood 112). Sonority is not the aim, character is; and the key to it here is a troubled intellectuality.

In another instance, he seized on a moment from Irving's

performance as a way of both characterizing Hamlet and getting the maximum dramatic impact from the scene. When Hamlet greets Horatio, who has come to tell him about the appearance of the Ghost, he does so abstractedly, musing about seeing his father in his mind's eye. Horatio's 'My lord, I think I saw him yesternight' falls at first on 'unhearing ears'. Gielgud's response ('Saw, who?' is all there is in the script) begins in abstraction, 'Saw?' almost automatic, then a pause in which a whole world is opened up, a 'flashing realization' burns out, he 'leaps to his feet', grasping Horatio and pinning his life and all his attention to the sequel (Gilder 34-5, and Gielgud in Gilder 126-7). Taking his cue from Irving, Gielgud made the moment distinctly his, and, as he wrote, found 'a guide to the playing of the scene which seems to me still so perfect that I have never veered a step from it' (127). What arises from this is not the sense of a fine speaker of verse (though of course he is that), but of an actor on the lookout for character, alert to momentary shifts, theatrical reactions, the shape of a scene, vivid contrast – in short, dramatic power.

The moment described also fixes for us a link between character and actor. A remarkable feature of Gielgud's own personality as it appears from his autobiography and from the numerous sketches, testimonials, encomia and the like that have been published about him, is his quickness – quickness of impulse, of intelligence, of tongue. That such a trait is especially suited to Hamlet goes without saying. Seizing on the particular moment from Irving's performance as he did shows the man matching himself to the character, making Hamlet his own, as he did from the time he first began rehearsing the part.

At the same time, Gielgud knew he was part of a line. His notes on the play, significantly titled 'The Hamlet Tradition', stress the continuity between himself and the legion of actors who preceded him. But it is Irving who most of all occupies his attention. Partly because of the family connection (he was Ellen Terry's nephew), but mostly because of the pre-eminence of Irving in British theatrical consciousness during the early decades of the century, Gielgud learned from the master. This means not only theatrical exploitation of certain strong moments, though those are crucial, but, at least in the later productions that he himself directed, a reliance on an overall conception that seems to have derived from Irving. In general during the reign of the actor-managers, there was more concentration on what an actor could do to an audience at key points than on meaning or directorial concept – perhaps because there was more agreement about the overall meaning of particular plays than there is today, less restless experimentation. Nowadays, performance practice and literary criticism have subverted the humanist consensus that prevailed for generations.

In the case of *Hamlet*, what Gielgud took from Irving, and others in his line, was the basic idea of the change to fullness and maturity at the end, so that tragic loss is compensated by spiritual gain. Hamlet emerges spiritually triumphant in death. In Gielgud's reading, he returns in the fifth act 'an integrated personality. Quiet, courteous, occasionally almost gay, with the tender lightness of those who, loving life, have accepted death, the Hamlet of the last scenes has discovered the springs of his own being' (Gilder 10). Not every critic saw it in exactly this light of course, but the ideological stress on integration, wholeness, and tragic closure that underlines the conception is clear enough. The sense of integration was rather wonderfully marked in the New York production by 'the ghost of a smile' that crossed his face as he received news and obeisance from Osric at the end, and most especially by the directorial decision to have him stand, gently supported by Horatio, right through 'The rest is silence' to his very death, when he simply collapsed into Horatio's arms. Standing upright among the corpses bespoke his spiritual power. In the London production that he himself directed the previous year, he died more conventionally, flanked by Laertes and the Queen, who had collapsed on thrones on either side, with Claudius in 'a swirl of red robes' up centre. But the triumph was marked there also by a display of verticality: 'Fortinbras and his army [so frequently left out of earlier productions, including Irving's] in grey cloaks and banners came from above over a kind of battlement and dipped their flags at the final curtain' (Gielgud in Gilder 167). Fortinbras's worldly power thus bowed to the dead prince's more complex spiritual victory.

Perhaps it is in that word 'prince' that we can find the best clue to Gielgud's approach to the role, though it is a word that has lost much of the range and power of connotation that it once had. When Ophelia says, after the cruelty and distraction of the 'nunnery' scene, 'O what a noble mind is here o'erthrown! / The courtier's, soldier's, scholar's, eye, tongue, sword ...' (III.i.150ff.), she is describing some of the characteristics of Renaissance princeliness, and Gielgud understood that clearly. But Ophelia's nostalgic encomium leaves out the less lovely aspects of princeliness, notably the tendency to arrogance and insensitive, even violent, exploitation of power, which she has just been subjected to.

In the 1930 production, Gielgud's approach tended to stress those unlovely aspects, which were gradually winnowed out over the next fifteen years. Nevertheless, in keeping with the sense of variety that was his hallmark, responding always to what he calls the 'truth' of the text (Actor 81), Gielgud's first 'Get thee to a nunnery' was delivered 'with maximum pathos as though Hamlet would draw out of that refuge its power to heal as well as mortify' (James Agate, *Sunday Times*, 11 May 1930). In later productions, under the influence of Dover Wilson's suggestion that Hamlet has overheard the earlier plan to 'loose' Ophelia to him, Gielgud began the scene warily, understandably suspicious of her presence before him.[3] He is seeking to get her to speak honestly to him, holding her arms, pulling her forward. Sincere on 'I did love you once', harsh on 'You should not have believ'd me', tender (as in 1930) on the first 'Get thee to a nunnery', he seems only half in control, struggling to win her over. At one point, 'their bodies sway toward each other', but the chance of an erotic breakthrough is cut off by 'Go thy ways to a nunnery', at which she retreats. Hamlet bounds after her down a few steps, grabs her, forces nose to nose contact, 'Where's your father?' She lies, he knows it and throws her off, furious, hurling down the string of pearls she has earlier returned to him. A few minutes of high anger lead to exhaustion, and, in a development of Kean and Irving, he begins to crumple: his 'hands go up ... denying the last faint shadow of hope that lies in that once-loved face ... "To a nunnery, go" is broken, spent.' And he exits, feeling blindly for support, leaving Ophelia to lament his loss.

Here we have a splendid example of the quick shifts in mood that Gielgud was so good at rendering and that seem such an inescapable part of Hamlet. But the other point is that his behaviour here is perfectly consistent with the complex princeliness that he adopted from Irving. Unassailable power is part of it; he can treat her as he wants, he can threaten, cajole, rant. The active intelligence is very much in evidence too, the desire to make Ophelia see what he sees, which gives meaningful shape to the scene as a whole. And underneath there is the developing sense that he is caught in a game of power: he remembers the 'set-up'; he has already commissioned and revised 'The Mousetrap', and he is formulating his line of attack against his mighty opposite. If Claudius can use Ophelia as a decoy, so can he. Personal feeling gives way to royal exigency. He puts his love aside, crushing it under the weight of responsibility that his exposed position fastens upon him.

If one runs through the reviews of all Gielgud's performances, it is the sheer intelligence of his Hamlet (another characteristic he shares with Irving) that emerges as the most outstanding trait. *The Times*, for example, was delighted and gratified by the way Gielgud's interpretation (in his own 1934 production at the New Theatre) matched the reviewer's ideal: the actor does not 'throw up passionate mists ... to conceal confusions' in the text itself. He lets them stand for examination. He curbs emotions, even fear and apprehension. Not that he is without feeling, but rather that he keeps it at bay. Hamlet's delay is the result not of fear, nor of weakness, but of intelligence: he knows the *futility* of action, he has read and assessed the situation, plumbed its depths. Had he been less intelligent, he would have acted. This provides the 'seed' of Gielgud's interpretation, giving it its characteristic 'lucidity' (*Times*, 15 Nov. 1934, 12). The same point, less admiringly stated, can be found in a number of other responses. Raymond Mortimer, for example, saw Gielgud as an intellectual averse to passion, a man no more likely 'to kill his uncle than Montaigne or Spinoza' (*New Statesman and Nation*, 24 Nov. 1934, 754). Though Mortimer (who preferred Olivier's approach to the part) felt there was too little of the athlete, the courtier, even the passionate actor who feigns madness, he stressed the positive: 'I can imagine a more moving Hamlet, but I never expect to see another so intelligent.'

The design of that production, created by Motley, fit precisely into the conception. Motley, a design team that frequently collaborated with Gielgud, comprising Elizabeth Montgomery, and Audrey and Margaret Harris, worked together for nearly thirty years. During that period, their work

3 John Gielgud strikes a classic pose during the 1934 production at the New Theatre which he directed.

was perhaps 'the most influential until the formation of the RSC ... [and] certainly was the most characteristically English in its practicality and restraint' (Kennedy, *Looking* 134). Their decision, as in the Old Vic staging four years earlier, was to evoke Renaissance costumes and décor, in the manner of Cranach and Dürer, rather than reproduce the old Gothic. But now the effort was to integrate the look more carefully than had been done in the past. The result was a 'symphony of bronze and grey and silver' (*Observer*, 18 Nov. 1934), which enhanced the slightly subdued but thoroughly considered rendering of the text. The design was built around an array of movable steps with a substantial raised platform upstage left, and a dais, used for the throneroom scenes, in front of the platform, marked off by rich curtains and a sensational banner directly behind the throne. The hangings were used in a variety of ways to define different spaces, while the soft Cranach colours provided continuity. The whole thing allowed for rhythmic simplicity and ease of movement.

Some reviewers felt a falling off from Gielgud's previous performance in 1930. Herbert Farjeon noted that 'Something vital has gone out of the performance' (*Sunday Pictorial*, 18 Nov. 1934) and Mortimer and Agate complained of the failure to simulate madness. 'What seemed to be ... markedly diminished was the molten anger of thwarted youth ... ugliness had been banished in favour of a chaste representation of the beautiful' (Mills 213). But there were gains as well. For one thing, the pathos evoked by this Hamlet's obvious love for his father impressed both Farjeon and Agate. And the soliloquies, especially the two central ones, were handled with grace, intelligence and tenderness. *Time and Tide* regarded the 'rogue and peasant slave' as a 'keynote', which showed that Hamlet 'would act, and act decisively, if any form that revenge could take had a lasting validity for a mind reflecting in its own disillusionment a spiritual world of contending forces' (quoted. in Mills 215).

In the New York production (directed by Guthrie McClintic in 1936), much of the same 'tortured cerebration' was in evidence (W. P. Eaton, *Atlantic* 159, April 1937, 476), and several of the American critics, while noting the thoughtfulness and intellectual grasp, felt they missed some of the strong emotion, the 'command, power and storm of Elizabethan tragedy', its 'harrowing horror' (Atkinson, *New York Times*, 9 Oct. 1936, 30; see also G. Vernon, *Commonweal*, 23 Oct. 1936, 617). Clearly some American critics were still in the grip of melodramatic conceptions of the play, and were perhaps less open to the relatively relaxed and informal style that had developed in the wake of the new stagecraft.

However, what they got may still sound to us like melo-drama (which suggests we have to read the reviews against a background of tradition different from our own more austere tastes). Take, for example, the 'O, what a rogue and peasant slave am I' soliloquy at the end of Act II, as described by Rosamund Gilder, from whose book much of the detail can be reconstructed (though her purpose is so obviously laudatory that some of her readings have to be approached with caution). In mid-speech, Hamlet is 'trembling with fury, his body shak-ing ... [On] "O Vengeance", he snatches his dagger ... rushes to the doorway', but the 'wave of futile fury' subsides, his raised arm falls, the dagger drops and 'he sinks, almost crouching, on the step' (64). Intellectual detachment or passionate melo-drama? The speech moves to self-condemnation and then to elation about his plan to trap the King. His voice 'is broken with a sob of humiliation' but lifts up a little on 'I'll have these players / Play something like the murder of my father before my uncle'. The tempo, though, is still 'uncertain', the voice 'hoarse [and] whispered'. He is 'absolutely still' upon consider-ing the possibility of his own delusion – '"I'll have grounds more relative than this" is a cry of despair and defiance' and the final rhyming lines ('The play's the thing / Wherein I'll catch the conscience of the King') are spoken in 'a frenzy of excitement'. He then 'hurls himself across ... to the chair [by] the table ... pulls the paper toward him, seizes a pen, the light catches his wildly excited face, then blacks out as he bends forward writing frantically' (65-6). The similarity to Barrymore (though more frenzied and without the pauses), and especially to Irving, could hardly be more striking.

Gielgud, in discussing this scene, notes the tendency of the actor in the theatre of his day, despite the new influences that had made their mark on the overall style, to play for applause at this climactic moment. He records a conflict, the feeling first that he is not succeeding unless he gets a strong burst of applause and the later irritation at his 'actor's desire to make such a "curtain" of it' (144). He had read and appreciated Granville-Barker, he knew that the scenes were meant to flow into one another, that there should be no curtain here, that the King's entrance should follow hard upon, even overlap with, the famous lines, which should then be echoing in our ears as we witness the King's interrogation of Rosencrantz and

Guildenstern. But the tradition of which he writes both sustains and inhibits him:

> I have never been either sufficiently experienced or sufficiently original to dare to direct or play *Hamlet* without including a great deal of this kind of theatricalism, for fear of being unable to hold the interest of the audience by a more classical and simple statement of the written text. (145)

There are a number of important if contradictory assumptions here. The first, from Granville-Barker and the new stagecraft, is that the text demands an approach based on what we can surmise about Elizabethan stage practice – fast pace, continuous playing – and on painstaking reconstruction of authorial intention. Another is that the audience controls the performance. They should get what they expect, otherwise they will stay away and the commercial venture will fail. To force a new way of seeing upon an audience was simply too risky. A third assumption, which shows up elsewhere in Gielgud's 'Notes', and which he knew from his years at the Old Vic, is that Shakespeare's plays require ensemble playing – they have been distorted by the actor-manager tradition and the stage business it generated. But despite this and despite the fact that he did everything he could to get the best supporting actors available, he could not resist the star actor's 'turn'.

When he came to play the part a fourth time, in June and July 1939, just before the outbreak of war, he had an opportunity to meet with Granville-Barker a few days before the opening (Hayman 117-18). The result was what Desmond MacCarthy called a more 'austere' version of *Hamlet* (*New Statesman*, 8 July 1939, 48) and Rosamond Gilder agreed that it was a stripped-down, more focused performance, done in a more explicitly 'Elizabethan' style. Perhaps the shadow of imminent war had a sobering effect. The production was designed (by Motley) for outdoor performance at Elsinore palace in Denmark, Hamlet's home base, which made possible the use of a large forestage (mostly for intermediary scenes), and a freedom of movement not available on the conventional proscenium stage.

There was, too, a difference in the interpretive focus. Gilder remarked that Hamlet was now a 'Prince who had been deprived of his rights even more than a son who had lost a father' (*Theatre Arts Monthly* 23, Oct. 1939, 711). MacCarthy, in detailing the austerity, notes that much of the traditional business was cut (*New Statesman*, 8 July 1939). Hamlet, for example, no longer broke the flute across his knee in the scene with Rosencrantz and Guildenstern after the play; this bit of melodrama had come down to Gielgud from Booth via Irving (Sprague, *Actors* 160-1), and its abandonment here marks a decisive move away from nineteenth-century style. Nor did Hamlet take the praying King's sword from a chair during the 'Now might I do it pat' soliloquy (a bit of business that led to a provocative 'take' when Claudius rose from his fruitless orisons and noticed the sword was missing). Gielgud had himself invented this telling stroke in 1934, and its jettisoning here shows the influence of Granville-Barker, who sought a leaner characterization and a less distracting flow to the action.

This production introduced an interesting innovation in the casting – doubling the Ghost and Claudius. In the New York production, Malcolm Keen, playing Claudius, had spoken the Ghost's lines from offstage (*Time* commented on the 'spooky, silent presence' of the Ghost 'whose voice croaks hollowly from an offstage microphone' – 19 Oct. 1936, 44), but this, as Gielgud observes, is 'not quite the same thing' as doubling, where the physical likeness would be 'very effective from my point of view as Hamlet' (in Gilder 138). In the Elsinore version, Jack Hawkins played both parts, an idea that has been used occasionally since (for example in the Peter Hall/Albert Finney production at the National in 1976 with Denis Quilley as Claudius/Ghost). Lest we go away with the impression that this was an overly controlled and disciplined production, however, MacCarthy's stern admonition about one particular moment might help us imagine something about the flavour of at least some of the playing. Osric, he writes, 'should not blow Hamlet a kiss upon retiring' (*New Statesman*, 8 July 1939, 48).

Gielgud played Hamlet one more time, at the Haymarket in 1944.[4] The magisterial James Agate, who for years had held critical court in the pages of the *Sunday Times*, had this to say:

Hamlet is not a young man's part. Consider how ill it becomes a stripling to hold forth on the life after death, the propriety of suicide, the nature of man, the exuberance or restraint of matrons ... Mr. Gielgud could not be at a better age [he was forty] ... The too-young Hamlet takes one's thoughts off this play in the way the concert hall's infant prodigy takes them off the music ... Mr.

> Gielgud is now completely and authoritatively master of this tre-
> mendous part ... [he is] the best Hamlet of our time.

Now this is patently absurd – it is in the very nature of strip-
lings to hold forth on the meaning of life and death, and to
lecture their elders. But it tells us something of the hold that
Gielgud now had on the role, the position he had inherited
from Irving, whom Agate cites affectionately in his review as
the Old Man. We can also detect how success in the role had to
some extent locked him into a conception and a style that were
essentially conservative and old-fashioned. The production
was fast-paced and intelligible, though some critics were both-
ered by its heavy and gaudy visual features. There were as well
those who regarded Gielgud's final performance as unduly
histrionic and studied (*Times*, 14 Oct. 1944, 2); in so far as this
is true, it is another sign of the hold that tradition had upon
him. Still, in many respects, the approach that Gielgud took to
the part was similar to what he had developed over the past
fifteen years. Mellow, intelligent, quick witted, and changeable,
at first tender with Ophelia and then bitter and aggressive, wild
at moments of high passion, meditative at others, and intelligent throughout, Gielgud handled the part with the masterly
authority that his experience and his talent had earned him.
But there was a competitor in the wings, an unruly one with
sleeves rolled up and chest bared.

Olivier at the Old Vic

Laurence Olivier played Hamlet on stage only once, at the Old
Vic in 1937 (followed by a memorable stint at Elsinore), but the
extraordinary success of his 1948 film has made his Hamlet the
most widely recognized portrayal of the part in history. In
1937, however, he was an upstart, a challenge to his colleague
and rival (with whom he had recently shared top billing in
Romeo and Juliet, alternating the parts of Romeo and
Mercutio). Here is how Olivier described the circumstances
many years later:

> I was the outsider and John was the jewel ... John still has the most
> beautiful voice, but I felt in those days he allowed it to dominate his
> performances ... I thought his first Hamlet was wonderful, because
> he didn't allow himself to do that, he didn't sing. But as time went

by I believe he sang it more and more ... Of course his voice was musical enough to sell it ... He was giving the familiar tradition fresh life, whereas I was completely disregarding the old in favour of something new. (*On Acting* 44)

Here of course Olivier is constructing himself as the rebel, shaking the foundations of the established order, and Gielgud is cast as the bastion of conservatism. And it is true that Gielgud's patrician style, his heritage and status as a scion of the famous Terry family, his dedication to tradition, combined to make the contrast vivid enough. But at the same time there is a certain interest discernible not far below the surface of Olivier's remarks. He is intent on establishing the 'truth' of his performance, based not on 'music' but on something more substantial – the physical and emotional presence of the 'real' Hamlet. 'Beyond any other Hamlet in my experience he is a credible and living individual', said Raymond Mortimer (*New Statesman*, 16 Jan. 1937), a remark that must have pleased the young would-be iconoclast. Olivier's rhetoric reveals him as determined to position himself as an innovator, sparking a trend away from honeyed verse speaking and posturing towards a more vigorous and individualized style of impersonation.

The differences in style between the two performances are visible even in the way the actors write about them: Gielgud elegant, tentative, self-critical, deferential to tradition; Olivier staccato, self-justifying and fierce. Where Gielgud ponders a problem (such as Hamlet's past relation to Ophelia) and thinks it through deliberately and rationally, Olivier simply pronounces upon it, often punctuating his text with calculated vulgarisms ('You're not supposed to tell the audience with every wink and nod that part of the reason for your present predicament is that you still wish you were hanging on your mother's tits').[5] Gielgud says nothing about Hamlet's relation with his mother (indeed his whole performance was much more directed towards his father), but on Ophelia he concludes quite reasonably that she is pure and innocent and does not lie to her father when he questions her about her relationship with Hamlet (for her to do so would reduce the effectiveness of her first (and reluctant) lie, to Hamlet in the nunnery scene). For Olivier, on the other hand, the matter is clear-cut: 'Hamlet is not just imagining what is beneath Ophelia's skirts, he has found out for himself – country matters – for certain' (*On*

Acting 51). Olivier writes with his fists – he is pugnacious and raw; Gielgud, his measured tones audible even on the page, is considered and well-balanced. It is easy to see how each of them 'has looked for himself in the part and for the part in himself' as *The Times* said of Olivier's performance (6 Jan. 1937).

The 1937 Old Vic production, directed by Tyrone Guthrie, used the full text; it was played on a stage built up with platforms and ramps that gave full scope to its hero's athleticism, and with an apron that was used, among other things, for the soliloquies. The show's most distinctive feature, for which it is now well known, was its reliance on the Freudian theory, promulgated by Ernest Jones, of Hamlet's Oedipus complex. Although, ironically, few critics picked up on the Freudian overtones, especially early in the run (after a while, word began to get around), Guthrie's choice is nevertheless significant. To interpret the play according to an overriding concept was itself a new strategy, one that heralded the 'director's theatre' that was to develop into the most dominant feature of Shakespearean production by the 1960s. Furthermore, the Freudian reading gave the actors, especially Olivier, a way to get a grip on this elusive text.

At the time, however, the oddity of the overall concept attracted less attention than the use of the full text, the wayward verse speaking ('Mr. Olivier does not speak poetry badly', wrote Agate, 'He does not speak it at all' – *Sunday Times*, 10 Jan. 1937), and the weakness of the design (which included awkward hangings to suggest different rooms, carried around by 'young ladies dressed in black' (Mortimer)). Of course, what everyone noticed was the energetic drive and physical power of Olivier. Mortimer, acknowledging that most Hamlets 'look a little like governesses', found his imagination captivated by a prince as 'elegant and vivid as a Botticelli portrait' (*New Statesman*, 16 Jan. 1937). Ivor Brown praised Olivier's 'magnetism and muscularity', but pointed to a problem: 'the weakness here is that you begin to suspect that such a Hamlet would have put through his murderous work without so much self-scrutiny and hesitation' (*Observer*, 10 Jan. 1937). But precisely here was the core of the Guthrie/Olivier reading. A man who is constitutionally active, virile, determined and energetic becomes *unaccountably* melancholy and passive. If Hamlet were always as inactive as he appears in the play, would he be continually castigating himself for following what he must by then surely have recognized as his 'natural' bent? So the Oedipus complex is brought forward as an explanation for the muddying of a determined current, for the blockage of what is normally an active and vital approach to life. Mortimer noticed and named Hamlet's 'mother-fixation', and used it to explain the shifts in Hamlet's feelings for Ophelia and his idolization of his father. But for him the dominant characteristic of Olivier's Hamlet was its very inconsistency, the force with which he played each moment, each persona: 'in this particular role an actor who plays line by line may prove wiser than all the scholars and critics.' Hamlet is a multiplicity of personae – a 'whole troupe of players', and Olivier's performance embodied them successively and successfully (*New Statesman*, 16 Jan. 1937).

The production as a whole lacked the polish of most of Gielgud's versions, some of the minor actors were weak, and the design was uncomely; but the full text elicited positive comment from some – *The Times* found there to be less of a strain on the audience because there were no gaps to be filled in, and the expanded text, handled with verve and speed (the whole thing lasted less than four hours) produced a feeling of 'spaciousness', of 'being led, not driven' (*Times*, 6 Jan. 1937, 10). And there were acute performances from George Howe, who played Polonius, as he had for Gielgud in 1934, as a sharp-witted counsellor rather than a simpleton, and Michael Redgrave as a strong and honourable Laertes.

The professional troupe that comes to perform at Elsinore was transformed into a band of comic incompetents, hardly superior to the mechanicals of *A Midsummer Night's Dream*, a serious misjudgment on Guthrie's part. The play-within does draw a contrast between the artificial style and rhetoric of these players and the presumably more naturalistic style used by Shakespeare's own troupe. This contrast is based partly on changes in theatrical fashion between the blood and thunder that Shakespeare probably witnessed as a child in a provincial town and the more sophisticated offerings of the professional theatres of his maturity. But the point is that Hamlet is interested in these Players, thinks highly of their skill and is impressed by their power to make the King blench. Furthermore, the First Player's speech about Hecuba (II.ii.468ff.), though written in a vein of affectionate parody, displays the sort of power that such emotionally charged, Marlovian rhetoric can have in the theatre. So to make fun of the actors does not really work.

Like Gielgud, Guthrie took up Dover Wilson's suggestion that Hamlet should overhear the plan to 'loose' Ophelia to him, thus helping to motivate his fury at her. But those critics who noticed failed to be impressed by it. He was less tender than Gielgud with Ophelia, both in the nunnery scene and the play scene, where his suggestive jokes were, characteristically, loud and raw, designed to provoke both the women on stage and, it seemed, the audience. And in the scene with his mother, Hamlet was unrepentantly torrid, so much so that, according to Olivier, it 'went about as far in this direction as I dared suggest, or the Ghost's complaints would have been on a different score' (*On Acting* 51).

Olivier was nothing if not physical. After the play he made a 'tremendous leap' from the throne down on to the makeshift stage[6] and, in the final scene, the protracted and splendid duel between Olivier and Redgrave (an event that Gielgud handled with caution and even reluctance) was a high point, though Agate thought the death scene lacked pathos (*Sunday Times*, 10 Jan. 1937). Athletic rush and impulsive heedlessness marked the whole sequence, punctuated by Dorothy Dix (as Gertrude) taking a backwards fall 'from a high rostrum on to the ladies of the court' (*Observer*, 10 Jan. 1937) and culminating in the King's 'splendidly horrible end' (the phrase is Mortimer's).

Olivier's voice, without the suppleness, mellifluousness or subtlety of Gielgud's, had nevertheless a 'marvelous ringing baritone brilliance at the top' (Guthrie, *Life* 187), and he used it to powerful advantage at key moments. J. C. Trewin remembered the last soliloquy as an 'emphatic cry, half-wailed, half-proclaimed [and] the mounting desperation of "I do not know / Why yet I live to say this thing's to do ..." (*English Stage* 164) with its 'sudden agonized, spaced emphasis' on each word – 'do-not-know' (Sprague and Trewin 66). Agate described the same speech as 'trumpet-moaned as though it has at last broken in on the young man that indecision is his bane' (*Sunday Times*, 10 Jan. 1937). Again Agate's comment is helpful even if his perception is wrong; the force of the moment in the context of Olivier's interpretation is not that Hamlet has realized that he is by nature plagued by indecision, but that he does not understand why his usual energetic decisiveness is failing him in this instance: 'I do not know … .' This painful awareness broke out at another key moment – on 'Now might I do it pat', which Mortimer saw as 'an obvious excuse':

> Olivier lifted his sword … with all the demoniac intention of assassination: then his sword-arm dropped as if dragged down by some unseen leaden force, and throughout the … rest of the speech … he paced the stage with a restless and uncomprehending exasperation. (Williamson 84)

In a move that had long-term consequences, the production, with a few cast changes, visited the courtyard of Elsinore castle for a brief run in early June (Gielgud's Danish sojourn two years later was no doubt inspired by the well-publicized success of this venture). Guthrie's autobiography tells a delightful story of Danish helps and hindrances, complete with nesting birds impeding the opening of important doors and the wayward maritime weather nearly drowning the production. Forced to rehearse every night, since the castle was open to the public during the day, the company braved constant rain and shrewd biting air, but on opening night the weather was too fierce to contemplate going on. Royalty, however, had arrived, the audience was on its way – what to do? The solution was a quick change to the ballroom of the Marienlyst Hotel, where the company had been staying. A makeshift stage in the centre, chairs hurriedly placed around it, a lightning rehearsal directed by Olivier, and they were ready. In an article published shortly after, Guthrie recreated the atmosphere:

> The actors felt it was an adventure and I think the audience did too. They sat, packed densely, round three sides of a small clear space on the ballroom floor, on which most of the action passed, with the steps and little stage used for occasional scenes. The effect aimed at was the atmosphere of a café chantant with the audience in the most informal and the closest possible contact with the actors. For two-thirds of the evening, with the actors performing miracles of improvisation, this effect was … excitingly achieved. Towards the end the actors' invention began to flag and the finale became a mêlée of unrehearsed positions which caused the evening to end too much in the key of a charade. (Guthrie, 'Elsinore' 248).

The liveliness generated by the occasion (what Brecht liked to call *Spass*) confirmed for Guthrie that 'intimacy between the audience and the players is the first essential' (ibid.), and taught him the value of the open stage that he was later to champion at Stratford, Ontario, and elsewhere. His experience was part of a growing realization on the part of a number of directors and actors that the open stage allowed actors to approximate the conditions of the Elizabethan stage without being slavishly antiquarian. Fuelled by the experiments of William Poel and encouraged by Granville-Barker's writings, theatre people were now coming to believe that such a stage could, more easily than the proscenium, provide not only the intimacy, but also the Elizabethan flexibility, the freedom from the conventions of realistic illusion, and the opportunity for continuous performance that many felt had been swamped by the Romantic verisimilitude of the Victorians and Edwardians. This view has, by now, come to prevail, so that today's productions, even in conventional proscenium theatres, almost always gesture towards 'Elizabethan' models.

By the end of the 1930s, if Gielgud was the unquestioned star among British actors, Olivier was a bright rival; but, lest we lean too heavily on what distinguishes them, we might do well to establish some parallels. Both were committed to rapid, quickly responsive delivery, both sought to rethink the characters they played, both favoured full texts, both approached Shakespeare in intellectual as well as emotional or musical terms. Both were 'modern', though in different ways. Gielgud was heralded as having 'the quick spontaneity of a modern man' (Atkinson, *New York Times*, 9 Oct. 1936, 30); by some, he was seen as bringing the play up to date (Ashley Dukes, *Theatre Arts Monthly*, 19 Feb. 1935, 105). Olivier, more obviously, was regarded as modern in the restless athleticism of his performance, his unconventional, often dislocated verse speaking, his refusal of tradition. In 1930, Gielgud's rendering was praised for its 'impassioned recklessness', a phrase that might strike us as more appropriate to Olivier. Their Hamlets both displayed a heightened passion and instability, a fierceness struck down by melancholic paralysis (a psychological condition pertinent to 1930s depression culture). There were, to be sure, telling differences between them – the very ones that have hardened into orthodoxy. Gielgud *was* more hesitant, more poetic, more tender, better with the soliloquies, weaker in the prose sections and with the physical demands of the part, especially the duel. Olivier was unsurpassed in the flow of brilliant energy, the physical power, the bite and harshness of the part. More soldier than scholar, more clown than courtier, he shifted the meaning of 'Prince' just enough to legitimate a rival claim, but not enough to dislodge it completely. The two actors together defined the range and meaning of pre-war Hamlets in England, but of course they did not come close to exhausting the role, any more than the productions of which they were a part managed to encompass what was at the time available to artists who wanted to re-think *Hamlet* in modern terms.

To see this, it is necessary only to glance beyond not only the West End but the Old Vic or even the Birmingham Rep, to the rise of expressionism and the politicization of *Hamlet* apparent in central Europe between the wars, where the experience of devastation during World War I and the breakdown of the Austro-Hungarian Empire led to modernist experimentation beyond anything that was happening in Britain. In 1926, for example, Leopold Jessner in Berlin mounted the play as an attack on monarchy, militarism and the abuse of power, and 'created a storm in the provincial assembly' (Kennedy, *Looking* 92). Claudius's shortened arm and uniform with 'shoulder brushes and breastplate' recalled Kaiser Wilhelm, mad Ophelia became the prey and whore of Laertes' savage soldiers, the whole royal household was turned into a swarming, whispering mass of eavesdroppers. The play scene was done as in a real baroque theatre with a 'sharply lit royal box in the background where the guilty couple [could] be observed by everyone' (Stahl 611). Hamlet (Fritz Kortner) was an utterly isolated rebel who embodied the expressionist theme of 'the sensitive individual crushed by the mindless machine of authority' (Kennedy).

In the same year, director Karel Hilar and designer Vlatislav Hofman teamed up in Prague to stage a visually striking version that moved away from naturalism altogether. 'It was particularly noteworthy for the use of changeable screens and high chiaroscuro which conveyed the feeling of events taking shape out of darkness' (Kennedy, *Looking* 92, 98). The lighting was harsh, there was almost no colour, and pieces of massive furniture on movable platforms slid out of the black space (Burian 198). The scenery was matched by the staging, which followed a 'revue format, a series of rapidly changing scenes that deliberately accentuated contrasts in tone between the comic and the serious'. Actors entered abruptly from behind the screens and furniture. Though the style was expressionist,

Hilar's main concern was with daily life after the devastations of war. Eduard Kohout played Hamlet as a melancholy youth, 'impotent within the hostile, often grotesque world of the Danish court ... an inexperienced boy, alternately confused and vehement' (Burian 197), an approach strikingly similar to that of Peter Hall and David Warner at Stratford in 1965. The idea was to speak to the alienation and resentment of the post-war generation, again in the same vein as Hall's production. The costumes too, Hamlet in vest, sweater and Basque cap, for example, or Gertrude in an evening gown, were designed to strike a contemporary chord, and to convey Hamlet's wayward distance from the centre of power.

In the context of such political and theatrical radicalism, Gielgud and Olivier can best be seen as complementary rather than opposed; each in his own way created the role in terms of the relatively narrow culture from which they both emerged. The bite and aggressiveness they each brought to the part suggests a commonalty deriving, perhaps, from the high hopes and dazzling youth culture of the 1920s (the 'recklessness' of the flapper), dashed by the depression and leavened by 1930s political ferment. But both of them lived within the encoded British traditions handed down from previous centuries. Even in their attempts to distance themselves from that tradition, they remained within its psychological and domestic borders.

CHAPTER V

Post-war *Hamlet*s at Stratford-upon-Avon: 1948 and 1965

During the 1930s and the war years, Stratford remained a provincial backwater. That was to change in the post-war period, when, even before the establishment of the RSC in 1960, and the re-naming and refurbishing of the Shakespeare Memorial Theatre (after 1960 to be called the Royal Shakespeare Theatre), Stratford became the centre of the Shakespeare industry. In 1945, the redoubtable Barry Jackson (by then Sir Barry), who had sought to revitalize Shakespeare twenty years earlier at the Birmingham Rep, was called in to rescue Stratford's illustrious native son from what Peter Brook called 'deadly sentimentality and complacent worthiness – a traditionalism approved largely by town, scholar, and press' (46). Jackson's tenure as artistic director was short, but it was decisive in moving the old theatre on to the road that would lead eventually to Peter Hall's largely successful efforts in the early 1960s to make the RSC not only the leading Shakespeare company in the world, but also the most intensely, and relevantly, up-to-date. The results of that move included Brook's boldly innovative and immensely influential productions of *King Lear* (1962) and *A Midsummer Night's Dream* (1970), as well as Hall's own work, along with designer John Bury, on the history plays (1963-64) and *Hamlet* (1964).

Hamlet was chosen as the 'birthday play' in 1948, Jackson's final year, opening on 23 April. The moment was much heralded in the press; Stratford, condescended to by fashionable Londoners since Garrick's time, was not only making itself felt as a major force in British post-war theatre, but becoming a focus of British cultural identity. National pride, despite problems in India and Palestine, was high, the modern welfare state was being legislated into being, new cultural horizons were looming, and Dover Wilson, that very afternoon, had proposed a birthday toast to William Shakespeare that placed the national author in a global perspective. One of Britain's foremost Shakespearean scholars and editors, the author of *What Happens in Hamlet*, a book that influenced both Gielgud and Olivier in their productions, Wilson used his speech to forge allegorical links between Shakespeare's characters and various modern nations. It is worth pausing over.

Shakespeare's, he said, was the 'greatest name in the world, a name so universally revered that the nations and denominations jostle each other to prove that he belongs to them' (*Stratford Herald*, 30 April 1948). English at root and core, Shakespeare has nevertheless 'outgrown us' and speaks to all the continents in a 'winning voice', not as a conqueror but as a 'friend and brother'; his is 'the one human spirit, his plays the only sacred book that the warring peoples on this distracted globe unite to reverence'. Wilson cites the 'compassion which breathes from *King Lear*' as 'characteristic of the English race', but hopes that it can extend beyond the cliffs of Dover as a 'salvation for our [i.e. European] society'. He regards the plays as 'myths': *Hamlet* as the 'adolescent' and 'perplexed' Germany of the nineteenth century, *Macbeth* as that nation's twentieth-century descent from nobility into crime and damnation, *The Merchant of Venice* as not only an exposure of the disease of race hatred, but also, in its 'impartiality,' a prefiguring of the 'sons of Shylock' in modern Palestine, 'who, fleeing from the Ghettos and concentration camps of Eastern Europe, are ready to murder any Christians that come in sight'. Finally, he finds in Shakespeare's 'two portraits of the dictator,' the parodic Jack Cade and the serious Julius Caesar, a sign of what he calls Shakespeare's 'English abhorrence of tyranny' (he omits, significantly, any English monarchs from this gallery, even though Richard III, for example, fits the bill rather nicely). It is all too easy to mock the self-serving chauvinism in some of this, not to mention the contradiction in, for example, the praise of impartiality in *Merchant* followed immediately by a statement of faith: 'Yet I have little doubt that Shakespeare hated racial hatred'. And of course not everyone shared Wilson's confidence or sense of patriotic mission. Even so, we should not entirely ignore it as a background to the production of *Hamlet* that opened that evening, nor fail to see it in context. If England's role on the world stage was diminishing, was it not fitting that an idealized representative of what was best in Englishness should arise to replace political with spiritual hegemony? One can sense the need to find some way of expressing English pre-eminence in a changed and rapidly changing world that no longer bought into the myth of that pre-eminence. Hence arises the construction of a universal Shakespeare who could humanize the world in concert with the unchallenged values of his native land.

Because of this, Shakespearean production, especially at Stratford, was seen to have international implications. Critics of different political stripes were quick to suggest this. Not wanting to be outdone by the Russians who had claimed that theirs was Shakespeare's 'spiritual home', John Garret wrote in the *Spectator* of the Memorial Theatre's 'national and international responsibilities' (24 Sept. 1948), and T. C. Worsley, in *New Statesman*, of Stratford's 'national venture [that] we can be thoroughly proud of' (1 May 1948). Britain, hard-pressed and plucky during the war, like Olivier's band of brothers in *Henry V*, its empire decidedly on the wane in the late 1940s, was understandably keen on laying hold of greatness. And in the universalizing of the peculiarly English genius of Shakespeare, many saw that greatness embodied. By the early 1960s, when the designation 'Royal' was added to both the theatre and the company (one wit remarked that with the names Shakespeare and Royal in the title, the only term missing was God), that process of universalizing Shakespeare was complete; but at the same time, it paradoxically began to fulfil a very different purpose. That is a point I shall explore later in this chapter.

Victorian chiaroscuro

Thus the opening of *Hamlet* on 23 April, 1948 can clearly be construed as a cultural gesture. It gave weight to the Stratford mission and perhaps carried with it some of the prophetic implications hinted at by Dover Wilson in his talk. But little of this was carried over directly into production values. The text used was as determinedly non-political as ever, all the international ramifications having been excised. Nor was there a clear effort to give a political turn to the plot or the characters. Of course, the refusal to politicize the play was itself an affirmation of the English tradition, a move not without ideological

[121]

weight given the contradictions between the shrinkage of Britain's political power and the attempt to secure its cultural hegemony. As well, certain innovative moves reveal an awareness of some of the issues facing the theatre at that moment.

Once again, the *look* of the production led the way. Costumes and set were firmly Victorian, though Elsinore was conceived of as Victorian Gothic, allowing for chiaroscuro lighting of veiled and receding archways. Through these vaulted spaces moved princes and courtiers sporting the frock coats, crinolines and crisp military uniforms adorned with gold cording and shining buttons of a not yet forgotten era. If Barry Jackson, in the 1920s, had sought a contemporary *Hamlet*, he now, along with director Michael Benthall, was inspired to move the play back a generation or two. The Victorian look, which from our present point of view in the 1990s has become almost commonplace, was novel – at Stratford, 'modern dress' of any kind, even Victorian, was an innovation. But the choice to dress the production in a style that reminded many theatregoers of their great aunts and uncles was not arbitrary, and the payoff was real. What it allowed, as some critics recognized, was a clearer sense of 'court precedence, rank and relationship' (*Wolverhampton Express and Star*, 24 April) than was normally possible, simply because audiences could recognize the various gradations. It gave to Claudius (Anthony Quayle) a weight and heartiness to offset the traditional villainy (though some objected to his resemblance to Albert the Good), and indeed endowed the whole production with the solidity of High Property. Moreover, it underlined the 'social nuances and the horror of the diplomatic pressure brought to bear on the untidy prince' more sharply than was possible in a doublet-and-hose court (*Time and Tide*, 1 May). Another gain from the setting was atmosphere. The dark arches of the single set were enhanced by effective additions for particular scenes (hanging, cobwebbed chains for the swearing scene with the Ghost, leaves for the graveyard, carved tables and chairs, a screen). The result was a mix of remoteness and familiarity within a space that allowed for the sort of speed and economy of movement from scene to scene that audiences had by now come to expect in Shakespearean production. And the lighting, like brief candle flames in the darkness, hinted effectively at the webbed life of the struggling and pained prince.

4 Paul Scofield snuffs the candles at the close of Act II (Stratford, 1948).

The choice of *Hamlet* as the birthday play was in some ways equivocal, given that Hamlet was, as we have seen, so often portrayed as indecisive, poetic and melancholy; perhaps the combination of sensitive fragility and unquestioned cultural pre-eminence expressed something of the doubleness of the

English self-image at the time. (In the same year Olivier was to release his well-known film which announces at the outset that *Hamlet* is the story of a man unable to make up his mind, while at the same time depicting Hamlet in primarily active terms.) The choice could even be seen as doubly equivocal in that, for the first time to my knowledge, the part of Hamlet was to be alternated between two actors, Robert Helpmann and Paul Scofield.

This move to use two actors, one older and more established, the other young and rising, had important consequences. The most notable was the new emphasis it placed on the production as a whole, giving more weight to the entire play than to the psyche of the hero and at the same time revealing the differences that can arise from the 'hearts and minds' of different actors, even when the other players, the blocking, the production values, even the emotional stresses, are all identical (T. C. Kemp, *Birmingham Post*, 26 April 1948). The verdict of the critics was generally that Scofield's interpretation was richer and more varied, a 'spirit in anguish no less profound than his father's … stricken to the soul, his grief and horror mingled with tenderness' (*Observer*, 25 April). He was the noble heart, the sweet prince of Horatio's encomium, with 'a lenitive cadence and a curious moth-like fragility' (*Time and Tide*, 1 May). 'On him the right sadness sits,' wrote Kenneth Tynan, 'but also the right spleen' (121). Helpmann was more rational, more settled and mature, better with the sardonic bits, less mercurial and emotional, hence less moving, though also better spoken than his young colleague. But their precise differences mattered less than the kinds of understandings brought to bear on the text as a whole.

Let us take as an example the end of the second soliloquy that closes Act II. Elaborate candelabra are set on a rich and imposing French writing desk, where the King has sat to carry out state business. Hamlet, alone, devises the scheme to use the play to catch the conscience of the King; as he speaks, he pinches the candles out, one by one, so that darkness comes with the final words of the soliloquy, and the curtain falls for the interval. This nicely etched moment might serve as an emblem for the whole production. For it highlighted several key facets – foremost the atmospheric concern with light and darkness, emphasized by James Bailey's arched Gothic set. The effect for most viewers, even those who found the Victorian setting incongruous, was visually captivating. The moment also captured something of the clarity of the production, its sharp intellectuality, as the extinguished candles not only bespoke for Hamlet the inescapable grip of his project but also suggested to an alert audience something of the darkness that would ensue, for Hamlet as well as for the bloat king whose conscience he sought to entrap. And it gave Scofield's frail and youthful Hamlet a moment of concentrated purpose, rising above the haunted suffering that was one of the hallmarks of his performance. For Helpmann, the move crystallized a performance that was characterized by a precision of movement and physical grace, the heritage of his training as a dancer, and also helped to underline the cerebral exactness that accompanied the physical deftness.

Such concentration of scenic and psychic effect seems to have been Benthall's primary intention. The many cuts in the prompt copy indicate a desire to give as clear and precise a rendering of the text as possible. They etch a sharp dramatic line, cutting down on the digressiveness, and hence to some extent on the discursive fascinations that the play can offer, and quickening the pace; not many of the cuts seem to have been ideologically motivated, though Hamlet's abrasiveness and extremity are curbed at a few points. A good example of the general approach is the way the elaborate plotting between Claudius and Laertes in the fourth act was managed. As it usually had been, Laertes's abortive rebellion – he is not just an outraged son but a would-be usurper who has whipped up the common people against the tyrant – was reduced to a minor scuffle easily handled by the skilful King. The conspiracy, which begins after Ophelia's mad scene and is fully elaborated just before the announcement of Ophelia's death (IV.v and IV.vii), was shifted to the graveyard, *after* Hamlet's return and tussle with Laertes at the grave-side (interestingly, the Olivier film adopts the same approach and traces an almost identical trajectory). Exclusive focus on Ophelia's plight and Laertes' reaction to it thus modulated smoothly and without interruption to the latter's revenge. The transposition also removed the need for the dramatically awkward letters announcing Hamlet's arrival on Danish soil (IV.vi and vii), and gave an urgency to the plotting, which was itself judiciously trimmed.

The sombre Victorian costumes added their effect – Quayle's Claudius, standing at the grave-side, ran his fingers over the top hat in his hand, smoothing it gracefully and with an edge of menace. After the plot was laid, Laertes paused to look at the grave that the sexton was filling in and was interrupted by the King tapping him on the shoulder, reminding him again of his deadly mission. Altogether, the scene, which can lean toward sentimentality, was given an ominous twist and led the play quickly and logically to its climax.

Claudius emerged as a man to be reckoned with, a 'genial Victorian man of the world with whom it would be a pleasure to dine' (*Times*, 26 April). For *The Guardian*, Quayle 'almost' gave the play another hero; he is a 'mutton-chopped *pater*' who made a wrong turn but seems 'entitled to lecture Hamlet on the error of his ways'. The *Times* reviewer, like others who objected to Quayle's 'almost sympathetic' portrayal, seemed reluctant to admit the sympathy he felt for Claudius, but this can give us a clue both to audience expectation and to changing conceptions. In the traditional conception, Claudius was an oily villain and tyrant, though we have noted that, in many earlier stagings, he was a worthy adversary for the prince and even, as at the Birmingham Rep, a sympathetic figure. Here the audience was presented with a 'bluff, rubious intriguer, a six bottle man ... given to churchyard conspiracies' (*Observer*, 25 April). This yielded a nicely ambiguous moment in the prayer scene – Claudius sipping from a wineglass as he parleyed with Rosencrantz, Guildenstern and Polonius, his head still befuddled with drink as he knelt to pray. Thus emerge the complexities of the play, the added difficulty for Hamlet and for us if our villains don't conform to stereotype. Such a conception also tends to isolate Hamlet's own perceptions, giving credibility to his self-doubt and forcing our own judgments upon us as audience. By now, we have become more used to the sympathetic Claudius, one who loves his wife and seems at times justifiably irritated at his stepson's antics; but in 1948, although the conception was not new, it disturbed many reviewers and playgoers, who wanted their villains clearly marked.

Diane Wynyard's Queen and Claire Bloom's Ophelia were less obviously conceived in opposition to received opinion, but they too had their differences. *The Times* wrote that Wynyard 'only with an uphill effort suggests the natural sensuality of

Gertrude', the word 'natural' giving away the game, and indicating clearly the masculinist assumption – sensuality was the standard explanation for her behaviour. From other hints we can surmise that Wynyard was trying to move away from the stereotype, not failing in a struggle to achieve it. *The Sunday Times* wrote that her 'discreetly opulent costumes give especial point to her mock modesty at some of Hamlet's less guarded references' (25 April), suggesting a more complex reading, something like Pinero's Mrs Tanqueray perhaps, a rather knowing woman of the world who is aware at the same time of the expectations that hem her in and takes pains to meet them. And Bloom's Ophelia, very young and innocent (the actress was only seventeen), took the audience by surprise when her madness showed an unaccustomed vehemence and wildness, a 'haunting distraction' (*Birmingham Gazette*, 26 April), after which the audience was 'too moved to applaud' (Roger Page, *Peace News*, 7 May). She was able to combine madness with a keen perception of the realities around her, pointing to an imaginary grave on 'Pray you mark', eyeing the King on 'My brother shall know of it', curtseying to the ladies in waiting (who had replaced the gentleman and Horatio in the scene) on 'Good night, ladies', collapsing, weeping, suddenly rushing across the stage. The effect was to heighten the incongruity, while at the same time making sense of individual lines. Instead of a picturesque and sentimental absorption in her own world, Bloom was disconcertingly between worlds; she handed out weeds, rather brazenly accosted the king, then flickered back to her personal plight on 'pansies – that's for *thoughts*', touching the necklace that Hamlet had given her, the same one we had seen her touch when she first mentioned his 'tenders of affection' to her father, and which she had sought to return to him in the nunnery scene.

How a production handles the Ghost is one mark of its comfort with the text, since in our century the Ghost can be a bit of an embarrassment. Of the various strategies that have been attempted, the least successful, I think, are those that shy away from a solid spectre to eerie lighting effects or amplified spooky voices with no material presence whatever. What is frightening about the Ghost for those who see him is precisely that he is *there*, even though they know he is dead. His presence is ineluctable. But a spectre can be too solid, and Esmond

Knight's did lean that way. He 'should thaw and resolve himself into a dew' wrote *The Observer* (25 April). He wound himself up into a terrific rage, yelling out key words like 'revenge' and 'murder' which were then echoed around the battlements. He also indulged in an 'asthmatic wheeze' when he was not speaking, giving him too melodramatic an air (*Peace News*, 7 May). But one can see the idea – how to make the Ghost both palpable and different, otherworldly and yet recognizably human, passionate and angry. Something 'majestical' was lost by this, but there were gains. In both the first scene and again in I.iv, he *tried* to speak but had difficulty, as though the wheeze were a condition of purgatory. The amplified echoes caused Hamlet, when he first heard them, to look around in wonder, again in an effort to suggest a different world.

The conception of Hamlet on the part of both actors seemed to fit with the production's overall dedication to clarity. Neither actor developed a unique or odd reading; while Scofield's was more touching, Helpmann's was more deliberate and harsh. In the nunnery scene, Hamlet knew about the eavesdroppers – he had overheard the plot in the previous scene (this idea, along with several other details, derived from Dover Wilson, via Gielgud). Even so, Scofield in particular was gentle at the outset, closing Ophelia's book without a snap, stroking her hair on 'Go thy ways to a nunnery', only rising to anger later, having seen the shadows of the spies and turning harshly on 'Where's your father?' The attack once mounted, Hamlet kept it up, but directed his fiercest venom at the hidden lords, threatening them directly. After he left, Ophelia collapsed; Polonius, after conferring with the King, helped her up, but then abandoned her as he went off with Claudius. She stood for a moment and then exited slowly into the black, ending the scene and heightening the contrast with the bustling opening of the play scene that followed immediately.

In general, Scofield played the part with a profound sense of being haunted – he seemed a 'spiritual fugitive' who was seeking his own death as a relief from the pain of his imagination. 'His skill in smelling falseness extend[ed] to himself, thereby breeding self-disgust' (Tynan 121). For the *Times* reviewer, his 'inner distractions [had] ... such intense dramatic reality that the melodramatic bustle of the Court appear[ed] unreal' (26 April). This gave even to the active moments a painfulness and uncertainty, a mix of horror and softness that captured some of the Prince's complexity. Throughout the crucial Act III sequence, for example, from the bitter scene with Ophelia through to the confrontation with his mother, Scofield's playing transformed the action into a doomed quest for 'spiritual certitude' (*The Times*, 26 April).

At the opening of the play scene, the actors were milling about, some setting the stage, others applying make-up; Lucianus was learning the lines Hamlet had penned for him. A sense of fellowship prevailed which Hamlet's purposeful lecture on acting did nothing to dissipate (the Clown executed a comic turn while Hamlet warned against clownish excess); but the Prince remained a little aloof, bent on his project. During the play (formally presented without the dumb-show), the court reacted to the pointed comments, and Hamlet, in an old and cumbersome bit of business invented (as we saw) by Kean, crawled across the floor from Ophelia to Claudius while Lucianus spoke the melodramatic speech the prince had presumably written. In this we can see some hankering for Victorian production values going along with the Victorian setting. It is as though the reverence for Shakespeare that Stratford was designed to inculcate was itself distinguished by reverence for theatrical tradition. Here was the true English *Hamlet*. This kind of obviously theatrical gesture may have cranked Hamlet up but went against the more sensitive and subtle playing Scofield displayed elsewhere. Perhaps, though, it served to even things out between himself and Claudius, since the taut moment after the play is halted was played as a stand-off. Claudius turned sharply on Hamlet after calling for light, and Hamlet backed slowly away. Then Claudius rushed off with the court following helter-skelter. Ophelia was left standing bewildered at centre stage till she was led off by her father and Hamlet moved into triumphant, if eruptive, movement. The scene with Rosencrantz and Guildenstern he handled with authority, snapping the recorder to the floor at the climax (here too the production was adapting Victorian stage business), but the adrenaline had thinned by the time he got to Claudius's private study. There, in a move invented by Gielgud in the 1930s and then dropped by him in 1939 (under Granville-Barker's simplifying influence), Hamlet picked up the sword that the King had carried in and laid down, but then retreated sword in hand. Not even the death and damnation of Claudius, it seemed, would satisfy his spiritual hunger.

With his mother, there was again the combination of determination, tenderness, and pain. He came in with Claudius's sword, startling the Queen as she turned from brushing her hair at the table. Her cry led to Polonius's shout, and then a key moment. As Polonius called out, the Queen rose toward him but Hamlet stopped her deliberately, moved sharply to the arras, jumped on a bench, and plunged the sword home. He was not impulsive here, but knew what he was doing, and was disappointed when he discovered the identity of his victim. The inconsistency with his hesitation a moment before became part of the characterization. He dropped the sword, turned to his mother and sat her firmly on the 'pouffe' (a round couch-like object but emphatically not a bed – there was no trace of the Olivier Oedipal motive). From there the scene modulated to tenderness (the promptbook indicates, interestingly, that after comparing the two miniatures, father and uncle, only Helpmann tore the locket from his mother's neck). After the Ghost's exit, Hamlet leaned on his mother's breast and some of the harsher lines (Hamlet's self-characterization as heaven's 'scourge and minister' and his irreverent reference to Polonius's corpse, 'I'll lug the guts into the neighbour room') were cut. Even when the lines could be played harshly, they were not: on 'I must be cruel only to be kind', it was 'kind' that received the emphasis, as Hamlet knelt in front of his mother, his head on her lap. There was even a lingering thought and a glance towards Polonius as the unlucky victim of the clash of two crafts. And the exit was decorous and sad.

Immediately after the closet scene comes Hamlet's arrest, a scene that was frequently cut in nineteenth- and early twentieth-century revivals (such as those of Irving and Barrymore); but it can be a key moment in a production since it helps to establish just how level is the balance of power between the two 'mighty opposites'. Here it was staged as a gradual closing in, the pain of it intensified by involving Hamlet's former allies as part of the police team: Francisco, Barnardo, and Marcellus were all there, along with Rosencrantz and Guildenstern, a palace guard incongruously but effectively armed with swords. Hamlet was brought in under guard, before an audience of footmen, councillors, and the ubiquitous Osric. With swords pointed at his back and midriff, Hamlet's distress was the more pronounced, his sardonic joking more desperate, and his isolation more evident.

The final scene brought some redress at last. The plotters spread their nets, Osric handing the unbated sword to Laertes as part of a plan, and the King acknowledging the poisoned cup to Osric and Laertes, though too late to save the hapless Queen. But Hamlet now took charge. Laertes, unable to hit him legitimately, took the coward's way out and stabbed him in the back. (The text here has no clear directions as to how the duel is to be handled, or how or when Hamlet gets hold of the poisoned sword.) Treachery renewed Hamlet's energy, and, after a vigourous chase, Laertes was dispatched while the failing Queen and frightened King looked on. The whole court reacted in fear while the Queen, standing stage centre, warned her son, who then leapt to the rostrum to prevent the King's escape, stabbed him, and, grabbing the poisoned cup from a terrified page, forced him to drink. As Hamlet staggered back, his now fallen mother held out her hand, and he took it just before collapsing into Horatio's arms. Again at the last, a sweetness of feeling prevailed despite the bloodshed, and his death was quiet and noble. The court, however, was in turmoil, uncertain, until suddenly everyone was arrested by the ominous entry of Fortinbras; all retreated in panic and silence ensued, except for a page on his knees at centre, sobbing. New power has taken over from old, the straightforward man from the complex one, a contrast that had been nicely suggested earlier when, behind Hamlet's probing conversation with the Norwegian captain (IV.iv) and the subsequent soliloquy questioning the value of military exploits, Fortinbras sat studying his maps, an occasional strategic rustle reminding the audience of his presence. At the end, Fortinbras has won, but the moment was neither ironic nor forbidding. What was paramount was the sense of loss.

Marking this emblematically was the weeping page. His presence throughout was in fact a kind of symbolic marker. He had run in with the Players bursting with excitement, grinned at the Player's recitation, listened while Hamlet spoke feelingly of the theatre and been a keen spectator at the play, lying in front of the enthroned Queen, sharp as a ferret. Re-entering with the Players to clear away props after the festivities were curtailed, he ran afoul of Guildenstern, who slapped him hard.

At the climactic duel, he was again an eager observer, little realizing that it would end in a mutual silence punctuated only by his own sobs. He thus became a kind of stand-in for Hamlet's own predicament, a wordless but eloquent chorus. He was pure theatrical invention, but such is both the liberty and the power of the theatre's way with texts.

Anti-establishment *Hamlet*: Peter Hall and David Warner

In the late 1950s, the ethos of the British theatre shifted radically. The Angry Young Men took centre stage: regional accents, lower-class heroes (or anti-heroes), Brechtian alienation, and existentialist angst – all of them in the wake of Osborne's *Look Back in Anger* (1956) and the unexpected success of Peter Hall's production of Beckett's *Waiting for Godot* (1955) – emerged as the dominant mode. In 1960, Hall became director of the new RSC, determined to mould what had been an ad hoc group into a recognizable company, and to give it a social and political meaningfulness (relevance was the era's buzz word) that Shakespeare had seemed hitherto to lack. A major success, though a controversial one, followed in 1962, when Peter Brook directed Paul Scofield in an 'absurdist' *King Lear* influenced by Jan Kott, the Polish director and critic whose *Shakespeare our Contemporary* was making inroads into *avant garde* pockets of the academy, as well as into English-speaking theatres on both sides of the Atlantic.

Stratford had by now come into its own, an achievement marked, rather ironically as it seemed to some, by the adoption of the 'Royal' epithet mentioned earlier. The irony is worth stressing, since Hall's work with the company as the militant 1960s gained momentum was deliberately to challenge the political and social status quo. So, even as Shakespeare and Stratford had, in the previous generation, been constructed as a universalizing and hegemonic cultural force, a counter-movement set in, but a paradoxical one with no less universalizing tendencies: Shakespeare as oppositional and anti-establishment. This move can now, from our present vantage point, be seen as less radical than it seemed at the time (see Sinfield 159-60). Based on a similar humanistic notion of the bard, 'royal' Shakespeare in the 1960s more or less inverted Dover Wilson's missionary image of the civilizing Shakespeare by re-imagin-

5 David Warner's scruffy undergraduate Hamlet, scarf around neck, confronts his mother (Elizabeth Spriggs) in her boudoir (Stratford, 1965).

ing the plays as critiques of the established values that propped up oppressive social and political structures. But the Shakespeare thus constructed was still one who believed in a humane and egalitarian order – a benevolent liberal.

By 1965, Hall was ready to take on *Hamlet*, and he had both the concept and the actor he wanted. The idea of the production revolved around the by now much quoted idea that his was to be a *Hamlet* for the 1960s, with a particular ideological slant: 'For our decade I think the play will be about the disillusionment which produces an apathy of the will so deep that commitment to politics, to religion or to life is impossible' (programme note). The actor was David Warner, age twenty-four, tall, gangly, unformed, distinctly non-heroic, the perfect image of the scruffy undergraduate, ready to play Trilby to Hall's Svengali (or so some of the press reports darkly hinted). Hall's most important idea was to place Hamlet firmly within an oppressive social milieu, to represent Elsinore as a smooth-functioning, efficient and dominating court – leaving little room for Hamlet to manoeuvre. The entrapment of the prince was imaginatively caught in the opening image of the second scene, with Hamlet not brooding in traditional isolation at the side but seated rigid at a table, flanked by Polonius to his left, Claudius and his mother to his right, locked in a 'cage of circumstance' (Robert Speaight, *Shakespeare Quarterly* 16 (1965), 320). Table and chairs, with the principals already seated, were on a small dais that rolled silently in from the back as the scene opened; this non-illusionary entry suggested immediately the well-oiled machinery of Claudius's reign. The bright patina of the inlaid table, the cold reflective gleam of the parquet floors, the dark shiny walls all added a sinister lustre to the 'Establishment' court, emphasizing the 'self-conscious inadequacy of the figure trapped inside it' (Wells 29). Here, as in all the court scenes, efficient councillors, milling ambassadors, and sharp-eyed sycophants swelled the scene, giving weight to the political process and point to Hamlet's apathy. And Brewster Mason's Claudius was no 'bloat king', even if he did, like Anthony Quayle, carry a wine glass to prayer; rather, 'completely in tune with the general atmosphere' (W. A. Darlington, *Daily Telegraph*, 20 Aug.), he was efficient and effective, dispatching the ambassadors with an air that made it clear he could manage the cold war with Norway, or quietly signing Hamlet's death warrant before dispatching him to England (IV.iii), thereby making clear that his plan is neither hasty nor unconsidered.

Such a King seemed the living embodiment of the sinister, gleaming world created by John Bury's settings. The basic material was black Formica, which the critics read variously as ebony or black marble, highlighted with glints of silver. The shiny patterned floor mirrored, as in a glass darkly, the determined steps and efficient gloss of the working court. Hamlet could not even escape his own reflection. There was a false proscenium, black, with walls on each side angled sharply inwards towards wide doors at the back; these were alternately opened, shut or hung with tapestries, but always claustrophobic. The walls had revolving panels, showing a bookcase for Polonius's study or Rubensesque nude murals for the court-chamber scenes concerned with the oppression of Ophelia (II.ii, III.i, IV.v). For the big court scenes (such as I.ii), there hung at the back an enormous tapestry of two huge, fully caparisoned horses, again suggesting the impinging danger without (Cockin 124). The lighting, dark and glinting, contributed to the feeling of entrapment, and the untroubled movements of the court produced a persistent sense of impenetrability. The set thus played a crucial role, not only in carrying the production's anti-establishment message, but in recruiting Shakespeare as a political ally.

Tony Church's Polonius fitted as smoothly into this shiny landscape as he did into the overall conception. He showed none of the traditional folly or fussiness but carried himself as the consummate politician, the King's right-hand man, president of the Privy Council, his pin-striped gown an effective bridge between the Tudor image of Lord Burleigh (Queen Elizabeth's chief minister and Church's model for the role) and the 1960s Tory insider. Some critics objected ('Polonius *is* a silly old man' – *The Times*, 20 Aug. 1965), but again the conception made consistent sense and was managed with very little manipulative cutting. Most of Polonius's 'silly' lines remained, but Church was able to turn them to the confident self-mockery of a man who can let himself be laughed at just in order to turn the wheel his way. Church had played the implacable and politic Cornwall in Brook's *King Lear* three years earlier, an interesting preparation for his reading of the dangerous, though more humorous and self-mocking, Polonius. He explained his approach by remarking that it is 'a well established device for Establishment politicians to laugh at themselves' (quoted in Addenbroke 130).

His control was sharply evoked in the sequence following Laertes' departure in I.iii. He dismissed his son fondly on 'Go, your servants tend', then took down a book from the shelf (the scene, domestic and confined, was set in his study), sat at a desk replete with state papers, ink, and a brandy glass, and settled down to read while his children exchanged goodbyes – oblivious, it seemed, to their chat. But all the while he kept an ear cocked. Laertes, on his way out, reminded Ophelia of what he had earlier said to her. There was a long pause before Polonius looked up from his book, but he had missed nothing: 'What is't, Ophelia, he hath said to you?' (Speaight 322, and promptbook). The general seriousness of the character was indicated by how other people reacted to him; the King, for instance, always listened to him with intense interest; Osric and Reynaldo made a point of respectfully imitating him, and Hamlet, though he mocked him, could not always stand up to him. In the 'fishmonger' dialogue (II.ii.169ff.), Hamlet's antics became a bit strained: he lay flat on his back between two benches for 'Out of the air ... into my grave' in a 'mad' enactment of what he was saying; but this didn't fool the old man. 'Though this be madness, yet there is method in't' was spoken not with comic amazement; rather, it 'meant "He cannot fool me" (Church in *Players* 108). Hamlet's inability to know what to do was especially pointed as Polonius took his leave: the repeated 'except my life' was spoken lying face down on the shiny parquet. The balance, as so often in this version, seemed tipped yet again against the sensitive but apathetic Prince.

Perhaps because of these stacked odds, the youth of the day loved it. Their readiness for a *Hamlet* of their own, promised by the advance publicity, is indicated by the fact that so many young people queued for two nights and days to secure tickets for the opening; and the popularity of the show only increased as the run got under way. Many older critics deplored the slow and broken verse speaking, the deliberately anti-Romantic, anti-heroic conception, the matter-of-factness and lack of 'excitement'. But their strictures had no effect on ticket sales. The generation gap that the performance set out specifically to dramatize, the sense of alienated youth in inchoate and ineffectual rebellion against an older generation that seemed to have everything in hand and whose very blandness was a weapon of oppression, was itself to some extent re-enacted in the responses to the production. But of course not all the older generation reacted negatively. Many of the best critics appreciated the new sense Hall's reading made of the text, partial as it necessarily was.

J. R. Brown gives a balanced analysis of Hall's and Warner's thorough re-thinking of the text and in the process helps to explain some of its wide appeal. Tiny details illuminated the sense of youthful alienation; for example, as Hamlet was being hunted down after the closet scene (a sequence given even more weight here than in Benthall's production), he entered wearily and knelt as if to pray (his stance ironically mirroring that of his hated uncle a few scenes before); as he did so, he 'hammer[ed] his sword into a crack in the flags' (Brown, *Shakespeare Survey* 19 (1966) and promptbook). His simple line, 'But soft, what noise? Who calls on Hamlet? O, here they come' (IV.ii.3-4), became a cry of ineffectual resistance: 'O here *they* come', the emphatic 'they' etching a 'composite description of restrictive and uncomprehending authority' (Brown 113). Later, indicted by Claudius and dispatched on a trumped-up diplomatic mission ('For England?' 'Ay, Hamlet'. 'Good'), he spoke the last word sharply, at the same moment rising from the prie-dieu where he had been kneeling, and striking it (promptbook). Brown saw this as a mixture of irony and tense nerves, the tone of 'Good' mocking the King 'with his own platitudes, but to no effective purpose' (113). So here was the disregarded youth, contemptuous and ironic in his attitude to the authority that binds him, but utterly unable to do anything about it.

A similar irony flickered over the final scene, most evidently when Hamlet spoke of the martial Fortinbras succeeding him, turning the traditional praise into a cynical joke which suggested that the young who follow in their elders' footsteps are as contemptible as those they replace (see W. H. W., *Birmingham Mail*, 20 Aug. 1965, and Harold Hobson, *Sunday Times*, 22 Aug.). The irony even extended to his own death, to the 'dazed triumph' (Trewin, *Birmingham Post*, 20 Aug.) he had finally effected; but, as Ronald Bryden argued, that irony was subject to multiple interpretation: though it could be read as 'an existentialist's discovery ... that the universe is absurd and history a trap, [it] makes more consistent sense ... as the ironic convulsion of a boy who has finally achieved the princeliness he aspired to by dying, and can find it funny' (*New Statesman*, 27 Aug.). His last gesture was to kiss 'lovingly and privately' (Brown, *Shakespeare Survey* 118) the medallion of his father that hung around his neck – so that a mix of deep feeling and ironic awareness of his failure sealed his performance and gave it its characteristic shading.

Both the depth and the inchoateness of his feeling were a

source of his appeal to the youth of the time. It was an appeal that the production deliberately sought to inculcate and politicize. In designing his version to be a mirror of youthful disillusionment and apathy, Hall was clearly seeking both to develop a young audience for his company and to awaken them politically. 'I am a radical and I could not work in the theatre if I were not', he declared the next year (quoted in Sinfield 159). In the production programme, he spoke sadly of the new apathy, of young intellectuals who have 'lost the ordinary, predictable radical impulses' which the young should manifest. 'There is a sense of what-the-hell anyway, over us looms the Mushroom Cloud. And politics are a game and a lie'. *Hamlet* , he felt, is less a tragedy than a 'clinical dissection of life', a 'shattering' play that leaves us in the end only with Fortinbras, 'the perfect military ruler. And I don't know about you, but I would not particularly like to live in Denmark under Fortinbras'. The problem was that in finding the perfect image (and the perfect actor) by which to gain youthful approval, Hall at the same time weakened his political project. The young audiences who took this Hamlet to their hearts were more likely to imitate him than to regard him as an example of what *not* to be. As a critique of apathy, the production in some way paradoxically espoused it, though it also succeeded in defining brilliantly the nature of the enemy.

The text used contributed strongly to the sense of the ubiquity and oppressiveness of Establishment politics. Turning his back on tradition, Hall retained almost all of the material concerning the international context: the wars with Norway, the Danish ambassadors and their mission, and both Fortinbras scenes, including the final moments with the entrance of the English ambassadors, who are almost always cut. In addition, Hall kept the Polonius–Reynaldo scene (II.i), usually excised but so useful as a sign of court intrigue; and he trimmed the Osric scene (in V.ii) so as to make the court fop into a menacing insider, adding to the general atmosphere of harsh and dangerous public pressure. There were plenty of cuts, about 730 lines in all (Wells 25-6), but most were directed towards passages of amplification and reflection, pointing and quickening several scenes, but never sacrificing their political weight.

International militarism was epitomized in the aggressive opening image: a massive cannon pointing directly at the audience. Here was a state prepared for war, hot or cold, a motif continued in the smooth diplomacy of the ambassadors, who were not only retained, but given their full textual presence. Still, the nervous sentries belied the official confidence – and no wonder. The Ghost was not only an errant spirit – he was huge, ten or twelve feet high (propelled on a trolley by a hidden stage hand) with the eerie, sepulchral voice of Patrick Magee. And when Hamlet finally met him, once again the sense of being outmanned was the dominant effect. The Ghost entered with raised arms through the doors at the back as the sentries and Prince huddled around the cannon downstage. Hamlet, facing forward, read his presence in the faces of his companions, but didn't move. 'Angels and ministers of grace ...', rather than the usual cry, was a soft prayer (Penelope Gilliat, *Observer*, 22 Aug.), followed by a pause where he steeled himself before turning. A sudden eruption of movement ensued as the guards tried to hinder him from following his father, Barnardo wielding two spears, one restraining Hamlet, the other challenging the Ghost. A sharp kick disposed of Barnardo, and Hamlet twisted away from Horatio's restrictive embrace. Moments later, he re-entered walking backwards from upstage, facing the towering, slow-moving Ghost. On 'sweep to my revenge', he swept, ironically, to the long arms of his father, to be cradled within them for the remainder of the scene. He seemed to be 'looking for the comforts of the nursery' (*The Times*, 20 Aug.), and it was clearly his father rather than his mother, here and throughout, that fired his imagination. But the gap between heroic parent and inadequate child was overtly underlined by the stage image, generated as it were by Hamlet's inner compulsions: the father huge and protective, the son comfortless and unfit. Even after the Ghost's departure under the stage, as he reeled about getting his friends to swear their secrecy, Hamlet kept falling on the ground as if 'attempting to return to his father's protective embrace' (Cockin 129). How could such a man effectively take on the polished King or his politic prime minister?

David Warner's Prince was reviled for not being princely, his condition of 'existentialist panic' (*Times*, 20 Aug.) thought unworthy of royal blood, and his general demeanour deemed unsuited to Ophelia's loving description of her courtier, soldier, scholar. But then again, as Harold Hobson noted, is a distraught

lover's description to be taken necessarily at face value? Furthermore, again in Hobson's words, few princes are conventionally princely – that is left for the sons of accountants 'from
good suburbs and lesser public schools' (*Sunday Times*, 22
Aug.). Warner may have been unsure of himself, but he was not
'socially insecure'; he did not care whether his inferiors approved of his strange clothes, but flouted convention with
aristocratic ease. He wore high boots and a succession of
weedy gowns and tunics, but the most telling sartorial mark of
his estrangement was a long knitted reddish scarf that dangled
from his burdened shoulders and became a kind of symbol of
his alienated selfhood. (It also led to some effective business, as
when Rosencrantz and Guildenstern, on their first appearance,
each took an end of it and tugged their 'friend' gently down
stage; this was countered by Hamlet's reeling them in conspira-
torially on 'Were you not sent for?'). For Hobson, Warner had
'inner authority' despite his bewilderment, expressed chiefly in
occasional, spare, controlled and deadly movement, as in the
duel scene where he stood utterly still, 'hardly bothering to
move his sword', while an 'active, sweating Laertes' tried to get
at him from different angles.

This economy of movement, contrasted sometimes by wild
and ungainly galloping, was a mark of the production as a
whole. Minimal but telling moves, sometimes slow but also
deliberate and thoughtful, can be traced in the promptbook, as
if the director wanted to centre and quieten the whole unfolding sequence. Hamlet simply sat, or stood, for most of the
soliloquies, directing them outwards, deliberately, to the audience, seeking as it were our help and counsel, using 'the Elizabethan convention with total literalness ... commun[ing] not
with himself but with [us]' (Ronald Bryden, *New Statesman*, 27
Aug.). So too he sat for much of the 'nunnery' scene; Polonius
sat quietly as he interrogated Ophelia about Hamlet's aberrant
behaviour, while she stood frightened and unmoving (II.i); the
Queen knelt at her husband's prie-dieu for the entire story of
Ophelia's drowning; Claudius sat to sign the papers that would
condemn his nephew to death and to arraign him when he
appeared. In such a context, sudden accented moves could gain
a new resonance. Polonius taking down a copy of Machiavelli's
Prince from the shelf, the King, in a repeated gesture, comforting himself with a glass of brandy, or Hamlet erupting into a

frenzy: kicking over the King's chair in the middle of the 'rogue and peasant slave' soliloquy or slapping Ophelia after slouching apathetically in that same chair during the nunnery scene – such moves punctuated the relative stillness into which they intruded.

The King's chair served in fact as a strong theatrical marker. After Rosencrantz and Guildenstern's first entrance, Hamlet sat provocatively in the chair, ironically registering for their benefit that perhaps he *is* ambitious. When the Players arrived, he deliberately set the Player-king on the chair and arranged the other actors around the table in a mock-up of the court, with the Player-queen taking Gertrude's spot; then he handed around goblets, which had been a conspicuous sign of the court's ease. When he shouted 'remorseless, treacherous villain' at the same chair a few minutes later, and then booted it across the stage, the audience could recognize an ambiguous symbolization, whereby the prop stood for the King and Hamlet's uneasy attitude toward him, but it was clear as well that Hamlet was more comfortable with self-dramatizing displays of bravado than with action. He thus turned the power of the theatre against himself, becoming as ineffectual as the unnoticed dumb-show.

This notion carried over into the play scene itself, and especially its famous aftermath. During the dumb-show, drinks were served, and general chatter covered the dangerous bits. There was an empty chair on the rostrum beside the King and Queen, but Hamlet preferred to remain below. He applauded loudly after the Player-queen's exit and Ophelia followed suit, but the rest of the court pointedly did not; then he moved to his empty chair to pose the question: 'Madam, how like you this play?' and the court chatter subsided. The sense was that Hamlet was being gratuitously offensive, and the court watched carefully for the royal cue. It came a few moments later when the King called for lights. Far from being a spontaneous manifestation of guilt, the interruption became, in Brewster Mason's hands, a mark of 'offended dignity'; he was publicly rebuking Hamlet for an impertinent 'social gaffe' (*Times*), i.e., for daring to enact a nephew's murderous inclinations toward his uncle. But there was also a flicker of fear in his eye, noticeable to Hamlet, if not to the rest of the court. This led to an electric moment when the two met 'eye to eye' with

Claudius 'silently accept[ing] the challenge of a duel to the death' (Mervyn Jones, *Tribune*, 27 Aug.). Here perhaps was Hamlet's strongest moment before the finale, but the King had clearly won nevertheless, by turning his nephew's theatrical test into a public relations victory. Again the theme was the imperviousness of power.

In the graveyard, there was a moment of ironic rest. There were realistic bones to accompany the often unnaturally isolated skull. The gravedigger nonchalantly poked mud from poor Yorick's eye sockets, and, while Hamlet caressed the skull, there was still earth caught between its teeth ('Where be those lips ...?'). On telling Yorick to 'Get thee to my lady's chamber', a 'lightening in his voice tells you he has not taught himself to face the shock, just a minute away, of Ophelia's burial' (*New Statesman*, 27 Aug.). It was raining and the court party entered with umbrellas and a canopy. As the gravedigger sprinkled dirt on the coffin, Laertes came forward, raised the lid and threw himself into his sister's grave. Hamlet was more reticent, refraining from the controversial leap, which would in any case have been quite out of character. Instead, Laertes emerged from the grave to tackle his adversary, clutching his legs and upending him. But despite Laertes' violence, the struggle ended inconclusively.

Later, contemplating the possibility of death and the shaping force of divinity ('There is special providence in the fall of a sparrow' V.ii.219ff.), Hamlet appeared not to believe in such a providence for *himself*; his face quivered on 'Readiness is all' though he mastered it and walked off, 'condemned but not now afraid' (*Sunday Times*, 22 Aug.). This led directly into the last scene, in which Warner's Hamlet finally achieved a measure of victory. Ronald Bryden describes the complex effect of the final image, Hamlet's body hoisted aloft on the shoulders of four captains who filed slowly back over the darkening stage, as a 'halo of luminosity' clung to 'the receding arched throat and hanging head' (*New Statesman*, 27 Aug.). This of course is the traditional image, but Hall evoked it with a difference. The duel, as I mentioned, began calmly, Hamlet remaining still and secure. At an unexpected thrust from Laertes, which drew blood, there was a shocked silence while Hamlet deliberately, intensely, showed the wound to the assembled onlookers. Suddenly the fight erupted into a scuffling brawl, with the combatants clawing and punching at each other (Jan Kott, *Sunday Times* 31 Oct.), Hamlet finally liberated into action. With Laertes down, the Queen stumbled downstage centre, warned Hamlet ('The drink, the drink! I am pois'ned') and collapsed in a stream of her own vomit (a touch of graphic realism that not everybody noticed). And Hamlet, dazed but deadly, turned at last to his adversary. He advanced on Claudius, nicked him almost playfully on the neck with the envenomed sword, then stabbed him in earnest, kneed him, and in a final symbolic flourish, poured the poisoned drink slowly into his ear – a reminder of the fratricide that is the source of all this carnage. Hamlet has little left to do but give Fortinbras, the glistening militarist, his 'dying voice', but he did so with a distinctly ironic tone, and then kissed his father's miniature, having fulfilled the Ghost's injunction, albeit with dazed relief rather than conscious determination. Meanwhile the court had reacted with horror at his initial approach to Claudius (the line in which 'All' shout 'Treason, Treason!' was not cut), and was ready quickly to make its obeisance to Fortinbras when the time arrived; the whole court, the troop of councillors and hangers-on who have been there from the beginning, went to its knees when Fortinbras announced his 'Vantage', with the menacing Osric taking the lead (he was, fittingly, no simpleton in this production but a knowing courtier who was implicated in the plot to kill Hamlet and who rapidly established a liaison with Fortinbras).

The presentation of the women in the production was consistent with the overall concept, the generation gap as prominent as in the treatment of the men. Gertrude was seen as if through Hamlet's own eyes, rather weak and too acquiescent, untroubled by moral problems, and a bit blowzy and vulgar (Wells 31). Her look confirmed the image: a bit too much flash in the dress, 'peroxide curls, dolly make-up' (Gilliat, *Observer*, 22 Aug.). At the same time, she had a vulnerable side, evident especially when she removed her wig upon getting ready for bed, which gave her a rather drab, vaguely pathetic, washed out look; 'shorn of dignity and finery' (Anthony Mervyn, *Liverpool Post*, 20 August), she shed as well her public face of strained glamour and her gestures of a slightly desperate suburban matron. The closet scene was played mostly on a huge bed with a substantial curtain behind it. But the sexual element suggested by the bed, so frequently seen since Olivier played it for all it was worth in his 1948 film, was little evident; this Hamlet's Oedipal feelings were directed mostly toward his father, to whom it seemed impossible to measure up. Still, the murder of Polonius, which adds a desperate and macabre air to Hamlet's confrontation with his mother, suggested a transformation of sexual feeling into violence. Hamlet stabbed through the arras while he stood on the bed astride his prostrate mother and the old man fell beside the bed, remaining visible throughout the rest of the scene. Later, as his interview with Gertrude heated up, she once again lay back, her head downstage, as he leaned over her. The entrance of the Ghost, from behind the same arras that had concealed Polonius, suggested a link between Hamlet's various father figures and drove the prince away from his mother. So the scene as a whole can perhaps be read as a narrative of how this sensitive young man is violently wrenched away from an attachment to his mother and forced into a world inhabited by successful and *large* men whom he cannot match.

Gertrude's forlorn physicality was an extension of and perhaps a commentary on the traditional idea of her as the ordinary sensual woman. It was put into most emphatic relief by her grotesque vomiting at the end, but she also had her moment of quiet dignity when she spoke the beautiful, sad account of Ophelia's death, kneeling unaffectedly at a prie-dieu. Her connection with Ophelia had been effectively suggested earlier as well, when she retrieved the mad girl's lute, after Ophelia had gone out in a dream of herbs and grace.

Glenda Jackson, who played Ophelia, had recently appeared as Charlotte Corday in Hall's powerful and influential production of the *Marat–Sade* and could therefore be said to be acquainted with madness. Hers was one of the production's most controversial interpretations. Most of the critics, unfamiliar with the idea of a harsh and turbulent Ophelia, did not know what to do with her. She was supposed to be innocent and hurt, a wounded dove, but Jackson's Ophelia was more a bird of prey. Though the comments varied, they were similar in tone: 'Very strong-willed' (*Guardian*), a 'tough confident deb' (*Financial Times*), 'frigidly spinsterish' (*Birmingham Mail*), a 'tough strident miss driven to suicide ... [by] sexual frustration' (*Glasgow Herald*), an 'old maid turned shrewish at Hamlet's breach of promise' (*Daily Mail*). Even Ronald Bryden's extremely warm review found her 'wrong'. Penelope Gilliat of the *Observer*, the only female critic in this large band, had, interestingly, a rather different view. Noting Jackson's hardness, the 'real, shrivelled, shrewish roots of madness' in her, Gilliat praised the deliberate blurring of the traditional boundaries of gender. She thought that this Ophelia 'should play Hamlet'. In the mad scene, there was no wispiness; on 'Pray you mark', just before her song, for example, she drummed her heel on the floor and lifted her upper lip in contempt. After the nunnery scene, the madness already beginning to manifest itself, she plucked at her dress, gulped the air, and barked out 'Courtier, soldier, scholar'. Her 'scornful authority full of Hamlet's own self-distaste' was discernible even in her initial scene with her father, where she sat rigid, resistant to his advice, defiant and loud on 'He hath, my lord, of late made many tenders / Of his affection to me' (Gilliat). Jan Kott also admired this Ophelia. For him, she was 'very upper class ... very English'. She consciously opts for 'disengagement' and ends up unfaithful to both Hamlet and her father. Her 'silent revolt' is thus ineffectual and her unsentimental suicide is a rebellious gesture which goes nowhere (*Sunday Times*, 31 Oct.). This establishes a link with Hamlet's own situation, suiting the wary lovers to each other, and connecting them to the inchoate rebellion of mid-1960s youth that the production as a whole aimed to reflect.

In the advance publicity for the production, in the programme, in the reviews, there was endless repetition of the idea that this was to be the *Hamlet* for the times, the 'mirror' of the decade, a record of the plight of youth in post-welfare state Britain. Hall's insistence on disillusion and apathy struck an obvious chord, but he accompanied it with a curiously conventional, even contradictory claim about Shakespeare's meaning: 'Shakespeare is asserting, as he always does, that the balanced government of oneself, or of one's family, or of the state, is the defined responsibility of living' (programme). Such a statement seems surprisingly conservative from a director who sees himself as a 'radical'; it places Shakespeare squarely in the bourgeois humanist camp that he had occupied for well over a hundred years, as well as implying a critique of the unsettled Hamlet that he and Warner had invented and made so appealing. 'Balanced government' could even be regarded as a fair description of the court of Elsinore under the Claudius of this production. Of course Hall had meant to question Hamlet's apathy; but he had also clearly set out to castigate the oppressive 'Establishment'. In his statement, Hall is giving to Shakespeare the very authority and legitimacy that his production sought so deftly and successfully to interrogate in the realm of the political. Perhaps it was inevitable, but this *Hamlet* of the time was itself blinded by the time. Hall could not see how his version of Shakespeare was itself politically inflected, and in some crucial ways *part* of the status quo – since it upheld a vision of self and society that underlay the political arrangements Hall wanted to resist. There is a further irony. For how could Hall know that the lack of commitment that he both appealed to and deplored, along with his tendency to overload his critique with existentialist alienation ('we need to discover and understand the universe in anguish' – programme), would in a few short years seem well out of date, of the 1950s more than the 1960s? Ironically, that disillusion was about to find a way to make a mark politically – apathy was about to be transformed into activism, a shift that might itself have been registered by the very committed response on the part of the youth of the time to this crucial and contradictory production.

CHAPTER VI

Royal Shakespeare and Royal Court in 1980

The Prince and the Player

1980 saw the opening of two important productions of *Hamlet*, both of which announced themselves in different ways as representative of the new decade. In April came the more surprising and more radical of the two, featuring Jonathan Pryce and staged by Richard Eyre at a bastion of oppositional theatre, the Royal Court, while in the summer the RSC mounted their first production of the play since 1970, directed by John Barton and starring Michael Pennington, who had played Fortinbras to David Warner's Hamlet in the 1960s. Where the Royal Court version was political and critical, and centred its attention on the actor's body, Stratford's was metaphysical and speculative, concentrating on the blurred lines between the play-acted and the real.

Since Pennington's *Hamlet* was the first at Stratford in ten years, there was plenty of talk of its being a new *Hamlet* for the new decade – what would this 1980s Hamlet turn out to be like? But in interviews before the show opened, Pennington was at pains to shrug off this particular responsibility. The idea was to present a classic 'scholar Prince, rather than a redbrick, Yahoo Prince'; he saw Hamlet as a 'very conservative rebel' (interview with John Higgins, *Times*, 2 July). This deliberate turning away from timeliness may have been prompted partly by the response earlier in the year to Pryce's Royal Court Hamlet. As Robert Cushman wrote of Pryce in *The Observer* (6 April), 'for the first time since David Warner played the role 15 years ago, a generation has found and crowned its prince'. The differences between the two 1980 productions might stand as a warning against any facile, if tempting, generalizations about the relation of a particular interpretation to the culture from which it emerges. That culture is far from simple or uniform, and particular productions are likely to respond to separate strands in a complicated network. If a version such as Hall's in 1965 manages to find a few of the most prominent and colourful strands, then it is likely to be hailed as peculiarly characteristic, even though it is of course highly selective in the ways it mediates the 'form and pressure' of its time. This becomes obvious if we look at the vivid contrasts between Barton's and Eyre's interpretations, each developed within the same subculture and mounted within a few months of each other.

They were of course presented in different theatres, and this certainly matters. The Royal Shakespeare Theatre in Stratford, the capital of the worldwide Shakespeare industry, has, despite the efforts of a string of directors to combat it, an atmosphere of worship. Shakespeare is its mission, and the place a focus of pilgrimage – even though by 1980 the tone had changed from 1948, when Dover Wilson gave his plea for Shakespearean and British moral leadership. Despite the attempts in the 1960s and 1970s to undermine the established iconography, Stratford still carried cultural weight. (Paradoxically, the fact that the RSC led the struggle against 'establishment Shakespeare' reinforced its own centrality.) That the emphasis of this 1980 *Hamlet* was to be on the power of theatre, and its Prince a scholar and a gentleman, might not surprise us in such a milieu. The Royal Court, on the other hand, had not come to its 'Royal' designation with quite the same authority, the name having been adopted by Maria Britton in 1871 as an attempt to upgrade the theatre's image and sell more tickets. Since the days of Shaw and Granville-Barker, the theatre had been associated with a taste for controversy and radical experiment. Neither 'Shakespeare' nor the classics generally had been in its repertoire, and the cultural establishment was as much its target as its support. Home base of the Angry Young Men in the 1950s, the Royal Court had been deeply associated with the revival of British theatre that began with the production of *Look Back in Anger*. Hence this theatre, even though it could hardly be regarded as fringe, was a surprising venue for a major production of *Hamlet*.

The souvenir programmes tell us something of the story – that of the RSC glossy and impressive, making a telling contrast with the Court's smaller and pulpier, but also more combative, offering. The RSC cover shows a full-front chiaroscuro photograph of Pennington's face and upper body, handsome, sensitive, slightly pained, with an unbuttoned shirt, a dignified high forehead and a ring of slightly dishevelled hair. Its centre-fold features a long passage from Anne Barton's Introduction to the New Penguin edition of the play, just then about to appear, with a rehearsal photo of the play scene, and the phrase, 'actions that a man might play' in large type. Barton's essay stresses how '*Hamlet* as a whole is … concerned to question and cross the boundaries' between 'dramatic representation' and 'life'. Hamlet himself, she claims, cherishes a private 'under-standing of how art may acquire a temporary and unpredict-able dominion over life'.[1] Her views presumably influenced her husband's decision to mould the production as he did, a fruit-ful example of academic and theatre worlds meeting not only in the seminar room or rehearsal hall but over the breakfast table. The Royal Court cover offers a Magritte-like photo of a dark young man in a suit with his back to the viewer, facing what seems to be a mirror that reproduces an identical image, doubling the view from the back instead of giving us the ex-pected reflection of his face. On a shelf in front of him, between the two images, is an old edition of Burton's *Anatomy of Melan-choly*. The picture has a vaguely 'thirties, east European air – Kafka caught in one of his own surreal frames. Inside, there is an essay (written by Rob Ritchie) on 'Hamletism,' developing the traditional picture of Hamlet as a figure of melancholia (hence the reference to Burton), isolated from his own cultural context and indeed from life itself, a victim of his own intellect. The argument runs that this romantic view of the character has produced an image of inertia deriving from a sense of alienated superiority. Rather coyly, the essay refuses to place itself in relation to the production, but the implication is clear: *this* version will not reproduce the same old image. Instead of giving us an idea of the direction the interpretation will take, as Anne Barton's thematic analysis does for the RSC, this piece merely clears the ground.

To see how the Bartons' ideas worked out in relation to both text and performance, let us glance at a moment when acting and the theatre's relation to personal reality take centre stage. The actors have arrived, greeted with enthusiasm by Hamlet and announced by Polonius in jester's cap and bells. Hamlet asks the leading Player for a sample of his art, a speech from an obscure, highbrow play reminiscent of Marlowe's *Dido, Queen of Carthage*. In most productions, Hamlet's motivation is unclear, but Barton and Pennington wanted to link his request directly to his dilemma. The speech concerns a Greek hero, Pyrrhus, who hesitates before acting, but then *acts*, and a grieving wife and mother, Hecuba, who, unlike the soft and untrustworthy Gertrude, is willing to follow her dead husband to the underworld. As the Player describes the scene, Pyrrhus stands frozen above the prostrate Priam, his fell sword 'Which was declining on the milky head / Of reverent Priam' seeming to stick in the air. Thus Pyrrhus, 'like a neutral to his will and matter, / Did nothing' (II.ii.478-82). Pennington's Hamlet, intent on this theatrical representation of his own situation, 'audibly anticipated' the last two climactic words (Warren, 152; the promptbook confirms that the phrase was spoken by Hamlet alone). This bold move helped to establish that intimate and unpredictable bond between the theatre and life that was the main theme of the production. But the analogy between Pyrrhus and Hamlet, highlighted by Anne Barton in her programme note and much commented on by reviewers, was itself purchased at a certain price. It was constructed, not found in the text. For what has caused Pyrrhus's hesitation? Is it pangs of conscience, melancholy, intellectual doubt, a wide-ranging consciousness of the sort typically associated with Hamlet? In Barton's version, there was no clear cause or motivation – and so, as with Hamlet, a certain mystery prevailed over the scene ('Pyrrhus hesitates *strangely* before letting his sword fall' says Anne Barton in the programme (emphasis added)). However, in the text there is a very clear and simple explanation for Pyrrhus's 'delay': there has been a deafening noise as 'senseless Ilium ... with flaming top / Stoops to his base, and with a hideous crash / Takes prisoner Pyrrhus' ear' (474-7). Although the collapse of Troy's walls draws off the murderous Greek's attention for an instant, he soon returns to his bloody task. But, wishing to emphasize the uncertainty of that crucial pause, Barton cut these explanatory lines and so propped up his reading.

There is nothing at all wrong with this procedure. As we have so often seen, the extreme length of *Hamlet* usually necessitates substantial performance cuts. Such cuts are rarely neutral, and, at moments like the one just described, can acquire special significance. What is important for our purposes is that the constructed nature of the 'fit' be recognized – there are no 'innocent' interpretations, particularly of a text like *Hamlet*. Barton wanted a strong way to link theatre and life, and to emphasize the ambiguous relation between them, as not only a crucial thematic element but a dilemma for Hamlet as a character. The whole production was designed to bring this out.

In III.i, in a famous soliloquy, Hamlet faces life and death. 'To be or not to be,' however, is rendered ambiguous in a context that dislodges the foundations of being, where playing is as real as truth. To mark the ambiguity, Pennington's Hamlet seized a prop from the players' basket at the side of the stage and contemplated suicide with a dagger of lath. If we are accustomed to forgetting that Hamlet is fictional, accustomed to accepting the stage prop as real, this production refused its audience such comforts and forced a consciousness of the constructions by which such 'reality effects' are produced. While this can fascinate, it can also, and in the eyes of some critics did, fail to excite. For if we are acutely aware of Hamlet's fictional status, will we care enough about the dilemma he faces to share the pangs of conscience that can make cowards of us all? But then again, *should* we lose ourselves in the excitement of a simple, fast-paced drama? Doesn't *Hamlet* force uncertainty upon us? The play is full of interrogatives.

Take the issue of Hamlet's madness. Always a key issue in criticism, the extent and nature of his antic disposition have been endlessly debated. Some see a Hamlet who is clearly sane, occasionally unorthodox or impulsive perhaps, but always in control. Others see him losing his grip at key moments: with Ophelia, perhaps, or his mother, on the platform after the Ghost scene, or after the play. One virtue of Barton's production was that it kept the ambiguity always before us. There was no question about Pennington's play-acting near the start: he donned an appropriate costume – a beret slapped on his head, with a quill behind the ear and an inkhorn slung over his shoulder, and short, ballooning trousers (B. A. Young, *Financial Times*, 3 July 1980); with Polonius he indulged in a kind of friendly mockery. But at other times, especially with Ophelia in the nunnery scene, the 'performance' began to 'take hold of the performer' (Peter Jenkins, *Spectator*, 12 July 1980). To play perhaps *is* to be. The one mode infiltrates the other.

As the plot developed, his behaviour became more erratic: he went so far as to knock Ophelia down in the nunnery scene; later, he stabbed Polonius repeatedly in his mother's closet but then bid him a tender farewell. So, when he insisted to his mother that he was 'essentially ... not in madness / But mad in craft', it was unclear whether he was to be believed. Even at the end, when traditional Hamlets generally reassert their spiritual heroism, uncertainty hovered around Pennington's pained Prince. On the point of gaining his long-sought-for revenge, there was a hollowed-out moment when the act of killing the King, to which of course the whole plot has been moving, seemed exposed as a theatrical gesture – Hamlet rattling his sword at Claudius who contemptuously brushed it aside as an exercise in false heroics (*Jewish Chronicle*, 11 July).

Ralph Koltai's simple acting platform and stage props for the RSC matched Barton's conception by foregrounding the theatrical. The platform occupied only a part of the large, mostly empty stage; there were a few benches around the platform (sometimes used by 'offstage' actors) and various theatrical accoutrements, such as a thundersheet and costume racks, but there was no attempt to provide a 'set'. In such an atmosphere, the Players must necessarily loom large. 'Brief chronicles of the time' as well as purveyors of artifice, they were professionals in a world of amateurs. Barton treated them soberly. They played 'The Mousetrap' straight, as though they had taken Hamlet's advice to heart. The idea was to make them seem more substantial than Hamlet's dream-like problems, closer to some intrinsic 'reality' than the fictional world that they to some extent represent; this was to reverse the usual hierarchy in which 'reality' prevails over fiction. The arrival of the Players was low-key despite Polonius's comic announcement; they merely set their prop-basket down and moved to the sides. For the Pyrrhus speech the First Player moved to the platform and as he built the speech from softness to intensity, his fellow Players joined in; on 'anon the dreadful thunder / Doth rend the region', one rattled the thundersheet, another a drum, while a chorus of wailing arose to simulate the stricken Hecuba's 'instant burst of clamour'. The audience was to witness how performance is born, how the 'real' is not only represented but constructed. As he finished, the Player, in tears, deliberately held the mood until a sympathetic Polonius broke in quietly with 'Pray you no more', a solicitous hand on his shoulder. At that, the actor 'smiled and switched off the performance to Polonius's laughing admiration' (Warren 152). This sequence, including Hamlet's echoing of Pyrrhus's suspended animation, marked most thoroughly the interpenetration of theatre and life that the production was designed to illustrate. Here was a patently fictional situation being gradually charged with life, and in the process linking to and illuminating a 'real' situation (that of Hamlet), which is itself fictional.

Hamlet himself begins the recitation, and to do so here he went to the players' prop-basket and took out a sword and cloak which then, together with a white mask, became markers of theatrical 'reality'. As he finished his bit, he threw down the sword and cloak. The Player advanced, knelt by the discarded props, and then used them in his performance, the sword first ('For lo, his sword ...'), then the cloak and mask for Hecuba ('the mobled queen'). Afterwards, as he left, the Player slid the sword to Hamlet, providing a visual transition to the remarkable soliloquy in which Hamlet's tortured analysis seems both to tighten and untie the knots that link theatrical and real. As he mused how the Player could feel so deeply 'For Hecuba', he knelt and touched her cloak, then picked up the enigmatic mask. If the Player were to enact *his* story (so he says), the stage would be awash with tears – and here was Hamlet marking his emphasis with acknowledged stage props, on an improvised platform, Hamlet himself only a poor player strutting and fretting. He became all the more an *actor* in the next part of the speech, where he whirled and tossed, flung down the cloak, brandished the sword, and then, crouching, suddenly caught himself in the embarrassment of playing the part of the conventional wild revenger: 'Why, what an ass am I'. Having determined on a play to catch the conscience of the king, he left carrying the various props. This was a clear departure from the Irving/Barrymore/Gielgud style of intense melodrama. Such details illustrate the way theatrical meaning can be delivered, abstract notions given concrete embodiment. All truth is provisional and tied to representation – or that at least is how this production sought to explain how the theatre remakes the world we call real.

The play scene itself was, fittingly, mounted on the main platform, the very space in which the action of *Hamlet* was played, the court audience seated on the benches that flanked the platform. Done quietly, it was also highly pointed. The Player-queen cast accusing glances at her 'real-life' counterpart, which, along with Hamlet's abusive comments, made Gertrude increasingly uncomfortable until, provoked by the needling, she interrupted the play: 'The lady doth protest too much, methinks' (III.ii.230). The Player-king died aggressively, rolling in agony to the very feet of Claudius. At this the real King stood, 'contemptuously breaking up the play, his chest resting against Hamlet's prop sword' (Warren 152). There was, perhaps, an insufficient sense of danger here, the play metaphor reducing rather than enhancing the moment's power. Certainly Hamlet's own triumph was somewhat undercut by what followed: as he expressed his elation to Horatio, the players began to unpack their performance, moving their basket and props upstage and changing their costumes. Hamlet's 'half a share' in a 'cry of players' was thus ironically revealed as precisely that, a merely theatrical accomplishment, well removed from the sources of actual power. There is no doubt that acting can suddenly illuminate, but it may also be revealed as ineffectual, disastrously divorced from action.

This consideration underlies a basic problem with the production: its failure to provide a fully realized social environment. Gone was the busy and oppressive court world of productions such as Peter Hall's; like everyone else, Claudius was an actor, and Elsinore was a stage, not a political milieu. Even though politics can be a highly theatrical practice, the sense of high stakes present in political struggle was largely missing. A production devoted to exploring the vagaries of what it means to act, of how the theatre interprets and remakes life, generating 'counter-illusions' to penetrate the 'illusions' of material reality (Anne Barton's terms), is almost bound to come up 'short on the public aspects of Elsinore' (Michael Billington, *Guardian*, 3 July). There was, it would seem, no attempt to establish the court as a political or administrative centre, or even as a court (Warren 151). Once again we are reminded that any production is bound to be partial; this one was openly so.

The production's theatrical self-reflexiveness did not always sit easily with the psychological emphasis in the acting. Michael Pennington is an actor who can project Romantic grace and charm, a characteristic much praised by critics and audiences who remembered Warner's puzzled and ungainly graduate student, or who wanted to draw a contrast with Pryce's tormented and brain-sick madman. Words like 'gentle', 'aristocratic', 'gracious' keep turning up in the reviews, and most especially 'sweet', a word used more often in this play than in any other of Shakespeare's and applied here to Pennington's conception, in tune with Horatio's and Ophelia's view of him. G. L. Evans noted how he greeted his inferiors with 'charmingly studious etiquette' (*Stratford Herald*, 1 July). Critics were more divided about Pennington's handling of the darker side of Hamlet. For Irving Wardle, Pennington's 'sweet, impish charm' was not so delicate as it first appeared; he 'encompasse[d] all the part's violence without surrender of its essential goodness' (*Times*, 3 July). But Roger Warren felt that the Romantic, princely Hamlet required the 'tailor[ing]' of certain key scenes where the harsher features of the character were not sufficiently in evidence. Pennington himself saw Hamlet as moving from passivity to violence, from a 'torpor [that] is deep and disturbing to watch' to 'an openly expressed viciousness' in both nunnery and closet scenes. During rehearsal, he discovered 'a strong current of violence [in Hamlet], particularly toward the women in his life' (Pennington 122-3), which emerged strongly in the nunnery and closet scenes.

The problem, however, is whether such psychological realism fits into the insistently fictional play-world created by the production. Compared with the thoroughgoing meta-theatrics of some contemporary European productions, Barton and Pennington's humanist emphasis might seem a tame compromise between post-modern play and traditional naturalism. In 1979, in Cologne, Hansgunther Heyme directed a version in which everything that happened on stage was subjected to electronic multiplication via a bank of TV monitors; the actors trained video cameras on each other, turning themselves and others into media images. The main part was split between two actors, one of whom remained on stage, lost in crude sexual fantasies, while the other spoke the sonorous lines of Schlegel's classic translation from the auditorium.[2] Such experiments externalized into theatrical imagery what in productions such as Barton's remained internal and character-oriented, despite the theatricalization.

A fine example of effective character acting was Barbara Leigh-Hunt's Gertrude. So long merely the stereotype of the weak and sensuous woman and even in 1965 not much more than a commentary on that stereotype, Gertrude at last developed some of the complexity afforded to Polonius and Claudius in many twentieth-century productions. The actual extent of her guiltiness was, like so much else in this version, left ambiguous, but that she was 'sensitive enough to suggest moral guilt' as well as 'powerful in sexual presence' was noted by several critics (Evans; see also Warren, Billington, Jenkins). In the play scene it was she who first interrupted, angrily cupping Hamlet's face in her hands for 'The lady doth protest too much' (Billington, *Guardian*, 3 July). In the closet scene, the Ghost's arrival occasioned a bold move: although invisible to Gertrude in the text and in virtually all previous productions, the Ghost here was not so easily dismissed. Pennington makes it clear that the intention was to have Gertrude see him (118), and most reviewers noted the innovation, though some stressed the ambiguity of the moment. Gertrude certainly tried to avoid the vision that was thrust upon her. She lay face down in terror, refusing to look again after a brief glance. She spoke her lines denying the vision as though 'trying not to admit [her] guilty realization' from earlier in the scene (on 'As kill a king?'), thereby making the vision and its denial part of a process of coming to terms with what she now knows (Warren). There was a pause as she lifted herself up from the floor (there was no Oedipal bed) and stood, as though to clear herself of the unwanted vision. 'This is the very coinage of your brain' seemed therefore like a doomed attempt to escape what she knows and return to normalcy. Afterwards, she greeted Claudius with an embrace, but their growing alienation was emphasized by their sitting on benches on opposite sides of the raised platform and exiting separately. Despite Claudius's exhortation, 'O, come away! / My soul is full of discord and dismay', she remained sitting, defeated and played out, her 'besotted love' for Claudius (Evans) now drowned. The guilt that possessed her persisted through her difficulties with Ophelia's madness and led to another bold moment at the end where she seemed to recognize her own complicity in the poison that laced the cup from which she drank (Jenkins). Leigh-Hunt's guilt and growing self-awareness thus seemed to develop in intricate relation to Pennington's intensity and barely repressed violence, the mother taking her cue from her son's perturbation.

It was appropriate that if Gertrude was to recognize him, the ghost should be 'exceptionally solid' and corporeal. On the battlements, with a 'dusty Napoleonic greatcoat' thrown over his shoulders, he simply sat 'on a bench and [told] Hamlet *quietly* what ha[d] happened' (Billington, his emphasis; the Zeffirelli film takes a similar approach). The Ghost's initial entry, hastened by extensive cutting of the first scene (including four of the already terse opening eleven lines),[3] didn't hide his theatrical status but combined it with a concrete physical presence. The play began with Francisco behind the platform 'getting ready for his entry rather than on patrol' (Warren). At Barnardo's entrance and first words, the simple rehearsal lighting (a few naked bulbs) shifted to stage lighting, signalling the beginning of the 'play', and a moment later Marcellus merely raised a trap and up climbed the Ghost. There was nothing heightened or spectacular, but no attempt either to deny the theatrical making of the ghost's reality. The paradox of theatrical reality, which amalgamates our awareness of fiction and our experience of physical, bodily sensations, was vividly etched by such a presentation. So too when the Ghost reappeared in Gertrude's closet, both its harrowing effect and Gertrude's frightened vision were enhanced by its ordinary physical actuality. This palpable but at the same time palpably fictional figure seemed more 'real' to many critics (though not to all), than the contrivances indulged in by many productions.

According to one critic, Gertrude's prominence in the production tended to turn 'Claudius into another player king, a usurper trying to live up to a part' (*Spectator*, 12 July). Her guilt was more complex and interesting than his. Certainly Derek Godfrey's King was a bit of a throwback to an earlier conception – a red-coated hussar, he was an 'extrovert half-way between old sport and bloody roué … impervious to guilt' (Evans, *Stratford Herald*, 1 July). Whether this made him the more dangerous for being 'so hail-fellow well met' (as Evans thought) or whether the tendency to melodrama and rant (Warren 152) reduced him to a caricature was left moot. The prayer scene, where the complexity of the character is given some scope, was reduced, not so much by the cuts, which were moderate, but by the stage business. As he spoke of his guilt, his distance from it was marked by his changing to a robe and slippers (promptbook), the cosy domesticity undercutting some of the sharpness of the feeling. Then, for the silent prayer, he lay face down on the platform, spread-eagled, as Hamlet entered from upstage. The exaggeration of the posture and the easy familiarity of the undressing suggested self-conscious play-acting. This may have been a deliberate device to provide an image of a villain correspondent to that of the revenger from which Hamlet shied away with embarrassment. However it was conceived, it led to a less than fully realized characterization, one that contrasted sharply with Tony Church's rich and rounded portrayal of Polonius.

Church had played the role years before, in Peter Hall's epochal production of 1965. He retained many of the subtleties of the part that he developed then, but certain elements had to be adjusted to fit the very different focus that Barton wanted to give this production. The shrewd politician had been the centre of the character, but now where the court world had faded into the world of the stage, that was no longer appropriate. Instead, looking closely at the story, Barton and Church decided to emphasize the effects of Polonius's death on his children – one goes mad, the other returns to Denmark, ready to lead a rebellion. 'Surely this must mean that there had been great love in the children for their father?' (Church 108-9). Accordingly, as in Noble's production in 1992-93, the first domestic scene (I.iii) was played to emphasize family harmony and understanding. Horseplay with Laertes, affection with Ophelia, a general air of tunefulness, marked the occasion. Laertes was packing his foils, so Polonius took one and made a fake thrust, Laertes pretending to die (adding an ominous foreshadowing to the fun). Polonius's long-winded advice to his son was played with genial self-awareness – he knew they were smiling at him behind his back and he didn't mind. After an affectionate farewell to Laertes, Ophelia played her lute and Polonius whistled an accompaniment – a tune that, in the mad scene, she would reprise in a darker key (once again suggesting the fragility of the happiness). Even the warning to Ophelia to avoid Hamlet was concerned rather than harsh, though by the end of the scene it was clear that Polonius was the kind of genial father who *must* be obeyed.

Later, after her troubled confession about Hamlet's strangeness, he comforted her by wrapping her in his robe, another motif picked up in the mad scene when she entered wearing it. (All these elements found an answering echo in Noble's version.) And after the nunnery scene, where his offhand lines to her ('How now Ophelia? / You need not tell us what Lord Hamlet said, / We heard it all') seem to indicate a callous indifference, he held her in his arms while addressing the King, and then helped her off. From this point, anger at Hamlet overwhelmed his earlier easy tolerance of the Prince. The first scenes of their interaction were marked by 'good natured banter' (Warren). In the scene with the players in II.ii, Polonius's comments were judicious, not philistine, and his obvious concern for the player's feelings after his Hecuba performance combined sympathy and admiration. But all this changed after the nunnery scene. Though with a different motive, his intention at this point merged with that of 1965 – get rid of Hamlet. And his death was unusually sympathetic: he hid behind the same simple blanket that he and Claudius had used to spy on Hamlet and Ophelia earlier, creating a visual link between his two eavesdropping scenes, and providing a focus in each case for Hamlet's violent outbursts. Here the deliberately theatrical nature of the production, where a prop could do double or triple duty free of the restrictions of naturalism, paid a dividend. Hamlet pounced upon Polonius and stabbed him three times, but then recoiled in remorse. Polonius, the 'arras' wrapped around him, staggered to an upstage bench beside the platform. As he slid to the floor, Hamlet took his hand and bid him a genuinely tender goodbye: 'Thou wretched, rash, intruding fool, farewell! / I took thee for thy better' (III.iv.31-2).

The treatment of Polonius illustrates some of the strengths of Barton's production – his concern for detail, his weighting of others' stories to balance that of Hamlet, his desire to unlock the complex human motives behind behaviour. But to some degree this aim conflicted with the other, more speculative, focus of the production on the theatre and its construction of reality. Barton's insistence on the blurring of the boundaries between theatre and life and on the ways that our lives are constructed according to theatrical modes of representation, has links to post-modern theory's emphasis on textuality and the all-encompassing reach of representation. But such theory tends to ignore the interest that the theatre generates in human persons and their dilemmas. In pursuing the theme of the infiltration of theatre into life, this production bypassed those very aspects of life that make it *not* theatre – its untidiness, for example, or, at a deeper level, the various political engagements and personal inevitabilities that impinge upon us. The theatre as an art form may render reality problematic, but it doesn't make reality disappear.

A paradise for eavesdroppers

Barton, in stressing the 'play' element, lost the sense of the social and political context, the feel of the palace as the working centre of a realized world. At the Royal Court, in keeping partly with that theatre's political interests, this side of the play was kept in the foreground – chiefly through the ingenious set designed by William Dudley who created a suggestive Renaissance interior, a *'studilo* of some Italianate palace' (James Fenton, *Sunday Times*, 6 April) with marquetry decoration and hinged pews attached to the side walls. The pews could then swing out to form narrow interiors. The overall feel, according to Michael Billington, was part Holbein and part Kafka (*Guardian*, 3 April), at once elegant and claustrophobic (the latter effect deriving in part from the narrowness of the Royal Court stage and the fact that the set tended to thrust the action forward on to the forestage). Painted *trompe l'oeil* doors with 'marquetry eavesdroppers' that then turned out to be the real thing, each with armed guards at the ready behind them, produced an uneasy ambiguity: 'what they depict[ed] they also conceal[ed]' (Fenton, *Sunday Times*, 6 April). When the whole palace was searching for Hamlet (IV.ii), the set came 'alive with treacherous possibilities ... all possible exits bristling with arms' (Fenton). Trying to escape his pursuers, Hamlet opened 'door after *trompe l' oeil* door' only to find behind each one an 'armed listener' (Lucy Hughes-Hallet, *Now*, 16 April). He could do nothing but 'yield meekly to the strait jacket' (Fenton). The set allowed for an assertion of power linked to a control of information. Power was evoked by the strategically placed guards – when, for example, Laertes raised his voice in the plotting scene with Claudius (IV.vii), posing a potential threat to the King, 'a servant appear[ed] from behind a panel' (Hughes-Hallet, *Now*, 16 April). Gathering information in such a space was facilitated by the possibilities of spying it provided.

6 Hamlet (Jonathan Pryce) mocks Polonius (Geoffrey Chater) in a scene showing the nooks and crannies of William Dudley's set for the Royal Court, 1980.

With its 'elegant series of adjoining timbered cubicles', this Elsinore was a 'burnished beehive ... a paradise for eavesdroppers' (Cushman, *Observer*, 6 April), ominously suggesting 'chambers and corridors beyond itself' (Christopher Edwards, *Cambridge Review*, 2 May).

The set was an indication of a desire to fit the personal and family drama into a believable, and ominous, political context. In this it was reminiscent of the Hall/Warner production of 1965. But here the power structure was less firmly established, more furtive and desperate. Despite a ceremonial pageant at the outset, apparently based on Holbein drawings (Hilary Spurling, Critics' Forum, Radio 3, 12 April), the court machinery was not particularly well-oiled, and the playing of both Claudius and Polonius added to the sense that the contest for power was less unequal than in Hall's production. Michael Elphick, as Claudius, succeeded in conveying 'that he, like Hamlet, [was] in over his head, lumbered with a destiny he would far rather escape' (Cushman). His anxiety grew during the performance, since he recognized clearly that the kind of prince created by Pryce (much more authoritative than Warner) could be extremely dangerous. Unconsciously, it seemed, he cast frequent furtive looks back over his shoulder. With Gertrude, he was alternately weary and affectionate. All in all he seemed obsessed with the insecurity of power (Colin Ludlow, *Plays and Players*, May 1980). Even the *trompe l'oeil* but real doors played their part in the ambiguity of power, since they induced a sense of enclosure and security that turned out to be partly false.

Geoffrey Chater's Polonius added to the sense of a nasty and brutish power structure rather than a comfortable and established one. Cushman thought him the very embodiment of the setting: 'prying, self-satisfied, rabbiting both to and about his children, but showing no affection for them whatsoever'. John Carey called him 'a bully, a sycophant [and] a miser' though he was no caricature (Critics' Forum). Very different from Tony Church's affectionate father in Barton's production, and different too from Church's earlier astute, but still genial, politician (in 1965), Chater inspired wariness rather than warmth. Pryce's gentleness after stabbing him derived from nothing intrinsic to Polonius's character, but rather from the shock that Hamlet himself felt at what he had done. This contrasted with Pennington's tender goodbye to Church's Polonius, which grew out of their earlier banter and Hamlet's appreciation of this Polonius's basic good humour.

From the moment it got started, Eyre's production made its iconoclastic intentions clear. The initial shock was the complete excision of the opening scene. The play began with a subdued reading of the court scene (I.ii), with Hamlet entering late into a roomful of courtiers. Pryce's was a 'spindly grief-stricken Prince, utterly without hostility or provocative reflexes' (Wardle, *Times*, 3 April); his figure was so 'palpably heartbroken' and his face so 'cadaverous' that one critic was prompted to wonder, 'how could he wear anything but black?' (*Observer*, 6 April). Before long, the reason for the missing first scene became plain. There was to be no visible Ghost. What exactly Horatio and the others might have seen on the battlements, if anything, never became clear, but what the audience witnessed certainly was. The Ghost was *inside* Hamlet. No longer an objective, if ambiguous, fact, he became an inner torment speaking in a strange, distorted voice, which was wrenched out of Hamlet in the midst of extreme pain and violent retching. Such innovation gave the critics rich opportunities for eloquence: Hamlet was 'a medium at an unlooked-for seance, half-booming, half-burping up the words of his father's spirit' (Nightingale, *New Statesman*, 11 April) and his voice 'an unearthly robot croak well[ing] up from his guts' (*Times*, 3 April); he 'struggles and retches as if in the grip of diabolic possession' (*Observer*, 6 April).

This crucial decision had several consequences. It made Hamlet's hesitancy about believing the ghost a matter of self-doubt, more a psychological than a metaphysical puzzle. It raised the stakes in the suspicions about Hamlet's madness; even his friends were unsure of his sanity, Horatio and Marcellus, for example, casting puzzled looks at him during the swearing scene. It also produced dividends in the closet scene, solving at a stroke the conundrum of Gertrude's not seeing the Ghost (which of course Barton solved by having her see it). In this instance, the invisible Ghost was silent as well, but Hamlet's violent retchings signalled its reappearance and had the added effect of raising the already feverish temperature of the interchange with his mother. And, climactically, it led to a poignant final moment when, on 'The rest is silence', a sudden epileptic shudder recalled the earlier possession and suggested the relief of exorcism (Alan Drury, *Listener*, 10 April and Jenkins, *Spectator*, 12 April). Nothing could have been further from the almost casual, wholly untheatrical ghost in Barton's production. Less happily, driving the ghost inside did violence to the text of the play, tending to reduce it to a merely psychological or even psychosomatic problem on Hamlet's part, rather than an external manifestation with some claim to objective reality. If Hamlet is possessed, how is it that what the demonic spirit speaks turns out to be correct? If he is mad, is he also clairvoyant?

That such questions did not in general come up is a tribute to the dynamism and momentum of Pryce's performance, 'unstoppable' in its drive and vitality (Benedict Nightingale, *New Statesman*, 11 April). Wild, dangerous, violent, erratic, menacing – such are the terms most often used to describe him. But, strangely, their seeming opposites came up almost as frequently – intelligent, reasonable, lucid. Abrupt veering from one pole to the other seemed to mark the interpretation. Jenkins felt Pryce had been 'deranged' by his father's murder and mother's remarriage: 'there is a revengeful method in his madness but mad he is, as likely to feign lucidity as lunacy' (*Spectator*). His behaviour in the nunnery scene offers an example. It began, in another much noted 'innovation' (though it is consistent with all the early texts and had been done only a few years before by Derek Jacobi at the Old Vic), with the 'To be or not to be' speech spoken in a perfectly reasonable way *to* Ophelia, a 'man talking to a friend in order to work something out in his mind' (*Listener*, 10 April), the two of them 'seated in adjacent alcoves' (*Spectator*, 12 April). Most observers saw this as a mistake, stripping from Hamlet the chance to explore and reveal a meditative and private inner life. But it also helped establish a companionable relation with Ophelia that was then developed in the first part of the nunnery dialogue, when he delivered his 'advice' in a gentle, affectionate and rueful way (*New Statesman*, 11 April), with an edge of self-mockery and even a touch of nostalgia ('I *did* love you once' quiet and sad – *Observer*, 6 April). All this was utterly broken when he realized she was in league with her eavesdropping father and the king behind the arras (here of course the production was following old theatrical traditions). In an abrupt switch, he turned on her with a sudden 'ravening frenzy' (*Guardian*, 3 April), a violent charge of erotic fury expressed in 'distraught grabbing [and] kissing' (*New Statesman*, 11 April), his hand thrust coarsely up her skirt in what looked to Irving Wardle like 'attempted rape' (*Times*, 3 April). In most respects, Pryce's unpredictable and eruptive manner contrasted with the sweet gentleness of Pennington's. But there was a strong similarity in their handling of the nunnery scene. Both started gentle and then broke into an anger that was inseparable from sexual desire. Can we hazard a generalization about the 'time' from such a consonance? It is certainly tempting to see a rather frightened male response to the new threat posed by the assertive woman of the 1970s, a response perhaps to a feminism that men fear may exclude or surpass them. Such a reading seems plausible, but it is troubled by the fact that, in 1925, Colin Keith-Johnstone's performance for the Birmingham Rep was characterized by much the same oscillation and the same confusion of anger and desire. Of course, that too might have sprung partly from an ambivalent recoil from a freer sort of woman, linking the 1920s and the late 1970s in their attitudes toward varying forms of emancipation. Although it is true that performances are not simple and clear reflections of their cultural milieu, the fact that each of these 1980 productions found a connection between sex and male anger at a moment when the independence of women was a major cultural issue can hardly be coincidental.

There was as well a parallel similarity in the two versions of the closet scene, despite the absolute opposition in the treatment of the ghost – seen and heard by Gertrude as well as Hamlet at the RSC, while invisible and silent at the Royal Court, present only in the twists of Hamlet's body. Both Pryce and Pennington played the scene with mounting intensity and violence, though Pryce was more unleashed and dangerous. At the same time, each reacted with sympathy and remorse to the murder of Polonius, and in both versions the dead body of the eavesdropping councillor was left in full view during the ensuing encounter between mother and son, keeping the fruits of violence directly and ominously before the audience. Pennington was touched by what he had done to Polonius and took his hand to bid him farewell. For Pryce, the moment was even more germane. In an interview before the opening, he explained the effect he was after: for Hamlet, the sudden 'shock and distress', the realization of the seriousness of what he has done, strikes him hard and he becomes very distraught (*Guardian*, 29 March). Accordingly, the following scene was played to the hilt, with both Hamlet and Gertrude 'in tears for a good ten minutes, tears of panic rather than remorse'; for a whole range of critics, the effect was 'ugly and disturbing' (Benedict Nightingale *Harper's*, June 1980) and at the same time 'totally involving' (*Listener*, 10 April). There was little holding back: when Hamlet produced the contrasting images of uncle and father to stun his mother into guilt, he did so with a 'hand red with blood', thrusting (in a neat solution to an old problem) different coins of the realm into the face of a 'whooping, groaning' Gertrude (Martin Dodsworth, *Times Literary Supplement*, 4 April). The scene was played as if from Gertrude's point of view – at least her conviction of Hamlet's madness could not but grow, especially when the 'ghost' made its epileptic appearance. So the audience's experience of the scene (since for it too the ghost was invisible) was aligned with Gertrude's bewilderment and pain. This to some extent made up for the fact that Jill Bennett did not trace the subtle development of Gertrude's guilty involvement as Barbara Leigh-Hunt managed to do in the RSC version, so that her performance stayed more on one level. She did, however, show a tender maternal side to Laertes when he burst in on Claudius in Act IV. In a warm and natural move such as she never displayed to Hamlet, she crossed to Laertes and held him till he suddenly dropped the aggressive bluff and wept on her shoulder. This added point to her later very gentle presentation of Ophelia's death to him (John Carey, Critics' Forum, Radio 3, 12 April).

In the family scene with Laertes and Polonius (I.iii), Ophelia (Harriet Walter) refused to take her brother's advice seriously, and generally showed herself 'full of spirit' (*Sunday Times*, 6 April). Her unhappy capitulation to her martinet father's commands almost immediately began to drain her of that spirit, so that the seeds of a possible madness were sown early on. Walter's choice to give us an Ophelia whose madness stems from some inner source rather than floating in operatically when the text suddenly demands it, was in line with most recent productions. Generated by twentieth-century commitment to psychology and by a desire to give as full range as possible to a woman's part that in the text is left truncated and undeveloped, this 'new' Ophelia (who began to make her appearance as early as

1925) is clearly a response to different ways of thinking about the place of women in society. In one recent version, directed by Derek Jacobi for the Renaissance Theatre Company in 1988, Ophelia made a number of unscripted appearances that enhanced her presence. She entered with the Players upon their arrival (II.ii) and was with them during their preparations; she remained on stage after the play for the recorder scene, and was even visible above the closet scene, a kind of hovering conscience reminding the audience of the consequences of male aggression.

Some sense of the continuity in the role as it is currently conceived by modern actresses may be gleaned from what Frances Barber has to say about playing Ophelia in today's world. It is no longer enough to see her as pretty, weak, and defenseless – a figure of pathos whose decorative madness reflects, and even contributes to, patriarchal control (see Showalter). Barber, who played the part for the RSC in 1984, remembered having seen Harriet Walter's performance four years earlier; that, she says, 'dispelled any traditional images of the weak, stupid girl which may have been lurking in the minds of the audience. I carried this memory with me for many weeks preparing for the role' (Barber 137). She seized on Walter's portrait of Ophelia as externally acquiescent but inwardly resentful, full of guilt, and as much as possible on Hamlet's side. Walter's characterization complemented the general sense of political and social pressure, and became one of the nodal points where that pressure was felt most acutely. Like several Ophelias since, she began to descend into madness with her soliloquy after the nunnery scene, her awareness of the blasting of Hamlet's mind seeming to extend to herself and 'her father's treatment of her as a manipulable chattel with no feelings' (*Listener*, 10 April). Her earlier defiance was thus revealed as less tough than it might have seemed, especially to herself. Overall, like most recent Ophelias, she did not just supplement Hamlet's tragedy, but shared it. Her madness dovetailed with his.

Madness was in fact one of the keynotes of the production. The old questions about the extent of Hamlet's madness have generated a wide range of answers; audiences have been witness on the one hand to the sanest and stateliest Hamlets (like John Phillip Kemble's or Ben Kingsley's) and on the other to the most mercurial and even demented (like Kean's or Pryce's). In tandem with Barton's pursuit of theatricality in his production, Pennington rendered Hamlet's madness ambiguous, a sort of comment on the whole critical tradition. Was it a theatrical ruse, or was it genuine? Could there be anything genuine within such a deliberately staged construction? Perhaps madness was simply another representation, and play-acted madness a representation of a representation? The endless reflexiveness of such possibilities framed the conception. In Eyre's production, madness was visceral, a matter of the body as much as the mind. Review after review stressed the physicality of Pryce's 'possession', both the guttural voice of his father's spirit and the brutal erotic tension that manifested itself in his dark groping after Ophelia.

If madness is an affliction of the spirit, it is also written on the body. As Michel Foucault has shown, the body of the madman, like that of the criminal, has always carried on the skin and in the defeated outline of the limbs the markings of authority. Ophelia's bowed person, her very crookedness in almost all recent renditions of the mad scene (like her Pre-Raphaelite wispiness in the nineteenth century), speaks not only of pathos, but of power, and it is first and foremost the power of men that she has no force ultimately to resist. Her father, Claudius, even Hamlet himself, *embody* patriarchy. But men's bodies, as well as women's, are subjected to the inscriptions of power. Pryce created a Hamlet whose possessed spirit left visible traces on the body – but whose body, the actor's or the character's? That ambiguity is always in play in theatrical representation, and this version highlighted it, theatricalizing the body in a unique way. In the script, Hamlet first of all performs madness – he acts and enacts it, in order to act against Claudius; but his performance comes perilously close to actuality. For Pryce to make his madness such a moment of sheer bravura acting while at the same time accentuating its authenticity was to stretch the paradox of madness in the play to its limit. Madness was rendered both absolutely theatrical, played for all it was worth, forcing thereby an awareness of the skill of the actor on the audience, and at the same time inescapably physical and, at the level of the body, utterly convincing.

In a sense, then, the two 1980 productions ended up in a similar paradoxical place. Both insisted on the authentic while asserting the performed, though in radically opposed ways – one, that of Barton and Pennington, by reminding us constantly of the fact of performance, the other by trying to make us forget. But in the latter case, because of the body's double commitment (it being both the actor's and the character's), that forgetting was rendered impossible; the *actor's* body was strongly foregounded. This could then lead, momentarily, to a privileged form of knowing – in the sense that audience awareness of the body's doubleness could become briefly an awareness of the paradox of performing itself. The theatre, that is, through the physical presence of the body on-stage and the institutional arrangements that make it culturally viable, brings together stage and world, actor and spectator, in an ongoing act of negotiated belief. The actor's body, in its double being as physical presence and fictional 'person,' is central to the persuasive process of convincing the spectators. Its rhetorical and instrumental force guarantees the truth of its *representational presence* to those who watch.

Although Pennington and Pryce brought out some similar features of their character – fear of and aggressiveness toward women, potential violence, theatrical assertiveness – their productions never converged into a single vision, nor could they have done. In seeking the crystallized version of the play 'for the 1980s,' if such a chimera exists at all, we would do well to combine features of the productions rather than select one as exemplary: violence and inwardness mixed with painful uncertainty; an awareness of the essential emptiness of political reality together with a feeling of the brutal oppressiveness of power; a sense of the ubiquitous invasion of privacy and a yearning, however nostalgic, for wholeness; and perhaps most of all a conviction of the theatrical construction of selfhood interwoven with an equally compelling sense of the truth of the self's vision of things. Such perhaps were some of the contradictions of the 'time' and its multiplex forms and pressures.

CHAPTER VII

Hamlet at the movies: Olivier and Kozintsev

Filming Shakespeare presents problems which the by now well-established, if minor, industry of Shakespearean film criticism has been quick to notice and explain. Against those who claim that it is impossible to film Shakespeare adequately because the text's imagistic language and the movies' strong visuals tend to make each other redundant, most Shakespeare-on-film critics respond that it is possible to find a cinematic language that encompasses both. Still, it is noteworthy that the most praised Shakespeare films tend either to be in a foreign language (Russian or Japanese) or to be the work of radically cinematic directors like Orson Welles whose willingness to let the visual crowd out the verbal is illustrated by his crackling, sometimes inaudible sound tracks, as well as by a keenly pragmatic attitude toward text. Another problem of translation from stage to screen is the question of 'theatrical' versus 'cinematic' space, the former being restricted architecturally in that the stage is part of a permanent building to which in most instances the audience has a fixed relationship. What happens on stage is contained and determined by the 'real' three-dimensional space in which it takes place, and each member of the audience can have only one perspective on the action. Film of course changes all that, providing multiple perspectives (long shot, middle shot, close-up, for example, or high angle and low angle), continuous space (where the frame contains only part of the scene that we know extends beyond what we see), simultaneity (as in cross-cutting), and a host of other possibilities. Filmed plays, such as the Olivier *Othello* or the Gielgud/Richard Burton *Hamlet*, tend to be boring. So how translate texts written to be performed within a theatrical space into a cinematic space, especially texts with the sacred potentialities of Shakespeare's, and none more than the holiest of all – *Hamlet*?

7 A classic Freudian moment from Laurence Olivier's film (1948), as Hamlet challenges his anxious mother (Eileen Herlie) on the ever-present bed.

Olivier and the Oedipal story of 'a man who could not make up his mind'

Such are some of the questions surrounding what is still the best known and most widely screened of *Hamlet* films (perhaps even of Shakespearean films generally), the Academy Award winner of 1948, Sir Laurence Olivier's tour de force portrayal of 'a man who could not make up his mind'. That infamous tag, spoken in voice-over at the beginning of the film as Hamlet is borne aloft by soldiers on the misty battlements, triumphant in death, suggests a problem: how does one render such a 'literary' notion in cinematic terms? The idea, if not the formulation, goes back at least as far as Coleridge, and is wholly in keeping with the intricately psychological interpretations focusing on Hamlet's interior life that have been the hallmark of British stage productions through the nineteenth and twentieth centuries. In many ways, Olivier's version reproduces the Romantic/Victorian Hamlet of cultural tradition, though there are distinctive 'modern' layers over the earlier strata.

Two of these modern elements, one ideological, the other technological, are ingeniously interwoven. The much discussed 'Freudian' motivation on which Olivier constructs the character of the hero is a new variant of the old psychological theme, and is given cinematic form by the obsessively restless camera movement which is the single most salient feature of the film's visual markers. The psychoanalytic model is suited to theatrical representation in that it belongs to the script and can be played upon a stage (as it was by Olivier himself in 1937); the second is obviously cinematic. But in the film the two are inextricable. The discursive notion that Hamlet is a man who cannot make up his mind is inscribed on celluloid initially in a literal way by the screened printing at the very outset of part of Hamlet's speech about nobility being undermined by the corrosive presence of a hidden 'fault':

> So oft it chances in particular men,
> That for some vicious mole of nature in them ...
> Their virtues else, be they as pure as grace ...
> Shall in the general censure take corruption
> From that particular fault. (I.iv.23ff., a Q2 only passage)

Meanwhile, a voice-over intones the words, rather in the manner of television newscasts, where bits of an important document are given on-screen presence while they are read aloud by earnest, but momentarily invisible, journalists. (Is this done for the benefit of illiterate viewers or for the sake of an audience whose aural capacities cannot be trusted?) Here the 'text' is given a reassuring presence and literalness that seem meant to assuage the anxieties of those who prefer their Shakespeare on paper or at most one remove away from paper, in the theatre.

The 'one particular fault', given such verbal/visual prominence, is of course the inability to make up one's mind – but the overt claim to explanatory power actually begs the question. What, we wonder, may in turn be the source of this mysterious failing? For the answer, cut to Freud and his disciple, Ernest Jones, whose theories about Hamlet's Oedipus complex, which Olivier had absorbed during his visits to Jones in the 1930s, had formed the basis of his and Tyrone Guthrie's stage production (see Chapter III, above).

The cinema, it now seemed to Olivier, offered a way, at once more intimate and more detached than was possible in the theatre, of rendering the unconscious visible. The obvious method would be a series of cuts establishing a chain of associations, but Olivier chose a different route: the serpentine tracking of the camera through Elsinore, up and down the ubiquitous staircases, past Romanesque columns and shadowy passageways, pausing here and there to gaze at, and then dolly expectantly towards, some salient feature, before retreating again to continue its interminable search. Of its various points of pause, none is more suggestive, nor more blatant, than the vast, slightly tousled, bed that *is* his mother's chamber. With its vaginal shaped canopy (Donaldson 31) and dark recesses, its symbolic emphasis seems almost comic, especially given the dearth of furniture in the rest of the castle. In the long establishing sequence following the first scene, the camera lavishes its slow, gradually advancing attention on it, before dissolving to an image of the King drinking from a huge chalice. Such is the prelude to our first sight of Hamlet, the prowling of the camera through the arched corridors of the castle clearly analogous to the restless wanderings of the melancholy prince, registering not his thoughts exactly, but his unconscious conflicts. In fact our view of him is withheld until it cannot be avoided ('But now, my cousin Hamlet, and my son ...' I.ii.64), so that the first section of the court scene (I.ii) is shot from Hamlet's point of view, sometimes literally (i.e. the camera occupies the space we later see is his), sometimes figuratively (as in the vaguely repellent portrayal of the 'bloat', and somewhat inebriated, King); this helps to establish the fluid but essential links between individual psychology and the camera.

All in all the inexorable tracking camera makes the castle – sparse, stony, and almost devoid of furniture – into a purely inner space, the inside of Hamlet's cranium; frequent shots, from the back, of Olivier's own blond head corroborate this sense. The most famous of these occurs immediately before the 'To be or not to be' soliloquy when Hamlet, high on the vertiginous parapet that seems to represent the apex of both his isolation and his vulnerability, is seen from above and behind, the camera gradually zooming in on the whorled crown of his hair and seeming to penetrate his skull – there ensues a misty, barely identifiable image of what looks like a human brain, before the camera moves around for a shot of his knitted brow and the beckoning beach far below (to which, a moment later, he lets his ineffectually phallic dagger fall). The inner space thus created seems the logical extension of an essentially theatrical evolution, developed in the nineteenth century and continuing through Barrymore, Gielgud and Olivier himself. Cinematic means are used to achieve what are, from the point of view of theatrical history, essentially conservative goals, focusing exclusively on Hamlet's psychology.

The psychoanalytic framework produces a way of privileging individual consciousness as the ultimate measure of reality. Again we find a development here of elements that had inhered in the *Hamlet* project for generations. Like so many of his predecessors, Olivier eliminated all traces of a *political* world, not just the international scene with Fortinbras and the various ambassadors, but Laertes' abortive rebellion as well: Laertes and Claudius are first heard and then seen from a distance in a large empty hall, all the while our attention being haunted by Ophelia's gentle madness and vacant wanderings. We thus focus on her inner plight and, briefly, Laertes' troubled personal reaction to it, the action remaining safely within the confines of mental, not political, disorder. Rosencrantz and Guildenstern also disappear totally from the action, robbing Hamlet of most of his opportunities to display his sardonic wit and lightning-fast perceptions of motive. But more importantly, their disappearance also reduces the political world of the play; what spying remains is purely personal (Polonius and Claudius behind the arras, Polonius in the Queen's closet). There is no sense of a network of spying, no 'secret service', no probing of Hamlet's 'ambition' in II.ii, little of the careful fawning before the King that is the sign of getting ahead at court. A key moment after the King breaks up the play with his call for lights might seem to contradict what I have just said, but in fact confirms it. The court explodes with horrified movement as the King rushes out in a whirlwind of fear and guilt, but the moment is purely symbolic; it does not register any actual social relations, but works as an allegory, an externalization of the King's feelings and Hamlet's elated response to the success of his plan.

All this is interesting given the post-war climate in which the film was conceived and produced. Olivier had moved from *Henry V*, which was shot during the Battle of Britain and deliberately planned as an encomium to the British people – memorialized in the small 'band of brothers' that defeated the foreign enemy at Agincourt. As Olivier put it later: 'My country was at war; I felt Shakespeare within me, I felt the cinema within him' (*On Acting* 190). 'Shakespeare' would speak to England through the double medium of actor and film. *Hamlet* derived from different imperatives. It was conceived in the context of the developing Cold War and produced as the British Empire was visibly losing its grip in the Middle East and India. Nationally, political life was active and prominent; after the election of the Labour government in 1945, social policy became increasingly collectivist and the transformation to the modern welfare state was quickly set into motion. Olivier's film turns away from both international and national politics towards an inner province of sovereign subjectivity. For an individualist like Olivier, who felt Shakespeare within him, Hamlet was the man to be, and cinema the medium best adapted to exploring the inside of his skull.

If the occasion derived partly from political circumstances, the precise contour and drive of the film may have been shaped by Olivier's own personal tensions. In a brilliant reading of Olivier's handling of the psychoanalytic framework in his movie, Peter Donaldson suggests that what was at stake was not only Hamlet's but Olivier's own Oedipal tensions and their irresolution. As is clear from his autobiography, Olivier looked upon acting, the sphere of his childhood power, as potentially 'feminizing'; it brought him closer to his mother and was connected to unwelcome sexual advances from older boys. His own sexual orientation was in question, and his masculinity in some danger. Lacking his father's support, he sought male mentors outside the family, who produced a 'nurturance' that was at the same time perceived as 'a kind of penetration of the self'. All this, plus a graphic incident of near rape by an older boy on a *staircase* with the nine-year-old Olivier dressed ambiguously in a kilt, is symbolically re-enacted in *Hamlet*. The strong male mentor reappears as the emasculating Ghost/father, whose eerie power robs his son of his sword and his upright posture both on the battlements and in his mother's bedroom, and whose figure is ambivalently linked with that of the abusive schoolboy. The sexual danger and the interplay of passivity and aggression reappear in both the violent/erotic treatment of Ophelia on the stairs at the end of the nunnery scene and in the complex dynamics of the closet scene, which begins with phallic aggression but modulates to a soft and tender reconciliation with the mother, culminating in a decidedly sexy kiss (Donaldson 19-25, 35-63). For Olivier, as for Hamlet, the question is, according to Donaldson, whether the 'theatrical' resolution to the Oedipus complex is a satisfactory one; does acting not retain its sexually ambiguous, feminized aspect? (Olivier begins his autobiography with the key moment when his father not only accepts but promises to promote his son's choice of an acting career, but the scene takes place while Olivier lies naked in the tub, in his father's second-hand bath water – *Confessions* 4-5.)[1] For Hamlet too, as Olivier presents him, the 'theatrical solution to the Oedipal dilemma ("the play's the thing ...") is a dubious one in which real mastery and narcissistic refuge are hard to distinguish' (Donaldson 57).

Hamlet won the 1948 Academy award for best picture, and Olivier got the Oscar for best actor, though he lost out as best director to John Huston, whose brilliant critique of untrammelled individual greed displacing collective interest, *Treasure of the Sierra Madre*, won him as well the award for best screenplay (Shakespeare wasn't nominated). In post-war Hollywood, radicalism and collectivism were gradually becoming suspect, despite movies like *Treasure* (which failed to win best picture), as was criticism, however veiled, of American society. Individualism, after the populism of the1930s and the many group-extolling propaganda pictures of the war years, was on the way in. So the success of *Hamlet*, which is almost devoid of social ramifications of any kind, at such a moment may not be entirely coincidental; it represents a move inward at a time when the social responsibilities of the artist were in retreat. William

[176]

Wyler, Olivier's mentor (another of those sadistic but supportive father-figures), remarked in 1948 that a populist-progressive film such as *The Grapes of Wrath* (1940) 'could no longer be made' (Neve 54). It was the time when the House Committee on Un-American Activities was first making inroads against the 'communists' and leftists in the film industry. In November 1947, ten Hollywood writers and directors, who had refused to co-operate with the Committee, were convicted of contempt of Congress; the same day executives from the major studios met in New York and decided not only to dismiss the so-called 'Hollywood Ten' but to refuse to employ anyone thought to be a communist (Neve 89-90). Even the kind of populist individualism that had characterized many of the films of Frank Capra, whose career was entering an impasse in the late 1940s, was no longer available; Capra's work had always been 'related to social responsibilities' and had emphasized the 'social constraints' on the development of human potentiality (Neve 55), but such a viewpoint was now under attack.

In 1946, *Henry V* had earned a special citation at the Academy Awards, a belated recognition of its wartime contribution. Its celebration of the earthy and stalwart British whose democratic camaraderie and love for their populist leader enable them to defeat the snobbish and effete French must have struck a chord in a Hollywood still devoted to the idea of community. It seems that, by 1948, the film industry was ready for a less overtly political vision, one in which the Shakespeare within Olivier was to be expressed in terms of a tortured subjectivity. *Hamlet* was the first non-American film ever to be honoured with the award for best picture. As for the actor, he comments that his 'Oscar' was not only good for his career but 'wise of the Academy; the Hollywood establishment had recognized an innovative screen performance which had sprung from one of them – Wyler' (*On Acting* 204). It also showed the desire of the Establishment to burnish the image of mass culture with a bit of Shakespearean polish; and, of course, *Hamlet*, then as always, could be relied on as a cultural marker, helping to define subjectivity in the era of the Cold War.

What was 'innovative' about Olivier's performance was chiefly the success with which he was able to suggest inwardness, to bring to the fore a brooding inner life. Throughout the whole first part of the film, he is almost motionless, sitting in the chair with which he has already become identified (it is shown empty during the long tracking shot through the castle which separates the first scene on the battlements from the ensuing court scene). He remains expressionless, rooted in melancholy. During the first soliloquy, ('O that this too too solid flesh would melt ...'), he moves around mechanically, leaning over the now-empty thrones of his mother and Claudius (the latter's usurped from Hamlet's father as we are made to recognize), and sinking into his chair again at the end, on 'But break my heart, for I must hold my tongue'. This line, which in the original is the cue for the entrance of Horatio and the others with their news of the Ghost, is strangely inappropriate, since we cut immediately to a cheery Laertes entering his sister's room from a sun-splashed gallery. The whole of I.iii follows (Laertes, Ophelia, Polonius) and we return to the rest of I.ii only afterwards. Hamlet, it seems, must hold his tongue not because of an external interruption but because of a mysterious inner compulsion. The nature of that compulsion is clarified by the transposition of scenes. We hear from Ophelia of Hamlet's 'tenders of affection' to her and we witness the warnings of Laertes and Polonius. At the end of this, as Ophelia and her father cross the gallery outside her room, Polonius looks out, starts slightly, and then strides into the room; Ophelia, following his gaze, sees Hamlet, still seated in the same pose, at the far end of an enormously long colonnade. He gestures to her feebly, his hand half raised. She is about to respond when her father calls her into the room, and Hamlet's hand falls, sad music emphasizing his loss. He never realizes that she is obeying her father against her own will. This famous sequence is filmed in alternating long shots down the corridor, the magic of 'deep focus' allowing the separated lovers both to remain in focus at the same time.[2] Olivier referred to it as 'the longest distance love-scene on record' (Cross 12).

The textual transposition, placing the Ophelia scene immediately after the first soliloquy, thus creates a direct link between his mother's betrayal, outlined in the soliloquy (she posts with such dexterity to incestuous sheets), and what Hamlet now perceives as Ophelia's similar disloyalty. His inner brooding is connected to the poisoning of the wellsprings of love in his defeated soul. All this is established *before* the news arrives of his father's ghost.

The Ghost scenes reinforce the Oedipal dilemma. Rejecting the tradition going back at least to Betterton, Olivier of course retains the speech about the one particular fault (its prominence in the prologue ensured that). A shot downwards from the battlements into a courtyard, where the 'heavy-headed revel' is in full swing, sets the scene; Hamlet turns from it, his hand on a symbolic cannon that seems to represent the phallic power of Claudius as well as the military prowess of his father, and lectures his companions on the psychology of inner contamination. On the word 'fault', the ghost sounds intervene (an ominous heartbeat that Olivier stole from Jean-Louis Barrault – *On Acting* 202), Hamlet reels, his face swimming in and out of focus, and he collapses on the cannon. Later, when he follows his father off, he holds his sword-hilt up like a cross (a borrowing from Edwin Booth), only to drop it later and then collapse backwards as the Ghost disappears into the mist. Like most of his nineteenth-century predecessors, he left out the 'tables' in which Hamlet writes of smiling villains, and he gave the ghost's 'O horrible, horrible ...' to Hamlet. More important, like Booth and a host of others, he avoided hysteria and madness, interpreting them as play-acted rather than real, and replaced them with brooding melancholy. The play-acting is evident, for instance, in the interpolated scene which accompanies Ophelia's description of Hamlet's visit to her in her chamber. One of several 'tableaux' designed to flesh out the poetry with visual cues, this one shows Hamlet going through the motions of hand to brow, perusal of Ophelia's face and shaking of her arm, all in an exaggerated theatrical manner calculated to alert us to his ploys.

If acting mad provides a refuge, the theatrical mode also helps to rescue this Hamlet from himself. What I mean is that there is a continuous edge of self-conscious play-acting in the presentation of the tortured inner life, a sense of pose and deliberate showiness that combines with the arty camera-work to render the self paradoxically hollow as well as full. These indeed 'are actions that a man might play'. Olivier seems ambivalent about this element – he eliminates almost the whole of the 'O what a rogue and peasant slave' soliloquy in which Hamlet ruminates on the deeply illusory basis of his own 'reality' and along with that most of the scene with the Players, including the whole of the Player's speech about Hecuba. All that remains is the famous final couplet of the soliloquy, 'The play's the thing / Wherein I'll catch the conscience of the king', which is thus detached not only from any clear plan or motivation on Hamlet's part, but from the anguished self-analysis that in the text leads up to his resolution. Olivier's Hamlet, despite the impulsions of Freudianism, is externalized and theatrical rather than introspective. The delivery of the couplet is extravagantly stagy: the prince gets a gleeful look in his eye, rushes down a pillared passage and up on to a raised dais that will serve as a stage for 'The Mousetrap' (the Players' props and masks are bunched carefully at the side), and shouts out the lines while performing an excited pirouette in a gradually narrowing spotlight, as the stirring show music builds to a climax.

The theatrical thread adds an odd texture to the film and its rendering of interiority. It is as though the psychoanalytic categories and insights are themselves theatrical constructs, put into play by the confrontation of actor and text. Interiority is something to be staged. This is where the element of modernism is most salient, where, despite the many throwbacks to Victorian staging and emotion, a more fragmented and alienated sense of personhood emerges, the self watching itself. A telling sign of the transformation of interiority into theatricality is the fact that in some prints of the film the fleeting view of a human brain before 'To be or not to be' gives way to an image of the masks of comedy and tragedy. The post-war period, marked by the recent experience of European deracination and the subsequent emergence of existentialism, produced a troubled individualism, one linked to Olivier's split vision.

Despite their mutual connection to Hamlet's Oedipal life, Ophelia and Gertrude are accorded contrasting treatment in the film. Ophelia is the nineteenth-century innocent, surrounded by light wherever she walks, her madness pretty, and her death a Pre-Raphaelite painting in motion. As played by the eighteen-year-old Jean Simmons, the character is as innocent of courtly machination as the actress was of Shakespeare. She tends to be framed in open windows, with garden or countryside in the distance, her blond braids a mark of her purity. The suggestive songs of her mad scene are distinctly played down – Olivier apparently no longer held his 1937 view that Ophelia and Hamlet knew each other all too well. One stroke, however, complicates the pretty portrait: as Hamlet finishes his advice to the players before the play scene, he approaches the company's boy actor and helps him with his wig – an exact replica of Ophelia's. Here again, the theatrical, constructed nature of 'reality' is hinted at (though not developed) along with the gender confusions implicit in Olivier's autobiography, Ophelia's blond innocence momentarily as much an act as that of the boy actor.

The Queen is altogether a different matter. Eileen Herlie was only twenty-seven when the film was made (Olivier was forty), and she brought with her a decidedly sexy presence. Although she graciously allowed herself to be photographed from unbecoming angles so as to add a few years to her looks (Cross 35), she remained young enough to be a plausible rival to Ophelia for her son's affections. More important, her story is given a prominence in the film that in some ways parallels Hamlet's. For both of them the turning point is the closet scene. Prior to that, despite the lingering kiss she plants on Hamlet's lips at the end of the first council scene (from which Claudius has visibly to pull her away), she is the usual thoughtless and sensuous woman of Victorian convention, the figure who lingers through most twentieth-century productions up to 1950.

The closet scene has been much commented on, mainly because of its steady Oedipal glow. The appearance of the Ghost has a similar effect on Hamlet as it had earlier, its signature heartbeat casting him to the floor in supplication. His mother's horror at the killing of Polonius and her vulnerability to her son's phallic aggression collapse at the sight of the prostrate Prince, and she breathes out 'Alas he's mad' with utter conviction, the camera carefully keeping the Ghost hidden from us as well as her. We get the merest glimpse of a ghostly shape in the doorway before the camera cuts back to Hamlet on the floor, reaching out, in the same pose as Ophelia on the stairs after the nunnery scene. So for a moment he *seems* mad, but, in bouncing back from that zone, he takes his mother with him and they become allies. 'Go not to my uncle's bed' leads to further reconciliation (much of the more unseemly part of the dialogue here is cut as it had been for centuries), and an alliance is struck that is sealed with a lovers' kiss and then, at the end, by Olivier's unceremonious treatment of Polonius's body ('I'll lug the guts into the neighbour room' is retained in defiance of tradition) and his mother's evident acquiescence.

[181]

From this point on, the Queen is definitely on Hamlet's side – almost as clearly as she is in the 'bad' quarto, Q1, where she is a party to Hamlet's revenge plot. Carefully avoiding Claudius's embraces, she seems as repelled by him now as she was drawn to him earlier. This is beautifully rendered in a moment between Ophelia's mad appearances, with Claudius acting very sympathetic and then seeking comfort from his wife, who turns from him on the stairs. Osric enters bringing letters from Hamlet for each of them. This is a subtle transposition of a scene which occurs somewhat later in the text itself; there, a messenger arrives with letters for Claudius as he plots with Laertes (IV.vii); the messenger mentions a letter for the Queen, but we hear nothing more about it. In the film, we see her receive it, and in a powerful visual moment the camera tracks back to a long shot of her and her husband exiting separately up two adjoining staircases, bent over their letters. Later she is not present when Laertes confronts the King (since the former's rebellious entrance is cut, their dispute reduced to a mild argument); hence the moment when Gertrude moves to protect her husband from danger (IV.v.110-30) disappears. All this suggests something of the Q1 sequence, where Horatio reports to the Queen what has happened with Hamlet, thus making her privy to the King's plot against her son. Nothing so overt happens in the film, but we are led to speculate on the contents of the letter, and certainly the final scene confirms Gertrude's commitment to exposing Claudius.

What happens is that Gertrude knowingly drinks the poison, in an effort, it seems, to sacrifice herself to save her son. She thus makes amends for her past sins and reveals Claudius's treachery, all in one strategic move. The sequence is carefully framed and intercut with the duel in order to highlight Gertrude's actions much more than would be possible on stage. When Claudius first drops the pearl in the goblet, she looks suspicious and unnerved; then, as the bout continues, she stares hard at the cup, making her fateful decision. She quickly seizes the wine, there is a quick cut to Claudius for 'Gertrude, do not drink', and then a cut back to her for 'I *will*, my lord'; her new self-mastery is audible in the voice, and the camera angle confirms it. We see her straight on, from slightly above so that she looks upward, full of light, as she holds the cup with both hands and drinks (Silviria 53-4). The goblet, the same one from which the King was first seen drinking at the opening (after the dissolve from the Queen's bed) works as a marker of the spiritual distance Gertrude has travelled. No longer a sign of corruption, it now carries communion overtones and speaks of redemption. This elaboration of Gertrude's role is made possible by the omission of a single line, Hamlet's 'I dare not drink yet madam – by and by', which indicates that she offers him the cup shortly after drinking from it herself, a move that would not be consistent with the knowledge of her husband's treachery that she displays here. So Olivier's reading diverges from Shakespeare's text in order to heighten Gertrude's stature and strongly emphasize the mother–son reconciliation. The last moment of the sequence brings Hamlet and his mother together for the last, and least ambiguous, time. He kneels before her when she says 'Come, let me wipe thy face' and she kisses him on the forehead, recalling, by contrast, those earlier, less motherly kisses (Silviria 54). A moment later, after the duel concludes with the fatal double wounding, the Queen warns her son directly and falls with a smile on her face (she of course does not know about the poisoned sword and so thinks she has saved him). This impels Hamlet to his most extraordinary effort yet, the man of melancholy galvanized into action: the famous Errol Flynn leap from the gallery on to a cowering Claudius. The resolved Oedipal tangle leads to manly self-assertion, but also to the possibility of self-destruction. In his autobiography, Olivier describes the dangers of a fourteen-foot head-first dive (with a sword in his hand). He was aware that he could permanently injure himself or even die; the shot was saved till the very last and everyone knew there could be no retakes. Even the stunt men he had engaged to show him how to do it refused to perform it more than once and what they did was too tame, so he varied it. In the event, the stand-in for Claudius was knocked unconscious but the hero rose up to invite everyone for a drink (*Confessions* 123-4). Peter Donaldson comments: 'The leap exemplifies a pattern in Olivier's life and art in which the fear of passivity and indecision is allayed by a masculine daring that offers only an equivocal solution because of its association with self-destruction' (61-2).

From this moment, the film moves to the final apotheosis. Hamlet takes the crown that the dying Claudius had struggled vainly to reach, bids farewell to his mother and sits on the throne, with Horatio kneeling in front; everything is very quiet down to 'The rest is silence' which is followed immediately (again recalling the nineteenth-century theatrical tradition) by Horatio's standing and speaking Fortinbras's final lines. The personal, private dimension is given its last emphasis when Horatio turns back to kiss Hamlet on the forehead as he bids him 'Good night, sweet prince, / And flights of angels sing thee to thy rest', the famous line transposed from its position earlier in the scene to climactic prominence. This is followed by the Prince's body being borne in procession back through the corridors and stairways of the castle, past Hamlet's chair with its bit of rosemary still there from Ophelia's mad scene, past the altar where Claudius prayed in vain, past the canopied bed and up to the top platform to end where the film began, with the dead Prince/King, his mind now and for ever made up, held in silhouette against the dying light and the silvered clouds.

Kozintsev, Ophelia and the prison-house

In 1964, during a 'thaw' in the restrictiveness of Soviet life and in east–west relations generally, Grigori Kozintsev produced his film of *Hamlet*, a version very much in the Russian tradition of the beleaguered individual imprisoned by an oppressive state apparatus. Like Olivier's, Kozintsev film ends with a procession up stairs and through gateways. But the differences are more important than the similarities. Now it is Fortinbras's bedraggled troops, not the court guard, that bear Hamlet like a soldier, and they take him *out* of the castle, not to its heights. Eschewing the old tradition, adopted by Olivier, of having Hamlet die on the throne that is now briefly his, Kozintsev moves the action out of doors, down to the omnipresent sea that has romantically defined the thoughtful prince from the beginning (we first see him on horseback galloping along the beach). The duel scene ends with Hamlet's effective dispatch of the tyrannical King who, the poison coursing through his system, rushes out of the hall past one of the many monumental statues that signified his 'Stalinist' cult of personality, screaming and pulling at his ruff. Then Hamlet heads to the sea, down the long, worn, outdoor staircase, to the stony shore. Here he dies against the rocks, accompanied by Horatio, all their explanatory lines reduced simply to 'The rest is silence'. Fortinbras and his troops arrive, a few lines of epitaph are spoken, and Hamlet is carried up the same worn steps. The procession moves out under the raised portcullis and across the lowered drawbridge, reversing Hamlet's entry into the castle at the beginning of the film when the drawbridge had swung ominously up, and the portcullis fallen with a clang. Denmark is a prison, from which the prince has now, finally, escaped.

The ending climaxes the double strain in the film, the pull between a Romantic vision of an isolated Hamlet and a precisely detailed evocation of social milieu. Here is no empty castle, dotted with bits of symbolic furniture and a sprinkling of allegorical courtiers, as in Olivier. Kozintsev's Elsinore is packed with people and things, courtiers going about their business in the background as unnoticed agonies unfold in front of them (Kenneth Tynan, *Observer*, 10 Jan. 1965). Ophelia dances awkwardly to a tune played on a celesta, there is the feel of a Dutch interior, augmented by Laertes' entrance with a large spotted dog. Hens and geese cackle behind the Player's speech about Hecuba. More significantly, Hamlet *thinks* his first soliloquy ('O that this too too solid flesh') as he wanders through a chamber crowded with busy courtiers and ambassadors (smatterings of foreign languages are heard) some of whom acknowledge the preoccupied figure while others fail to notice. This develops Olivier's device of the voice-over soliloquy, but uses it more consistently and with a different purpose. Olivier was alone and spoke certain key lines aloud, emphasizing their Oedipal content. Kozintsev's idea is to stress the tragedy of 'solitude in a crowd' (Kozintsev 258); for him, 'Hamlet ... thinks. There is nothing more dangerous' (250). This again catches the doubleness at the root of his conception. Hamlet's thinking is political. It threatens the state; but it is also a sign of his tragic-Romantic sensibility – his richer understanding, and hence his rejection, of all the busy comings and goings of his world. This doubleness comes partly out of the Russian tradition in which Kozintsev was working and partly out of his specific situation in post-Stalinist Soviet society, where a certain freedom of expression allows for some critique of an oppressive regime, but only when it is couched in the language of tragedy and set in a remote time and place.

In the nineteenth century, Germans and Russians vied for the dubious privilege of 'owning' *Hamlet*. 'Germany *is* Hamlet,' wrote the revolutionary poet Ferdinand Freiligrath, while the poet Heine and the Shakespearean scholar Gervinus echoed him in claiming that Hamlet was a mirror for Germans. The Russians, not to be outdone, saw themselves as Hamlet too, but it was a slightly different Hamlet – not simply the reflective figure invented by Goethe and developed by Schlegel, the man who thinks so much that action is crippled. Rather, the Russian Hamlet was – in the words of an important political writer of mid-century, Aleksandr Herzen – a man unable 'to act from the force of … thoughts which are carried away by a desire for action before they themselves are completely formulated' (quoted in Kozintsev 116; see also Rowe 59-60). The Slavic element here, according to Kozintsev, is the emphasis on 'the energy of ideas and a desire to act which has raced ahead of the completion of the ideas'. Herzen, significantly, links Hamlet's hesitation to 'an era when [men] are conscious of some sort of black deeds taking place nearby, some betrayal of the great in order to serve the insignificant' (ibid.). Such formulations give the Russian Hamlet an unmistakably social dimension and produce an emphasis on cultural responsibility and the collective spirit. Herzen's notion of the 'great' centres mainly on the ethical greatness that resists political oppression. Hamlet's isolation and alienation, usually positive features of his individuality in the West, are often seen more negatively in Russia (Rowe 178), which may go some distance to explain the more active figure that Kozintsev and actor Innokenti Smoktunovski portray.

In 1837, Pavel Mochalov, the Edmund Kean of Russian theatre, appeared in a production that became a hallmark of what 'Hamlet' meant to Russians. Imbued with a bitter, self-tormenting energy as well as a deep, *active* melancholy, one that 'concealed the "wing-spread of an eagle"' (Kozintsev 121, quoting Belinski), Mochalov defined a political Hamlet in an era of widespread repression of artists and intellectuals under Tsar Nicholas I, and the parallels with the Stalinist era a century later were not lost on Kozintsev and his contemporaries. The translation was by Nikolay Polevoi, an intellectual who a few years before had written an unfavourable review of a play that the tsar had enjoyed, a move that was interpreted as treasonous. As a result, Polevoi was brought from Moscow to St Petersburg in a courier's troika; the chief of the secret police conducted the investigation. His spirit was broken. The *Hamlet* that he later produced reflected the pain he felt at the compromises he had made, just as the production emphasized the stifling repressiveness of Claudius's regime and the powerlessness of the sensitive intellectual who sees through it but can do little. A famous interpolated line conveys the dominant note: 'Afraid, I am afraid for man' (Kozintsev 120-1, Rowe 43). At the same time, there was an element of energetic and sardonic comedy in Mochalov's performance, and a drive toward social purgation. 'Through waverings, doubts and struggles with himself, [he] arrived at the necessity of destroying evil and coercion'. He 'sounded revolutionary' and roused the souls of those who had 'become silent under the yoke of Nikolaevan despotism' (Y. Dmitriev, quoted in Rowe 45). It was precisely the 'destruction of silence' in the play that was most influential:

> A smallish man on the stage of the Petrovski Theatre grew to an immense height. Belinski wrote that his gigantic shadow scaled the very ceiling of the auditorium. This man proved that it was possible to break away from the system, disobey the command, tear off the suffocating uniform, and refuse to be silent. (Kozintsev 123).

All this sits in the background of Kozintsev's film. The busy, vigilant regime oppresses the Romantic, stifled hero. But Hamlet treats his jailers with sardonic insolence. There is the 'sublime moment' (Jorgens 225) when he pauses by a huge statue of Claudius to shake a pebble from his shoe as he is being hurried to the investigation chamber by Rosencrantz and Guildenstern; or his subsequent entrance into the chamber, which is crowded with ominous black-clad inquisitors perched on benches like ravens, when he thrusts a torch through the door with a histrionic flourish. The flame has obvious symbolic value, Hamlet bringing light to 'benighted councillors' (Jorgens 223), but the main point is to define the rebellious voice of the hero. The dialogue that follows ('Now Hamlet, where's Polonius? – At supper …') is handled with detached ease; there is no trace of madness – he is controlling *them*. He comes nose to nose with his enemy for 'Farewell, *mother*', using enigmatic speech to break the conspiracy of silence. This flavour is summed up best in the recorder dialogue, when Hamlet attacks Rosencrantz and Guildenstern for seeking to 'play upon' him, to know his 'stops' (III.ii.363ff.). In his notes on the play, Kozintsev comes back again and again to this moment; it is the still centre of the play for him, 'the most important passage in the tragedy' (224). Why? Because it defines the individual against, even in defiance of, the operations of the state and its informers, suggesting a personal 'mystery' the heart of which Rosencrantz and Guildenstern are unable to 'pluck out'; this is the essence of the Romantic Hamlet of Mochalov and Herzen, but with a slight existentialist tang, stemming perhaps from the philosophic milieu of Europe in the 1950s and early 1960s.

It is as well the creed of the artist in a repressive society, something that Kozintsev knew all too well. In 1971, he told Jan Kott that he had had only 'a few happy years' in his life, during the early 1920s, when he was a young revolutionary artist in 'the time of Eisenstein and Mayakovsky, and Essenin and Meyerhold. Mayakovsky and Essenin committed suicide, and Meyerhold, after the closing of his theatre in 1938, disappeared and died in prison' (quoted in Kott and Mirsky 385). Kozintsev himself survived the Stalin years, but not without scars, nor, one cannot help but surmise, some feelings of guilt and sense of self-betrayal. In 1941, an offhand remark by Stalin simply 'put an end to *Hamlet* rehearsals' (Rowe 135), a fact which gives us some idea of the repressive conditions under which theatre artists worked. The play was not performed until after Stalin's death in 1953 when the old Russian valuation of Hamlet as a hero who does not keep silent rose once more to prominence, not least because of a production directed by Kozintsev in 1954. Another production of the same period strongly marked the idea that 'Denmark [and by extension, Russia] is a prison', using a 'massive iron grill' to divide up the stage, and prison bars to block the passage of Laertes followers, who tried to scale them in order to break into the palace (Rowe 136-7).

By 1963, when the film was being shot, the Khrushchev era, which had introduced something of a 'thaw', was coming to an end, but the sense of hope was still visible in the film; visible but fragile, because, as Kott says, of the 'little sinister smile' of Claudius/Stalin (387). Kott detects a 'double track of allusion' in the film, a standard technique of skirting censorship in a regime of terror, allowing the audience to read hidden significations pertaining to the contemporary situation which itself is never directly alluded to. Fortinbras poses the problem nicely – what kind of future does he portend? The film remains uncertain whether he is Stalin or Khrushchev, but he is certainly not Hamlet.

The recorder scene gives full play to these feelings of the dedicated and heroic individual speaking out against the system, aware of the danger (he has, after all, just tipped off the King about what he knows), but unyielding. 'The Mousetrap' has been staged outdoors, but its aftermath takes place back in the great state chamber, reminding us of its political implications. The musicians play, Hamlet seizes the pipe and rounds in on the bewildered pair, once his friends but now, in a shift all too familiar to those who had lived through the Stalinist years, government informers. Here one wishes one knew Russian in order to get the full flavour of Boris Pasternak's translation, itself a reflection of the Russian poet and novelist's efforts to maintain his integrity through the long years of terror (see Rowe 151). As it is, one must content oneself with Smoktunovski's rich intonations, as he rises heroically to the occasion. It is the one place in the film where the voice reaches such fullness, and it is significant as a sign not only of Kozintsev's perspective but of the Russian understanding of Hamlet, going back to Polevoi and Mochalov under Nicholas I, as a man who *speaks*, who breaks the conspiracy of silence and refuses, in Herzen's words, to betray greatness 'in order to serve the insignificant'.

For that of course is what is going on all around him. Ordinary life proceeds as expected. There is the life of the people, first imaged in the sullen crowd who listen to the opening lines of Claudius's throne speech (I.ii.1-14) being declaimed by a herald, but marked more casually by the scratching hens and peasants passing with horse and dog as Hamlet thinks of his plot to use the play to catch the King, or by the rowboat that plies across the bay in the background while the play penetrates the King's defences (Jorgens 224). And there is the life of the court, alert always to the smile of the King: no one smiles unless Claudius does; 'eyes shift, sometimes cunningly, sometimes in fear' (Rhode 62); this is where the 'betrayal of the great' is going on, and only Hamlet seems to notice.

Ophelia may also notice, but she is powerless. Her presence is a repeated reminder of the power over bodies that the court can so easily summon. We first see her dancing, doll-like, to a lovely if slightly mechanical air, being coached by a rigid old woman in black. 'We want to show how they denaturalize the girl', wrote Kozintsev to Shostakovich, who composed the music (255). Warned by her shrewd and effective father to stay away from Hamlet, she returns to her dance at the end of the scene, more puppet-like than ever. Later, after an interpolated scene copied from Olivier in which Hamlet enters her chamber in silence, grips her hand and stares closely at her before retreating, she goes in tears to her father, kissing his hand, a gesture he but grudgingly acknowledges. He has just been instructing Reynaldo to keep an eye on Laertes, a scene that is almost universally cut in English-language theatre productions, as in Olivier's film, but which in the Soviet context made perfect sense. Here we have a Polonius who is never foolish, always wary, a fleshy, sharp-eyed councillor in a furred gown.

Ophelia meets Hamlet in a large bare room lit by a high stained glass window at the back. Since most of the castle is furnished and busy, the emptiness of this hall announces itself as symbolic: the main players are prisoners being observed not only by the hidden spies but by us as well. There is a wide staircase on the left, another echo of Olivier, but used differently. Hamlet watches his beloved through the balustrade, speaking through it as through a grille – a shadow of the prison-house. When she reaches to return his 'remembrances', he slaps a jewel from her hand and it echoes sadly across the wooden floor. He shifts between anger and softness, strong sexual attraction ('I did love you once') and suspicion. He never sees Polonius and Claudius, but he knows something is up. He leaves her on the staircase, her hand on the banister and her face lifted, distraught, once more the image of 'pure fragility' (Kozintsev 244). He goes away in anger but without a trace of madness. Ophelia loses her soliloquy ('O, what a noble mind is here o'erthrown'), not just because Hamlet is not mad, and not only because of cinematic redundancy, but as a way of further reducing her individuality and rendering her poignantly symbolic.

Kozintsev keeps coming back to her image in his notes. She is a 'girl of the north'; the 'strong lines of her face, hair, and dress' speak of the Middle Ages more than the Renaissance; she is 'utter naturalness' mutilated by 'artificiality' (241); she lives in 'a strange aerie ... painted with fabulous unicorns and birds' (244); her madness is to be conveyed in 'an almost religious key', though it takes place 'amidst iron' (270). When Laertes launches his 'meaningless' attack, there is 'only one happy person, already gathering dirty, broken branches instead of

8 The nunnery scene from Grigori Kozintsev's film (1964): Hamlet (Innokenti Smoktunovsky) broods in front of the bars of the balustrade which frame the doomed Ophelia (Anastasiya Vertinskaya).

little flowers – Ophelia' (259). The most arresting image of all enters the film after Polonius's death. Hamlet has been dispatched to England. As he rides off, Ophelia is silhouetted in her window and we cut to her being garbed for her father's funeral. Attended by dour and silent crones, she is girdled and hooped in iron, literally caged under her black dress; her face is impassive, but there is suffering in her eyes. Her madness thus becomes a kind of social product, a sign of oppression that has been written on her body, and though it paradoxically frees her, it also spells her end.

Not exactly pretty in the Pre-Raphaelite way that Olivier adopted from nineteenth-century tradition, Ophelia's madness is not harsh either. Rather, it is a telling social commentary. As a prelude, we see her in the same empty room used for the nunnery scene, all in black, her hands stretched out and her long trailing veil held by her women, reliving, perhaps, the pain of her father's funeral. But her earlier impassiveness has extended to vacancy. Again we view her through a balustrade – her external imprisonment has moved inward, social pathology made personal. This is further suggested by a touching reprise of the dance music from earlier on, when she breaks briefly and mechanically into her dance. She goes up the stairs, casting off her mourning dress as she leaves. When we next see her, it is after Laertes has invaded Elsinore with a troop of soldiers; her rigid black dress and iron corset are gone, replaced by a flowing grey cloak and shift; her once well-coifed hair is loose and her feet bare. She seems bizarrely happy as she picks up a few twigs by the fire and wanders among the stone-faced, iron-clad soldiers, offering her sticks like flowers – a 'white, crazed figure in a framework of metal' (Manvell 83).

The juxtaposition of Laertes' rebellion and Ophelia's madness, already present in Shakespeare's text but heightened through a brief interpolated scene of Laertes returning to Elsinore, solemnly taking a sword from the family coffer and swearing revenge at an altar, gives a particular angle to the 'theme of government', which, says Kozintsev, 'Olivier cut', but which he finds 'extremely interesting' (234). Laertes' troops batter down doors and overpower the palace guard, but the smiling Claudius easily placates his adversary. 'Government' is partly a matter of show, a way of wielding the appearance of innocence. Or perhaps thoughtless revolt is itself useless, another form of madness; only Hamlet's *thinking* is truly revolutionary, truly disturbing to the regime.

But Claudius is not untouched – his own reflection is abhorrent to him. As he seeks to pray after the play scene, his distorted image, lit by a flickering candle, is reflected in a mirror. He flings his wine against it, obliterating the image, as Hamlet's huge shadow is thrown on the stone wall beyond the wooden doors. Accosted by a guard, Hamlet passes his uncle by and goes straight to his mother; 'Now might I do it pat ...' is cut, as is the fourth act soliloquy, 'How all occasions do inform against me'. This Hamlet does not delay, but in a crowded world seizes what opportunity he can. He has no trouble making up his mind – 'he lacks not will but opportunity' (Arthur Knight, *Saturday Review*, 21 May 1966). He is hence a suitable adversary for Claudius, who shows his weakness only when he has to face himself. With Laertes after the burial of Ophelia (the plotting to kill Hamlet, as in Olivier's film, is moved to after the graveyard scene), Claudius easily exploits the young man's anger and naiveté, but catching sight of his own reflection, he again tosses his wine against a mirror. The familiar motif of the drinking Claudius, present in almost every version whether on stage or screen, is thus given a distinctive twist.

During the play scene, Claudius shows his mettle by controlling his reaction. Basil Sydney's melodramatic shriek and rushing exit in the Olivier version is turned into a shrewd political move, though there are again similarities in the way the two films establish the scene. Both versions feature an impressive procession on the way to the evening's entertainment, more formal in the Russian film, the elaborate Velázquez costumes adding to the picture of court life. The procession moves through the baroque halls and out into the Scandinavian twilight, where a kind of double stage has been set up, King and Queen facing Player-king and queen across a gap. They 'observe and play to each other' and 'Hamlet watches them both' (Jorgens 232), thus enacting the play's concern with the complex interrelations between theatre and life. Directly opposite to Olivier, Kozintsev eliminates the dumb-show and retains the play itself. The acting is exaggerated but effective, puffed just a little above the already slightly inflated (at least to Anglo-Saxon eyes) Russian style. Lucianus sweeps his cape villainously around himself in the manner of Ivan the Terrible in Eisenstein. Claudius, very jolly at first, becomes rapt, slowly and unconsciously rising as the reflective action plunges on. When the Player-king dies, he begins to applaud slowly and the rest of the court follows suit, bringing the performance to a premature end. He then turns quickly and rushes out, followed by the bustling courtiers, calling for 'Lights' only when he gets inside the castle; Polonius, in his haste to reach the King, thrusts Ophelia aside and she is left by the whirling crowd to stand alone and bewildered by a parapet. The play scene is thus made to mirror not only the events of the primordial murder, but the intricate social relations of the court.

The court world is inescapable. In Act I, just before the Ghost appears, there is wild revelry in the palace, with dancing satyrs and an overtly lustful Claudius. Horses stir in the royal stables, and then break out violently in conjunction with the appearance of the huge, portentous figure, 'his long cloak extending behind him in the gale' (Manvell 81). The spectre moves ominously in slow motion, and Hamlet follows him down toward the sea as the music swirls and the drum beats. Most of the ensuing scene is shot not up at the ghost striding the cliff but, unexpectedly, down toward Hamlet, who is dwarfed against the glinting sea. Occasional upward shots reveal a grotesque metallic mask, similar to that used in the Olivier film, with just a glimpse of sorrowful human eyes visible for an instant ('Nor let thy soul contrive / Against thy mother aught'). At the end, Hamlet is left prone on the rocky shore as a grey dawn breaks; there is no swearing scene, no talk of putting on an antic disposition. This is a troubled Hamlet, but not a mad one, either in play or in earnest – a Hamlet who is terribly alone, and whose friends, because they see so little, can offer little support. But we are made to care much less about his subjective stance than about the pressures upon it from outside forces. These are what count.

Kozintsev keeps finding ways to make those pressures visible. When Polonius falls behind the arras, victim of the Prince's impulsive dagger thrust, he tears away the curtain to reveal a line of tailor's dummies arrayed in Gertrude's finery. They stand on guard, like mute sentinels; spying seems to extend even to inanimate objects. Hamlet's aggressive strike is set against stacked odds. But the symbolism is not overt – it fits naturalistically into the developing plot. Prevented a moment before from stalking Claudius, Hamlet now, stabbing through the arras, seizes what he thinks is his chance to fulfil the ghost's command. Kozintsev's cutting of 'Now might I do it pat' makes perfect sense of this moment, lending the text a narrative drive and clarity that it does not always have in the original. The scene achieves what is really the film's signature: a combination of well-paced narrative and symbolic signification.

The confrontation with his mother ends with Gertrude quite easily won over, and Hamlet lugging out Polonius's guts with a maniacal laugh that echoes through the palace corridors. In general in this version, there is no attempt to soften the harsh edges of Hamlet's character. The Russian tradition has always included the biting laughter and ready cruelty of the Prince; unlike the German tradition stemming from Goethe, or the Anglo-American stage tradition epitomized in Booth, where the sweet ineffectuality of the Prince is uppermost, the Russians have typically included what Turgenev called 'negation', a kind of corrosive scepticism, in their conception of Hamlet (Rowe 66-7). Intelligence and sensitivity in the face of despotism and corruption seem almost to demand such an attitude.

This in turn helps to explain Hamlet's bitter treatment of Ophelia, his scorn of Polonius, his offhand dispatch of Rosencrantz and Guildenstern. This last is accomplished through a brief interpolated scene on board ship where Hamlet, hearing again his father's voice ('Remember me!') is led to break open the coffer and read his death warrant by a swinging lantern in which he then burns it, while Rosencrantz and Guildenstern snore. In the film, the lines from the end of the closet scene about the engineer being hoist with his own petard ('O 'tis most sweet / When in one line two crafts directly meet' – III.iv.209-10 (Q2 only)) are inserted here as he re-writes the commission, sending the luckless pair to their deaths. Sardonic delight in polishing off his enemies is in no way alien to this Hamlet.

Though there is plenty of room for barbed irony, there is little actual humour in the film, no evidence of Hamlet's floating wit or the aristocratic ease with which he spars with his school-fellows, mocks Polonius, trades jests with the gravedigger, or teases the befuddled Osric. English wit is not part of the Rus-sian tradition. There is, in fact, a tendency toward the porten-tous, a Dostoyevskian weightiness that could lend itself to satire (one thinks of Woody Allen's *Love and Death*). The bird that soars at such length after Ophelia's death, the little me-chanical chess figures which appear periodically under the tolling clock (the last of which is Death),[3] the return of the bird before Hamlet accepts the final challenge, the ubiquitous shad-ows, the repeated shots of the sea crashing on the rocks, all these are heavy with meaning, a little relentless in what they portend. The scene with Osric, handled lightly by Olivier, with Osric tripping over himself and waving his hat absurdly about, is as ominous as the conspiracy that immediately precedes it. There is no satire; Osric is a dangerous fop, one of many to emerge from the castle shadows. Osric, says Kozintsev, 'is a plurality' (258); and 'the architecture of Elsinore does not con-sist in walls, but in the ears which the walls have' (225).

The last part of the film proceeds inexorably to the defeat of both the tyranny and the heroic rebel. The duel is strong and athletic; Hamlet, once wounded, immediately realizes what's up and powerfully puts things right, closing in quickly on Laertes. He then turns to go, assuming that all is for the moment over, but the Queen's fainting brings him back. He rushes at the retreating King, who ends up staggering by his smiling statue, the sword still in his back. Despotism may be dead, but so, almost, is Hamlet, as he makes his slow way to the rocky coast. The future remains uncertain. As Jan Kott remarks, 'Kozintsev did not solve the problem of Fortinbras – but then, to be honest, neither did Shakespeare's play' (Kott and Mirsky 390). From the political perspective of post-Stalinist Russia, this is certainly true; the film is the product partly of the Khrushchev 'thaw', but colder weather was soon to ensue, under the wintry gaze of Leonid Brezhnev. Shakespeare may have seen it otherwise; for him Fortinbras is certainly a falling off, but there is nothing necessarily foreboding about him.

In contrast to Olivier, the resolution here is defined in terms of freedom: Hamlet dying on the rocky shore and being borne out of the castle as the portcullis rises. The whole last part of the film emphasizes the Romantic Hamlet, alone (Horatio, while present, loses most of his lines and remains a background figure), embattled, but far-seeing and ultimately triumphant. But it does so within the political context that has been its subject from the outset and that has established its ambiance throughout. If, for Olivier, the architecture of the castle points inward, a map of the psyche, for Kozintsev it remains external; it is not architecture that stifles Hamlet, but 'the organization of life and the spiritual atmosphere of the century' (255). That the century in question is the twentieth as much as the sixteenth, that the setting is Russia as much as Denmark or England, is made clear in the equivocal final line of Kozintsev's book: 'The play was written in 1600 and performed in the forty-sixth year after the October Revolution – *Leningrad, 1965*' (276).

CHAPTER VIII

Through the looking glass: Zeffirelli and the BBC

Zeffirelli's cinematic eye

If the empty castle and the tracking camera are what is most characteristic of Olivier's *Hamlet,* and the Romantic figure isolated in the crowd typifies Kozintsev's, the gesture that seems to define Franco Zeffirelli's vision of the play is the glance. The camera moves, bodies move, but more than anything in this film, *eyes* move. Glances are continually being exchanged. Whether it is Ophelia returning the Queen's look at the rowdy banquet and wanly raising her goblet in acknowledgment, Polonius a moment later cutting in on the Queen's glance, Gertrude urging the King with her eyes to make up with Hamlet or looking down at Hamlet arriving with the players, Hamlet eyeing Claudius at the grave-side or catching the Queen's eye just before the fatal finale of the duel and winking at her, the camera is always on the alert for looks. Beyond that, the film is full of suspicious glances, the sidelong look that registers wariness. Polonius (Ian Holm) is a master of this, his eye movement a sign of his love of spying. But one of Mel Gibson's most characteristic moves as Hamlet is also the stealthy glance – Zeffirelli rations the pleasure associated with gazing directly into Gibson's gorgeous baby blues. All in all, we get looks that register connection – some kind of intimacy – and looks that speak contrastingly of distrust and suspicion.

Hamlet – the director's third Shakespeare film, shot in Britain in 1990 – offers us an interpolated opening scene (like Kozintsev, Zeffirelli leaves out the first scene of Shakespeare's text) in which some of the meanings constructed by the glance are put into circulation. Instead of the Ghost on the battlements, or a ceremonial lead-in as in Olivier, there is an extended depiction of Hamlet's father's funeral. We begin with a gradual closing in on the castle, first seen from a distance on its promontory; we enter the large castle courtyard, where flags flutter and horsemen and soldiers stand at arms; there is a long pan interspersed with solemn close-ups until the camera settles on a sobbing Gertrude (Glenn Close – 'like Niobe all tears') in the castle crypt. Kneeling over the open sarcophagus, she sports a pair of striking blonde pigtails, the very sign of Scandinavian womanhood as defined in a thousand nineteenth-century productions. (The pigtails reappear again in the final scene, though during most of the action they are replaced by more modern and sexier hairstyles.) She tearfully lifts her veil, takes a brooch from her hair and lays it lovingly on the armoured body of her dead husband. A quick cut to Claudius (Alan Bates) gazing intently at the scene, and then we see a hand scattering dirt on the corpse. As the camera pulls back, we recognize the hand as Hamlet's, his fringed head and chin half hidden under a monkish cowl (another reminiscence of Kozintsev). Claudius assures Hamlet that he is 'the most immediate to our throne' (I.ii.108-12), though it is never explained how Claudius got to be king; the whole political theme of the play is as invisible here as it is in Olivier, despite the fact that the castle is a kind of working village, peasants and artisans hover around the frame of almost every outdoor scene, and constant sounds of ongoing life provide a realistic background. The marble lid of the sarcophagus is put in place. Claudius, standing at one end, raises a massive sword over the coffin and lays it on the lid, its phallic point aimed directly at the weeping Queen who has collapsed again at the other end. The camera moves from the sword to a close-up of Gertrude, who looks up at Claudius. A point of view shot follows her anxious gaze and we see Claudius looking down at her, his eyes impassive but ripe with meaning. Looking is tied to desire – the link between the ceremonial sword and Claudius's strong gaze could hardly be more obvious. The Queen's hesitant upward look, seeking comfort perhaps (what hidden, adulterous knowledge is there behind that gaze?), registers both desire and longing. But looking also threatens fulfilment: intercut with the King and Queen's reciprocal glances, Hamlet watches each of them, his eyes marking a triangular relationship, heavily tinged with Oedipal tones, where the seeming simplicity of sexual desire gets turned awry, its current muddied. In fact, much of Zeffirelli's conception of the narrative is contained in these opening minutes. Despite the royal panoply and the medieval robes, the emphasis in the film is relentlessly domestic, focusing on the emotional turmoil of a woman caught by the love she feels for two men, one her son, the other his stepfather, and on the increasingly sharp battle of wills between the two men. What the eyes register is *knowledge* (Polonius too keeps a sideways eye on them all, sizing up the new political-sexual situation), although what exactly is known remains uncertain.

The triangular configuration in the opening tableau recurs soon after the enactment of the actual play gets under way. The first part of I.ii, Claudius's speech to the assembled crowd, is delivered in the castle's huge hall, but what follows is broken up into smaller, more intimate moments played in more confined spaces. Space, as well as time, is domesticated. The sequence in which Laertes begs permission to return to his studies takes place, fittingly, in the palace library, and the colloquy with Hamlet is moved to his private room. The camera cuts away from the library to a wide outdoor staircase down which the buoyant Queen rushes to greet her new husband. After a big, sexy kiss, she entreats him with her eyes and he, his look tells us, reluctantly complies. They enter Hamlet's dark room together and Gertrude casts open the curtain, thus welcoming the brilliant sunlight that is the strangely inappropriate observer of all that happens in this Elsinore (the gesture also literalizes Hamlet's sardonic 'Not so, my lord, I am too much in the sun' (I.ii.67) at which the Queen fetches a weak laugh). The King, goblet in hand, says his (much shortened) piece about lost fathers to Hamlet, egged on by his wife's eyes, and then departs, leaving mother and son alone for the interchange about seeming and being ('I have that within which passes show ...,' transposed to after the King's speech) and her earnest entreaty that he should stay at Elsinore. His pointed reply, 'I shall in all my best obey you, madam' (I.ii.120), normally delivered in front of the whole court and spoken as an implied rebuke to Claudius, becomes merely a straightforward assent, and the scene ends as it began with a kiss. Gertrude kisses him on eyes and mouth, motherly enough, but with a touch of unacknowledged incestuous feeling, transferred perhaps from the earlier more passionate kiss with Claudius. Then she runs down exultantly to join her bloat husband and the two ride off on horseback, while Hamlet is left to gaze down at them from his sunlit window and launch into his dark soliloquy.

Thus what is public in Shakespeare becomes private in Zeffirelli, played out in little duologues, unobserved by courtiers or hangers-on. We alone get to witness these exchanges, which themselves emphasize intimacy and domesticity. The sharply triangular relationship of the three principals, with Gertrude at the apex, is marked by her optimistic dashing up and down stairs, by her vibrant kisses and anxious looks, even by the overtly symbolic, and ironic, gesture of welcoming the sunlight into the dark room. The battle is joined, and it will be waged over the body of this woman, just now prancing off on her white horse, while her son watches despondently. His soliloquy is cut in half, ending with the famous tag, 'Frailty, thy name is woman'. This alerts us to the centrality of Gertrude and her betrayal, which has been strongly stressed too in the contrast between her weeping in the tomb and her shy, royal caresses a moment later at the assembly, giving point to Hamlet's compression of time ('within a month ...'). As for that fourth figure in the family constellation, he that was 'Hyperion to a satyr,' he remains momentarily in the background, having been denied his initial ghostly manifestation. Before long, however, we hear of the eerie reappearance of this troublesome pilgrim.

One of the most memorable aspects of the film is the wonderfully palpable Ghost played by Paul Scofield. In contrast with the Romantic, distant ghosts of Olivier and Kozintsev, whose mask-like features are only briefly humanized by the sorrowful glint of eyes in the darkness, Scofield is simply there, a father talking sadly to his son. The impulse is purely domestic, the colloquy between them emphasizing a need to connect. Old Hamlet speaks to his son as though to a child and occasionally lapses into child-like tones himself when he complains of his prison-house.[1] Most of all, he is a father who wants recognition, *remembrance*. Since family relations most concern Zeffirelli in this version, it is perfectly appropriate that the Ghost should be so evidently a member of the family, a father. And yet there is one decidedly ghostly quality to this figure – its cinematic shifting between visibility and invisibility. Exactly as the cinema controls what we see and the point of view from which we see it, so the Ghost appears and disappears at will,

9   Glenn Close (Gertrude) and Mel Gibson (Hamlet) eye the invisible
Ghost during the closet scene from Franco Zeffirelli's film (1990).

like a kind of emblem of what the movies can do. It is a familiar
trick: we watch Hamlet following the Ghost down a vaulted
corridor (designed perhaps to recall Hamlet's special gallery in
Olivier's film), up a set of stairs to a high turret, but then losing
him; he wheels frantically this way and that before sensing the
ghostly presence and turning slowly to see (at the same time
dropping his sword with a clang, as Olivier had). In the context
of a film in which looking is the key gesture – a film of a text in
which spying, watching, and play-acting are central and recurrent motifs – such tricks with visibility and invisibility, with
what is seen and how it is seen, take on added meaning.

Over the last couple of decades, film theory, especially feminist film theory, has concerned itself with what is called the
'male gaze', referring to the way male viewers are privileged
and empowered by the visual pleasure that the handling of the
narrative makes available. To gaze becomes in itself a form of
power, and the theme is repeated in a million advertisements,
TV programmes, fashion photos etc., products all of a visual
culture which constructs the woman as the object of a consum-
ing look.[2] The politics of looking in *Hamlet* are centred on
Claudius, whose cool desiring gaze is first marked in the crypt

scene and reappears at intervals through the film, a sign of the consolidation of power. Hamlet's eyes flit between mother and stepfather, as in the sequence of the Players' arrival, when Hamlet, who has met them on the way, comes riding in motley triumph on their wagon, to be greeted by Claudius on the palace stairs and Gertrude at a window. Again there is a triangular exchange of glances, signalling rivalry. When, a bit later, Hamlet conceives of the plan to catch the conscience of the king with a play, he too watches from a window, looking down on the actors as they unload their wagon. The window serves as a kind of frame within a frame, obsessively calling attention to the act of viewing, which both spectators and characters are equally engaged in. The film thus reflects upon itself and its medium, finding a meta-cinematic means of rendering the meta-theatricality of the text.

The play scene, always the meta-theatrical high point, begins with an actor's face in a mirror. Clarifying the narrative line in a manner reminiscent of Q1, which separates the Ophelia plot and the plot involving the Players and 'The Mousetrap' into two distinct strands instead of interweaving them as in the received text, Zeffirelli ties the scenes with the players into a single sequence, beginning with Hamlet's encounter with Rosencrantz and Guildenstern on a grassy hillside, proceeding to the arrival of the actors, Hamlet's plan to use them (the whole Hecuba section, as well as the later advice to the Players, is cut), and thence directly to the play itself, which begins with a male actor (the player-queen) making himself up to look rather like a cruel caricature of Glenn Close. The film thus cuts directly from Hamlet framed in the window to a representation of his mother framed in a mirror.[3]

The 'male gaze' is fragmented and complicated, here and throughout the film, through a bank of references to framed looking, to the ambiguity of gender in the acting, and to the erotic currents set in motion by the play scene as a whole. Most of the banter that precedes the play is kept, including, of course, all the suggestive lines that nineteenth-century audiences were protected from. So too there is the expected exchange of glances, Hamlet (and Horatio) watchful, Claudius expansive and self-satisfied. A pair of masked tumblers of uncertain sex performs a grotesquely erotic routine, with heads between each other's legs and bums thrust out in rocking simulation of unconventional lovemaking. This is interspersed with close-ups of Hamlet moving in on Ophelia, telling her to make her way to a nunnery, the lines transposed from the earlier scene and spoken in all earnestness, shorn of the anger that would have attended them then, when Hamlet was aware of the spies in the doorway. This, we are led to believe, is the 'real' Hamlet speaking in the midst of play-acting. But what he says and when he says it forge a dialectical link between sexual liberty and innocence, much to the bewilderment of Ophelia.

As 'The Murder of Gonzago' proceeds, the power of the gaze is turned back on Claudius. His ebullience turns to caution (for 'Is there no offence in it?' Hamlet is at his ear, sizing him up with a sideways look), then to apprehension, and then, on the appearance of the poisoner, to utter confusion: he stands, drops his goblet (that ever-present sign of 'Claudius'), stumbles forward, staggering like a drunk, tries to cover up his reaction with a knowing laugh which quickly changes to a maniacal one, and then calls wildly for lights. As the court streams out, Gertrude has time for a watchful glance at Hamlet's elated response, but Ophelia is left still bewildered in her chair. Again Hamlet approaches her, and again we get transposed lines from the nunnery scene: 'We are arrant knaves all, believe none of us'. The last phrase is given paradoxical weight, as if to stress that, although he can now speak the truths that he was prevented from voicing when overheard, he himself is as untrustworthy as the knave he has just succeeded in exposing. He accosts her with an aggressive kiss and leaves her with a flippant 'Farewell', as her incipient madness begins to show itself in her oddly distorted look and welling tears. The effect of the whole scene is ambiguous: it confirms the hero's suspicions, but it also breaks Ophelia; 'truth' emerges, but in the context of theatrical representation becomes almost inextricable from falsehood; and sexual betrayal (Gertrude's, the Player-queen's, Hamlet's own, maybe even Ophelia's) is coupled with purity and innocence.

The text's concentration on watching and spying is abetted in the film by a network of catwalks and upper galleries that snake through the castle (actually three different British castles used for the location shots). From these, observers constantly look down on the action being played out below. The idea seems to derive from Olivier, whose labyrinthine castle corridors and staircases offered endless opportunity for the hero to observe his enemies from above. So Zeffirelli's Hamlet, walking on an upper level, overhears Polonius in the courtyard cautioning his daughter to avoid contact with the Prince (and Polonius catches a reciprocal glimpse of Hamlet before he ducks inside); later Hamlet and his companions watch the 'heavy-headed revel' from a gallery above the banquet hall and Hamlet comments on the soiled reputation resulting from such swinishness. After they have moved on to the cold battlements, he gazes in solitude down through a grille punctuated with spearheads at the continuing revels and, with the king's head 'sighted' telescopically between the points of the grille, reverts to his meditation on the 'vicious mole of nature'. (The speech, from Q2 only, is normally cut, but Olivier had included it as a kind of lecture on Claudius's, and his own, failings; in the Gibson/Zeffirelli reading, it lacks any direct reference and seems to waft quietly over the scene as a floating signifier, fraught with meaning, but conveniently vague.) In another example of non-textual watching, Polonius appears in an overhead gallery spying on Hamlet and Ophelia as she is 'sewing in her closet' (as in both Olivier and Kozintsev, this is an interpolated scene replacing her description of his bizarre approach to her); what he gleans then provides Polonius with the ammunition he needs to tell his tales to the King and Queen. Or, for another instance, Gertrude and Horatio look down from a window (again!) at the mad Ophelia twisting a stolid guard's leather jerkin in a dark sexual parody. Indeed, Ophelia is throughout her madness a spectacle to be watched: the open courtyards and stairways where she wanders 'distract' are dotted with observers, and there is a memorable symbolic shot of her framed against a huge central tower that is ringed and studded with wooden balconies and catwalks, a monumental watchtower defining the shadows of her, and Hamlet's, prison-house.

Ophelia's madness has a strong element of anger mixed in with the pathos. Always, it seems, on the edge of violence, she recurrently turns the aggression inward, wringing her hands and doubling over. Her madness is introduced by a shot of her fingers gripping a parapet, her hands twisted into the stone. Hands in Zeffirelli are charged with meaning – Peter Donaldson, in his analysis of Zeffirelli's *Romeo and Juliet*, relates them to disintegration and reintegration of the self. He refers to a story in Zeffirelli's autobiography in which the future film director becomes so intrigued and disturbed by a severed hand that is presented to his drawing class as a model that he searches the Florence morgue, tracing the hand back to its owner, a young girl (mourned only by a single old woman), her hands now reunited, 'both of them holding a little mother-of pearl spray' (Zeffirelli 21, Donaldson 150-2 and 174-84). Ophelia's hands seem to work independently of the rest of her – they become a sign of her mental breakdown. With the stalwart guard whom she accosts, they move around his body like sexual claws; they fly to her own mouth as she sings her risqué songs and again when she thinks of her brother ('My brother shall know of it'). As she departs she kisses Gertrude's hands and holds out her own for Claudius to kiss. Later, sitting curled on Gertrude's throne, she passes out her 'flowers', a few bones and wisps of grass. Twice, the camera focuses exclusively on her hand as she holds it out to Laertes, clutching a bone which would seem to carry associations with both violence and sex. Ophelia's earlier sexual confusions, her chafing under her father's prohibitions and her simple delight transformed into bewilderment at Hamlet's contradictory behaviour, her love for her brother and her general sense of the court being a place beyond her (all conveyed powerfully in Helena Bonham-Carter's intense performance), converge on her as she crouches before Laertes now, bone in hand. Her death is lyrical, another borrowing from Olivier, but we are spared the extended Pre-Raphaelite drift. We get only a glimpse of her in a pool, floating peacefully on her back, her hands folded around a small bouquet. As with the girl in the morgue, reintegration comes only through the immobility of death. This point is sealed in the graveyard, when Hamlet plucks a spray of white flowers, kisses them and lays them on her breast.

If Hamlet's relationship with Ophelia is riddled with ambivalence, it mirrors that with his mother. In choosing to stress the triangular relationships involving Prince, mother, and step-father, Zeffirelli may have been bowing to psychological imperatives (see Donaldson 146-50), but he was also responding to commercial exigencies. Casting Mel Gibson and Glenn Close, two major Hollywood stars, as mother and son was bound to create box office expectations: lethal weapon meets fatal attraction in what turns out to be a dangerous liaison indeed. Sex and violence, those staples of popular culture, could be represented as central to high culture as well, making 'Shakespeare' appropriate material for mass consumption and digestion. That the Hollywood imports were to be surrounded by a trio of English stage actors of impeccable credentials (Paul Scofield, Ian Holm, Alan Bates), supported by an array of distinctive young players, also English, the cream, as it were, of the Masterpiece Theatre crop, only added to the cultural cachet of the whole enterprise. British depth, sensitivity, familiarity with the classic tradition, could be joined to American (or, more accurately, 'new world') energy and erotic vitality in a straightforward tale of sexual obsession and physical action.

The closet scene brings the two stars together for a duet (the very closeness in their ages adding an edge to the film's incestuous arpeggios), a sequence that registers, in a kind of paradigm, the ambivalence, the watching, the murderous violence, erotic attraction, and Oedipal tangles that characterize the film as a whole. A fire in a huge stone fireplace bathes the scene in incongruous golden light, a domestic touch akin to the rich fur rug on which the Queen sinks at the end. But the events played out in this warm atmosphere are anything but cosy. Gertrude is furious – she slaps Hamlet at the top of the scene, and his vehement response leads rapidly to the demise of the spying Polonius, stabbed wildly through the heraldic arras. Hamlet lifts his boot against the arras to withdraw his sword, making a visible effort to pull it out of the resistant flesh. Blood flows on the stones, to be noted later by Claudius ('It had been so with us had we been there' – IV.i.13). But Hamlet is sensitive as well as manly, and weeps over the dead busybody even as he mocks him. Dropping the phallic sword but not the feelings that it implies, he advances to his mother's bed, flashing the lockets at her and then getting on top of her in a sequence where sex and anger, eros and aggression, become indistinguishable. As he rocks and thrusts at her in a parody of the primal scene (Zeffirelli reports in his autobiography on the fascination he felt witnessing his parents' lovemaking, the young child unable to distinguish between loving and hurting – see Donaldson 147, and Zeffirelli 6), she stops him in the only way she knows how, with a passionate kiss.[4] The Ghost's timely arrival completes the family triangle, and Hamlet leaps guiltily away from his father's place. But Scofield's quiet, fatherly Ghost seems to have noticed nothing; unlike Polonius, he is a benign watcher. The Queen's shock at Hamlet's seeming madness leads quickly to a reconciliation and an alliance on 'O Hamlet, thou hast cleft my heart in twain'. Her promise never to breathe what he has said is sealed by his giving her his locket, which she is left to gaze at as he hauls away the body. Collapsed on the bear rug at the end of her bed, she immediately puts her promise into action by hiding the locket and covering for her son as Claudius comes in to question her.

The alliance between them links this version, like Olivier's, with Q1 (see above, 182, and Campbell 7) and is confirmed by a moment transposed from the end of the closet scene to a later sequence, after Hamlet is dispatched overseas and Claudius has called upon England to do his dirty work for him (IV.iii). It is dawn, Hamlet is on horseback, ready to leave with the shifty Rosencrantz and Guildenstern, when Gertrude comes running down to say goodbye, and they share a conspiratorial moment. He lets her know that he is aware of the plot: 'I must to England, you know that?... But I will delve one yard below their mines / And blow them at the moon' (III.iv.199-209 – a Q2 only passage). What in the closet scene seems an idle boast is made into a clear statement of intention; Hamlet is in charge, and his mother is on his side. This simplifies and clarifies what in the text itself is murky and ambiguous. Hence a speech unique to Q2, the most 'introspective' of the early texts (see Ward), is made the paradoxical instrument by which the narrative is given the direction and drive associated with Q1.

Later we see Hamlet on board ship with the snoring Rosencrantz and Guildenstern. Like Kozintsev and Olivier, Zeffirelli enacts the substitution of the letters which in the text forms part of Hamlet's narration to Horatio – but with a significant difference. This Hamlet does not have to read the letters, nor to write a new one on the spot; he already knows their contents and has forged his own substitute *before* raiding his companions' dispatch case. He has successfully pre-empted the whole plot, a fact that is hammered home by the following shot, which shows us the hapless Rosencrantz and Guildenstern being led to execution, and the 'great axe' falling. Thus we have Hamlet as a sort of medieval Mad Max, an action hero polishing off his enemies with ease and aplomb. The trouble is, of course, that the text, which, despite all the changes, Zeffirelli is following, doesn't really allow for this approach. Thus what follows is inconsistent: when Hamlet returns, instead of confronting Claudius directly and finishing the job, he lapses again into passivity, even if it is a passivity with a religious tinge ('There's a special providence' is spoken with Hamlet again alone at a window as the setting sun drifts into the sea).

Zeffirelli was inspired to cast Mel Gibson as Hamlet after having seen him in *Lethal Weapon* (*New York Times*, 19 Dec. 1990). Good looks and box office appeal were clearly important in the decision, but equally so was the conception of *Hamlet* as an action drama, one which could negotiate between the late 1980s and the late 1590s.[5] In *Lethal Weapon*, Gibson plays a tough *and* sensitive cop on the verge of psychosis. There is a tense 'to be or not to be' sequence in which he toys lovingly with the muzzle of a gun, his suicidal mood having been brought on by the death of his young wife. One of the last moments in the film shows us the now restored and resigned hero leaving a bouquet of flowers on his wife's grave, an image that Zeffirelli picks up for *Hamlet*. Just as the heroic past in *Hamlet* is evoked nostalgically as a kind of golden age, so too in *Lethal Weapon* the past functions as a bizarre form of pastoral – bizarre because the lost golden age is the Vietnam War, now reconstructed as a time of quintessential male bonding and heroic achievement. The 'good guys' and the bad share the same past and their bonds derive from the same imperatives; the difference between them is that Gibson and his fellow cop, an older black man (Danny Glover) who becomes Gibson's surrogate father, have feelings! As a minor character at the beginning of the film remarks, it is now the late 1980s and a new version of masculinity is disturbing traditional boundaries – men of the '80s have to be able to cry. But the film does little to dislodge traditional gender politics; its climax is a bloody and absurd one-on-one battle between Gibson and Mr Bad which ends with both Gibson and his partner/father shooting the robot-like villain simultaneously. Meanwhile, there is a running gag about how badly the partner's wife cooks: the ultimate self-sacrifice (and index of male bonding) is revealed in the final shot of Gibson and Glover going into the house together to eat overcooked Christmas turkey. So the Vietnam War is really O.K. – it produced guys like this; and sensitivity is not incompatible with tough police work. This makes for a neat, and highly conservative, resolution of political contradictions that the film touches upon only obliquely. The film's appeal to Zeffirelli must have gone beyond the image of the hero, since so much of his *Hamlet* seems to resonate from the earlier picture.

If Q1 is any indication, one *Elizabethan* way of conceiving of *Hamlet* was as a taut narrative centred on revenge – but this did not preclude the intrusion of politics or ethical doubt into the equation, though of course there is much less of such complication than in the received texts. Fortinbras is present in Q1, as are the ambassadors, and there is an overarching sense of the presence of a working court. Zeffirelli's court, on the other hand, seems to have only one function – revelling. Like Olivier's, this version is relentless in its elimination of any political dimension to the action. Olivier was intent on a psychoanalytic agenda, and I have speculated on some of the reasons for his excision of politics. In Zeffirelli's case the motivation and meanings are similarly complex. As Donaldson has shown, Zeffirelli had his personal reasons for being interested in the intermingling of sex and violence and in the triangular structure of familial relationships (146-50), but I want to raise another set of questions. In the West, the 1980s were as profoundly apolitical as one could wish, with the rise of the acquisitive baby boomer and the heyday of the junk bond dealer standing as two of the decade's primary images. Only within such a context could the Vietnam War be recuperated as it was in *Lethal Weapon*. (In eastern Europe, of course, things were different; a series of tumultuous events in the late 1980s led to *perestroika* in the Soviet Union, to the falling dominoes of the various satellite states, and finally to the shattering of the Berlin Wall in November 1989.) By late 1990, when *Hamlet* was released, tension in the Persian Gulf had tightened to a knot, and Operation Desert Storm was about to be unleashed, and packaged, as a relief effort, with the hapless media contributing to the general impression that all of America was firmly behind it – uneasy memories of Vietnam no longer an obstacle. (One *Hamlet* reviewer lamented the elimination of the Fortinbras scene (IV.iv) and with it 'the contemporary political message that Americans need to hear right now' – referring specifically to Hamlet's meditation on soldiers who 'for a fantasy and trick of fame … fight for a plot / Whereon the numbers cannot try the cause, / Which is not tomb enough and continent

/ To hide the slain' (61-5); see Edward Quinn, *Shakespeare Film Newsletter*, April 1991.) In Britain, Margaret Thatcher's revolution, which had successfully reversed much of the welfare state legislation built up after World War II and blasted the collective mentality that had fostered the legislation in the first place, had driven a wedge between rich and poor, north and south, reminiscent to many of the Victorian period (Thatcher resigned in November 1990). Action films in such a context – and there was a massive wave of them, from Rambo to Schwarzenegger to Mad Max – may be regarded as paradigms of power. Muscle-flexing on the international diplomatic and monetary fronts was projected on to individualist heroes of the screen, representing, perhaps, the not so heroic moves of Bush or Thatcher in an oddly rosy light, transforming into mass entertainment the economic agendas of the rich and powerful. Given as well Zeffirelli's own generally conservative politics and the romance with British high culture which has characterized his artistic life, one can see why he steered clear of the rebellious politics implicit in a version of *Hamlet* such as Kozintsev's.

It is remarkable, indeed, that in his autobiography Zeffirelli cites his viewing of Olivier's *Henry V* as the turning point in his early life, the moment when he chose a theatrical and cinematic career. An illegitimate Italian lad at the end of the war, with a name that came from no one and nowhere, sees an English film glorifying England, Shakespeare, and the British war effort, and turns his mind to artistic endeavours that would seek to emulate somehow that glorious example (Donaldson, Zeffirelli). By a wonderful coincidence, Kenneth Branagh's film of *Henry V* itself so clearly competing with Olivier's for cultural sovereignty, came out at almost exactly the same time as Zeffirelli's *Hamlet* and can be viewed in something of the same light, as delivering a similar, even more overtly conservative message. Combining the image of the lonely Prince (he had consulted with Prince Charles on that question) and the sensitive warrior (Rambo with heart), Branagh made a glorious film designed, or so it seemed, to give Britain the uplift it sorely needed at the end of the Thatcher era. It is tempting, if a bit fanciful, to read the film's construction of a culturally aggressive foreign power in contemporary terms; once again, as it had in the days of Shakespeare's Henry, France was flaunting its cultural superiority – now, of course, within the

European Community about which so many Britons felt, and continue to feel, ambivalent. Fittingly, a symbolic break-through occurred at the end of the same year (1990), when French and English workers shook hands under the English channel, having successfully tunnelled from their respective sides; it was a moment of collaboration, but one laden with threat, uncannily akin to the precarious peace achieved at the end of *Henry V* and described in the gloomy epilogue that was, naturally, omitted from the film. It is interesting too that many of the same faces appear in *Hamlet* and *Henry V*, and none more memorable than that of Paul Scofield who in both portrays an enervated, though dignified, father – a marker of both weakness and knowledge – who yields his sway to an heroic son.

In keeping with the emphasis on action, the duel at the end of *Hamlet* bristles with physical power and flirts too with a fine self-conscious comedy suited to the swashbuckling style. There are three bouts, each with different weapons and protective gear. In a routine reminiscent of *Lethal Weapon*, Gibson clowns around through the first two, mocking Laertes' high serious-ness and demonstrating an easy superiority. The court laughs and the Queen is delighted. Hamlet, in a variation of the glance motif, winks at her. Much kissing of hands surrounds her taking of the fatal drink as a prelude to the final, and deadly, bout. The comic tone completely disappears as Laertes and Hamlet, each with two swords, close in on each other – we have seen Laertes unsheathe the poisoned weapon just before. As their struggle proceeds, there are frequent cuts to Gertrude fighting against her incomprehensible pain; again she looks and we see the goblet and pitcher on the table – she *realizes*, and exchanges glances with the King, hers knowing, his ex-pressing a kind of pained and sheepish shrug. (But, unlike in Olivier, there is here no radical extension of the alliance be-tween Gertrude and Hamlet – she does not take the drink knowingly and deliberately.) Meanwhile, Laertes has slashed Hamlet with a dishonourable hit from behind that is soon revenged. The Queen's revelation about the drink and Laertes' confession of complicity are both in close-up with a mourning Hamlet intimately involved: he lays his head lovingly on Gertrude's chest and, as she whispers of poisoning, his eye flashes a triangular glance at the King; a moment later, he cradles the dying Laertes in his arms.[6] These intimate moments lead directly to the climactic attack on the King. Rushing straight at him, Hamlet first stabs, and then, in a gruesome bit that recalls the blood on the floor in the Queen's bedroom, pours the poisoned wine down the King's gullet as he lies, the red liquid swilling over his beard and neck like gore. *His* revels now are clearly ended. Hamlet staggers first to his mother for a last adieu, once more kissing her hand, and then to the centre of the makeshift stage on which his final scene has been enacted, collapsing spread-eagled on the wooden floor. After Horatio's brief farewell, the camera retreats backward and upward, displaying a tableau of the assembled court with the dead scattered around Hamlet and Horatio at the centre. There is no procession, no evocation of a future, only the dead, frozen on the stage, pinned like moths. After all the watching, all the close-up glances, all the looking downwards, we are privileged with the long-range view, the pseudo-divine regard from on high as the credits roll.

In the end, the question of the significance of all this arises. What does it add up to? And no simple answer presents itself. The film seems to lack both a coherent sense of the text and a firm grasp of its own aims. Zeffirelli has stated that he wanted to present the play as Shakespeare 'meant' it to be performed: 'I'm going to break away from the notion that Hamlet must be a blond, brooding prince [a jab at Olivier and Kozintsev]. The story is full of blood and excitement and that is what I want to bring to the screen. I don't want to sound arrogant, but I want to tell the story the way Shakespeare meant it to be told. It's never really been done the way it should be done' (quoted in *Variety*, 7 Feb. 1990). Those are fighting words, and of course familiar ones, the battle-cry of almost all producers of this most malleable play – the 'way it should be done' being more a projection of the producer than an obvious textual imperative. In order to embody his notion of Hamlet as dark, unshaven, and active, as opposed to blond and brooding (though Gibson does his share of the latter), Zeffirelli adopts a naturalistic tone and stance. He presents the play as a kind of metaphysical thriller, a sixteenth-century John LeCarré entertainment. Aided in this by his choice of Gibson in the main role, he at the same time loses those essential elements which his actor cannot deliver. Gibson is too studied, too serious, too much in awe of the task; his performance, says one critic, 'is excessively

august, as if he were trying ... to live down the flightier conno-
tations of his usual image' (*Sight and Sound*, Jan. 1992). He
lacks the crucial ingredient: quick, razor-sharp *thinking*. That
mind is hardly ever in evidence. If other Hamlets can routinely
make words cut, 'Gibson's Prince makes incisions only with
cold steel' (Richard Alleva, *Commonweal*, 22 March 1991).

I think finally that this production is best understood as a
cultural projection. Launched during a period of relative stag-
nation in the West and upheaval in the East (how Kozintsev
would have deplored such a private *Hamlet*), the film presents
an apolitical, even smug, version of subjectivity, an uncompli-
cated sense of a firmly anchored – if pained and at times
uncertain – self on the sea of Oedipal discord. Something of a
cultural throwback, the film eschews the post-modern interrogation of the very possibility of a unitary self, despite the fact
that *Hamlet* has in many ways invited exactly such questioning
in a range of recent productions and spin-offs. At the end of the
scene between the Prince and his father's Ghost, there is a
moment of incomplete contact expressed in the characteristic
movement of hands that is almost as ubiquitous in the film as
that of eyes. Scofield's Ghost reaches out his arms as though to
embrace his son, but only the shadows of his hands appear on
Hamlet's face; then, as they recede, Hamlet raises his own
hands which cast a congruent shadow.[7] The father hands on
his heritage to the son, but the gesture is literally shadowy.
Such moments add a touch of the contemporary, a feeling for
the patched selfhood inflicted by post-modernism. But Hamlet
remains externalized and sharply active, especially in the second
half of the film, where his ability to manage the whole action is
unquestioned. I have mentioned the incongruous golden glow
that so frequently emanates from sun and flame in this film. It
is a signature of the director, and was appropriate and evocative for the southern passions of *Romeo and Juliet*. If it seems
out of place here, perhaps it may be read as a sign of would-be
integration, of a self renewed and settled – designed perhaps to
confirm and uphold cultural expectations. Shadows may be
cast, but they are, or so Zeffirelli seems to say, surrounded by a
warm and comforting light.

Small-screen *Hamlet*

In the widely circulated BBC television version of *Hamlet*, Derek Jacobi gives us a theatricalized, relentlessly histrionic Hamlet, in a production that fails to take the measure of the reflexivity it flirts with. Unlike Gibson or the redoubtable Schwarzenegger, Jacobi is a 'no action' hero, and as such is a variation on the old tormented Hamlet caught in the meshes of his own thinking. But here the psychological tradition, as in the exactly contemporary RSC production with Michael Pennington, sits uneasily with the incessant play of theatricality. In various ways, Rodney Bennett's production seeks to keep the theatrical, constructed reality of the play's fictional world before us, but this aim clashes with and ultimately succumbs to the power of psychological naturalism abetted by the intimacy of the medium.

From the outset, the BBC series of the complete Shakespearean canon was committed to delivering 'straight' productions that would, in the words of Cedric Messina, originator and first executive producer of the series, be both 'permanent' and 'accessible to audiences throughout the world'. He wanted directors to 'let the plays speak for themselves' (Bulman 50-1), although in response we might recall Peter Brook's warning: 'When I hear a director speaking glibly ... of letting a play speak for itself, my suspicions are aroused, because that is the hardest job of all ... if what you want is for the play to be heard, then you must conjure its sound from it' (Brook 43). One consequence of the BBC's choice, driven as it was by a mix of aesthetic and economic imperatives, as well as by a sense that Shakespeare's plays are to be understood in terms of universal, trans-historical meanings (Hodgdon 44-5), was the decision to eschew innovation and to work within the confines of an unthreatening TV naturalism. The hope was that such an approach would prove saleable, especially in the USA, where substantial investment from Time-Life, Exxon, Metropolitan Life, and Morgan Guaranty Trust had underwritten the project from the start. Such big financial 'players' would clearly not want to jeopardize their stake. So they insisted on a Shakespeare who would prove palatable to educational institutions everywhere. And now, fifteen years later, with BBC Shakespeare being played and re-played around the world, we know how successful the venture was, despite the many voices that have been raised against both the interpretive blandness and the socio-political complicity of the series as a whole.

Hamlet was produced in November 1980, at the end of the second season, the last play to be done before Messina handed over the reins to Jonathan Miller. It was also the first play to be released from the constraint of the original two and a half hour limit, running three and a half hours in its original American screening and even longer in its present video form. The reasons for this were presumably its status as one of the star Shakespeare plays, and the general uneasiness about heavy cutting that the series producers had occasionally voiced. The result is a very lightly cut version, with no transpositions and no visualizations of the sort that most film directors have used (such as the scene in Ophelia's chamber, Hamlet on board ship, or Ophelia's death scene). Furthermore, the restrictions and conventions of TV dictate the way we see the play – mostly in mid close-up or small groupings (one or two characters seen from the waist up, or three in a triangular position – two in the foreground, one behind). This means that long shots, pans and other effects of the moving camera, crowd scenes, and the kind of symbolic juxtaposition of background and foreground used by Zeffirelli and Olivier, are entirely missing. We have to be contented with almost four hours of talking heads, and the result is not merely monotony, but an effect of what Sheldon Zitner calls 'over-psychologization'. Especially in the soliloquies, the 'prolonged image' requires 'from the actor a facial pose and variations more elaborate than the relevant speech-time on stage'. This produces an increased emphasis on 'inwardness' at the expense of 'rhetorical art' or 'the connection of the words with plot and theme' (Zitner 36). In a way, we get to know these characters, especially Hamlet, too well – we are forced into an intimacy we may not want, while the larger context of the psychological struggle remains opaque.

The problem of context is exacerbated by the absence of a social scene. The stylized studio setting, consisting of a barren grey platform for most of Act I as well as for the Fortinbras and graveyard scenes (IV.iv and V.i), together with a group of sombre, almost interchangeable interiors demarcated by dark painted screens and unencumbered by furniture, was a departure for the BBC series, which had previously stuck to naturalism. Part of the motivation to move away from TV verisimilitude was, in director Rodney Bennett's words, to invoke a 'theatrical reality', starting with 'nothing and gradually feeding in only what's actually required' (BBC *Hamlet*). Hence features such as the panels with obviously painted vistas, the walls that don't reach the ceiling, the impossibly narrow passage where Ophelia is revealed to Hamlet before the nunnery scene, were designed as symbolic spaces meant perhaps to evoke a sense of 'False perspectives, of surfaces that disguise actuality' (Willis 213), in keeping with the play's themes. We may be reminded of the Royal Court production (also 1980) where the *trompe l'oeil* setting and the theme of dangerously smooth appearances were similarly knit together, though more subtly and imaginatively. But the closest link is once again to the Barton/Pennington version, where the set emphasized the fact of playing, rather than deflecting attention away from it. If, however, the attempt in the BBC *Hamlet* was to move the series beyond the constraints of naturalism, it was too half-hearted. Rather than encouraging imaginative re-creation or making us think about theatrical ways of remaking reality, the neutrality of the space tended to remind viewers of BBC parsimony (Rothwell 396). Although *Hamlet* was being treated mainly as a domestic drama, even more so than in Zeffirelli's film, the settings failed to provide the domestic feel so successfully reproduced in some of the best BBC productions, such as *All's Well*. The psychological emphasis in the playing was thus left to itself, while the production's look reminded us merely that we were watching a studio version of a play.

The most successful evocations of social and domestic life circled around the King and Queen (played by Patrick Stewart and Claire Bloom), whose relationship in many ways formed the core of the whole production, and around Polonius (Eric Porter). Fittingly, Polonius's office, with its books, desk, murals, etc., was the most fully realized setting; in it he attended to the only partly serious business of making sure his son was behaving himself in Paris (the little scene with Reynaldo (II.i) was retained and played for sympathetic comedy) and then listened with loving concern to his daughter's story about Hamlet. He frankly admitted his error in underestimating the force of the Prince's passion and apologized to Ophelia for his mistake. This diverged nicely from the usual modern Polonius, whose politic eagerness to please the King tends to overbear fatherly feeling. After the nunnery scene, Polonius was again tender, never leaving Ophelia's side, holding her gently throughout the dialogue with the King who himself, in a gesture hovering between fondness and threat, held Ophelia's chin between his fingers for 'Madness in great ones must not unwatch'd go' (III.i.188).

As for Stewart's Claudius and Bloom's Gertrude, they gave the impression of being in a relationship that *mattered*, not one cheapened by adolescent passion, as in Zeffirelli and many another recent version, nor overplayed in displays of anxiety or dependency. Several intimate moments solidified this impression. Gertrude's whisper to her husband as he is about to address the question of Hamlet's return to Wittenberg suggested his willingness to accede to her desires, perhaps against his own judgment, and he did so without ruffling the affable smoothness that marked his public role. Later, in a tiny colloquy stolen from the courtly round of diplomacy and politic probing (II.ii.54-8), their intimacy emerged in the light emphasis on 'sweet' in Claudius's addresses to her, and the intelligence of Bloom's considered judgment on her son's erratic behaviour: 'I doubt it is no other but the main, / His father's death and our o'erhasty marriage'. Bloom's watchful and thinking Queen brought her some criticism (she wasn't the sloppy sensualist of tradition), but it cast a searching light on every scene in which she appeared. Responding to Polonius's tale about Hamlet's love-madness, she spoke 'it may be – very like' (II.ii.152), with a concerned but sceptical air, and, when he proposed spying on Hamlet, the camera briefly registered her silent response – thoughtful reflection rather than acceptance.

After the closet scene, in a moment when Gertrude has often been seen to withdraw visibly from Claudius (as both Glenn Close and Eileen Herlie do in the Zeffirelli and Olivier films), Bloom's reading was again subtle. A silent look revealed a new hesitation with him, and on 'mad as the sea and wind', she had clearly decided to protect Hamlet. But she didn't back away from Claudius's embrace at the end of the scene. Their intimacy had not completely evaporated. And a few scenes later, horrified by the waste of Ophelia's madness, *she* embraced *him*, and then moved strongly to defend him when Laertes burst in. Their relationship was being prised apart more by the relentless course of events than by a growing conviction of her husband's villainy. At the end of Act IV, after the poignant tale of Ophelia's drowning, this sense was effectively rendered by the contrast between Claudius's continued determination to fight and her seeming defeat: on 'Let's follow, Gertrude ...' he strode out to calm Laertes' rekindled rage, while, for the first time, she lingered behind, her heart no longer in the struggle. She had not rejected him; rather, the breakdown between them was the sad result of a string of catastrophes. So, when he could not prevent her from taking the poisoned drink at the end – she was too independent to heed his warning – it seemed fitting that he walked calmly towards Hamlet for the final blow, the ghost of a smile on his enigmatic countenance. He had nothing left to live for.

This Claudius is one of the few who never, before the final scene, appears with a goblet or whisky glass. It is a mark of his seriousness and political competence, and sets him apart from the bloated villain of Alan Bates (Zeffirelli) or the shallow sensualist of Basil Sydney (Olivier). He is a good man who has committed a single crime to get what he desperately wanted, who feels the weight of remorse but cannot handle it with the same dispatch with which he manages court affairs. The eerie, blue-plated Ghost has nothing on him – nor has his hysterical, unbalanced nephew. Widely praised for his playing of the public side of Claudius, Stewart has been criticized for his flat rendering of the King's guilty inner life. But his soliloquy in the prayer scene, beginning with a sob but continuing at a rapid clip, gives us a glimpse of a man who has faced his dilemma a hundred times before. It is the vexed inner life of a man used to activity, uncomfortable with introspection, going over and over a problem that he knows he cannot solve with his usual decisiveness. In the whole speech, he pauses only once, just before 'my queen' as he is reminding himself of the reasons he committed the murder; he knows where he has garnered up his heart. For a man not normally introspective, it is a telling moment, made possible by the very features of television that produced difficulties with the portrayal of the hero.

From all this domestic interplay and personal intimacy, Hamlet was almost entirely isolated (see Kliman, 'BBC' 101-3). This of course seemed to be the intent of the production, but for me, and for many other viewers, it had a less positive and, one supposes, unintended effect: I cared much less either for or about Hamlet than I did about the other principals. The King and Queen seemed like adults struggling with adult problems, while Hamlet kept behaving like a troubled adolescent for whom one could feel only a mixture of exasperation and obligatory pity. Even his one friend, Horatio, it appeared, would rather read than engage in disturbingly jumpy conversations with Hamlet (Kliman, 'BBC' 102). As for other of his potential allies, Rosencrantz and Guildenstern were slimy from the outset, Ophelia was blandness itself, the First Player kept his distance from him, and his mother regarded him with a mixture of sympathy and detachment. She had other commanding loyalties.

Derek Jacobi came to the TV role fresh from a long stint as Hamlet in a production (directed by Toby Robertson) that originated at the Old Vic and then went on tour. He carried over his sense of the role's trajectory, as well as a number of details – reading the 'What a piece of work is a man' speech from his book, for example, and donning a rubbery Halloween skull-mask at the beginning of the play scene ('I must be idle'). He also, less happily, carried over his tendency to 'falsetto hysterics' (I. Wardle, *Times*, 31 May 1977), and was prevented, because of director Bennett's adherence to the BBC policy to play things straight, from speaking the 'To be or not to be' soliloquy directly to Ophelia, an innovation that had aroused a fair bit of attention at the Old Vic and which was picked up by the Royal Court production in 1980. An accomplished actor with a proven track record in the part, Jacobi was the kind of star the series wanted to attract, but for me his Hamlet remains misjudged and overwrought. Part of the problem, as I suggested, is that the production as a whole did not develop the meta-theatrical theme; it kept within the frame of psychological naturalism. Furthermore, the medium as it was used put us in uncomfortably close contact with Hamlet, so that effects that might work in the 'middle distance' of the theatre (Zitner) became too pressing, too obviously acted. Since Hamlet is a self-dramatizing and ironic figure, such histrionics can work, but too often here the effect was sabotaged by a tendency to go over the top. Jacobi's performance was so relentlessly mercurial and so crossed with giddy self-irony – his voice so flutey and his manner so insistently actorly – that there seemed no point of purchase, no way to place the interpretation in perspective. His madness, much noted by critics, became definable as having no place simply to rest.

In the 'rogue and peasant slave' speech that ends Act II, he started quietly, moved from a considered to a feverish tone, and then to deliberately histrionic fury on 'Bloody, bawdy ... kindless villain', which was hurled out with drawn sword held high, as though he were about to lunge, while at the same time the whole gesture was undercut by a knowing, self-consciously theatrical look. A certain discomfort in the fury makes sense, but Hamlet's immediate withdrawal to self-mockery, 'Why, what an ass am I ...,' loses its edge if the whole tirade has itself been riddled with irony. In other words, if the actor has already signalled his awareness of melodramatic excess, the purpose and effect of Hamlet's recoil, when he catches himself in the *act*, are blurred. At the end of the speech, Jacobi unaccountably accompanied the famous couplet ('The play's the thing ...') with a fit of hysterical laughter, a sense of ironic futility undermining his plan even as he devised it. Such moves served to reduce Hamlet to actorly self-parody instead of establishing differing ways of looking at or reading the character.

Some of Jacobi's most effective moments came in his witty by-play with people he despised, where his sense of irony could be given full rein without collapsing in on itself. In the best of these moments, the prelude to the play scene, a telling contrast between skull mask and deceptively innocent repartee added an edge to 'I eat the air, promise-cramm'd', or 'It was a brute part of him to kill so capital a calf there' (III.ii.95, 106). Here Hamlet had an advantage, but it was one he would soon dissipate. The whole rest of the scene seemed calculated to assure Claudius's victory. The dumb-show, played in front of an engaging, Italianate perspective set with a chequered floor and painted-sky ceiling (to which Hamlet would later point for his 'Do you see yonder cloud that's almost in the shape of a camel?'), was deliberately stagy, with *commedia*-style costumes and elaborate gestures pushed gently into comedy. The court reacted with delight, Claudius watching and laughing despite the poisoning and the murderer's exaggerated wooing of his queen with a golden chain. The play itself, with a different set of actors, evoked some discomfort in Gertrude, whose 'The lady doth protest too much' was nevertheless collected, spoken with a slight smile as if to suggest that she realizes what

Hamlet is up to and that he should quit it. Claudius's 'Have you heard the argument ...' was designed to protect her feelings. As the play proceeded, with the king giving nothing away, Hamlet became more and more desperate. Intruding on the action in an attempt to provoke the response he wanted, he began to shove the players aside, putting a special spin on words like 'nephew to the king', 'murderer', or 'revenge', suggesting a threat that he couldn't in fact back up. The meta-theatrical possibilities here, implicit in Hamlet's behaviour, were nevertheless played down in the concentration on psychological naturalism. Claudius remained totally cool, only the tiniest movement of a gloved hand near his face betraying any agitation. He rose and walked toward Hamlet, called calmly for 'light', took the proffered torch and held it out towards his nephew, who covered his face with his hands. Then, as Hamlet burst into crazed laughter (The play's the thing that sends him into hysterics!), Claudius simply shook his head, turned slowly with a slight smile, and brought the performance to an end – 'Away' was a quiet command rather than the usual disturbed cry. There was no doubt who had won this round.

The moment contrasted sharply with Zeffirelli's treatment of the scene (or indeed with Olivier's or Kozintsev's), where Claudius tries to cover up his anxiety, but fails. The key difference is that, in Zeffirelli, Claudius is seen always from Hamlet's point of view, whereas here he has a life of his own, one that commands respect and even admiration from the viewer. It is one more instance where we are made to care more for him than for the ostensible hero. Even in a production such as Peter Hall's (1965), which treated the end of the play scene in a similar way to the BBC, David Warner's baffled Prince held the high ground; Claudius's cool rebuke was politically astute but morally bankrupt (see Chapter V). The BBC reading, however, suggests that Claudius's refusal to be flustered is the *right* response in the circumstances. In Hall's version, Claudius's reaction confirmed Hamlet's perceptions but made his problem all the more difficult, thus underlining his morally unexceptionable helplessness; in the televised version, *Claudius's* behaviour seems unexceptionable, while Hamlet appears out of touch (Dawson, *Watching* 161). Hall's orientation of the play towards youth found no answering echo in 1980 – at least not at the BBC. Those uncertain kids of the 1960s, the very boomers whose successive ages have defined post-war culture in England and America, had grown up into emergent yuppies; Stewart's Claudius perhaps spoke to their concern with getting ahead and their impatience with adolescent angst. This may have been one way in which the BBC concern with 'accessibility', especially to American viewers, merged unobtrusively with corporate sponsorship.

What this reveals, as with so many of the BBC plays, is a mixed intention generating mixed effects. Especially in the early seasons, when Messina's guiding vision exerted control, the stress on delivering straight, definitive, even permanent Shakespeare clashed not only with the impossibility of actually doing that, but with the artistic aims of individual actors and directors (this dynamic changed when Jonathan Miller took over the series in 1981 – see Bulman 52-5). To reduce the likelihood of conflict, Messina chose directors who were familiar with television but unfamiliar with Shakespeare, his aim being to speak specifically to *television* audiences, to stress action and pace (Bulman 51). Hence what would emerge as 'definitive' must at the same time seem a little naive. Rodney Bennett had never directed Shakespeare before taking on his most complicated play. It is not entirely clear whether the unbalancing produced by the moral as well as political strength of Claudius, and the correspondent weakness of Hamlet, derives from interpretive choice or is the result of seasoned Shakespearean actors following their own distinctive agendas in a directorial void. This distinguishes it from the three films examined above, all of which derive from the choices of a particular *auteur*.

The author of the BBC *Hamlet* is more than anything television itself, its strengths and weaknesses. It is a much more verbal medium than film, having developed out of radio rather than silent pictures and still photography, so that not only is an almost uncut version of the play possible in a way it would never be on the large screen, but also the 'spoken words loom larger in the total sensory output' (Zitner 36) than they do in film, making television in that one way more suitable for Elizabethan plays. Furthermore, the naturalistic mode of TV generates specific strategies which, in the case of *Hamlet*, outflanked any intention of subverting them through meta-theatricality. Television, notoriously, also manages its viewers much more systematically than film or theatre, turning them into passive consumers prepared for the blandishments of commercial and aesthetic interests. Perhaps we are readier to admire Claudius just because, like figures in *Dallas* or *Dynasty*, he appears on television – it is part of what Scott McMillin calls the 'perversity' of the series. Quoting the London *Times* on the aim of the series to 'present Shakespeare ... to millions both across the globe and down the years to come', McMillin envisions the 'natives' who are 'waiting for Shakespeare, and natives had better not be given their Shakespeare without reinforced guidelines of correct interpretation'. He reminds us that 'monuments and profits' are motives that 'have been known to occur together before ... and the answer to the question of who will receive the enlightenment of these productions takes on global proportions'. The project is, he infers, a 'form of cultural control' (77), although the term suggests a more monolithic, less haphazard sort of control than is actually in play. It would probably be more accurate to conclude that ventures such as the BBC series follow in the wake of cultural and economic processes rather than drive them. The globalization of culture through television and the now thousands of channels soon to be bestowed on first and third world alike may induce some of us to retreat to Shakespeare as a sign and model of the cultural values we are losing, and hence to seek to impose our sense of him on others whom we regard as dangerously in the ascendant. But even if the BBC versions circulate in all those 'foreign' countries, the imperial message they bring will be filtered and re-defined through audiences and media that will inevitably re-shape what is seen and understood.

CHAPTER IX

Translations

Throughout the writing of this book I have been conscious that I have for the most part confined myself to the Anglo-American tradition of *Hamlet* performance, concentrating on those canonized performers who have a legendary relationship to Shakespeare's most famous role. In some ways this has been inevitable, given the nature of my own training and native language, the available evidence, the series of which this book forms a part, and the daunting breadth of the task of coming to terms with even the British stage tradition, let alone performances in other languages and media. But I do not want to leave the reader with the impression that there is no world elsewhere. As the globe shrinks and as Shakespeare is translated into more languages on a widening variety of 'foreign' stages, ideas about what 'Shakespeare' might be, or about what performing *Hamlet* can mean, are becoming increasingly diverse. Currently fashionable models concerning the use of Shakespeare in connection with some putative cultural hegemony need to be rethought in the context of the cultural exchanges and appropriations that are a distinctive mark of the post-modern world we inhabit. Shakespeare, perhaps at one time a British export with imperial implications, is now more properly seen as one part of an elaborate system of global interchange.

While recent cultural analysis has identified the institutional role of Shakespeare in Britain as conservative, even reactionary (see Sinfield, for example), on European stages Shakespeare has typically been seen as a liberating force. So too the conservatism of theatrical tradition has been less tenacious in countries where the freedom offered by translation has, especially in the twentieth century, been accompanied by an experimentalism with regard to scenography and performance style rarely seen in England or America. As I mentioned in Chapter IV, at the time when Gielgud was preparing to step firmly into the shoes of Henry Irving, Leopold Jessner and Karl Hilar were re-imagining *Hamlet* in expressionist terms. Later, during the 1970s (to take just one exemplary decade), several innovative productions challenged the conventions and pieties that still typified most English language productions.[1] In Germany Peter Zadek's provocative display of boldly discontinuous images (1977) and Hansgunther Heyme's wildly electronic, surveillance-oriented version (1979) extended the iconoclasm of Jessner or Brecht; in France, Daniel Mesguich mounted an 'intertextual' *Hamlet* (1977), strongly influenced by French literary theory, which spliced into the main text a series of other Hamlet-influenced literary and critical texts; in Czechoslovakia in 1978, a landmark production spoke to audiences of the bitter, anti-heroic, even grotesque deterioration of humanist ideals in the aftermath of the Prague spring; in the Soviet Union Yuri Lyubimov's 'poor theatre' revival starring the most famous of Russian balladeers reminded Moscow theatregoers throughout the 1970s of oppression, censorship and hope.[2]

Two German *Hamlet*s

Foreign Shakespeare properly begins with Germany, which, for two centuries now, has identified itself with Shakespeare and indeed with Hamlet ('Germany *is* Hamlet,' as Freiligrath said). The original appropriations on the part of Romantic writers like Schiller and Schlegel were carried out in the service of a revolutionary nationalistic vision. The great Schlegel–Tieck translations of Shakespeare's plays were a crucial part of the effort to construct a German *Volk*, a project spearheaded by Schiller's vision of 'a German theatre that would transcend the petty principalities of the Holy Roman Empire and define the essence of a people' (Kennedy, *Foreign* 3). By the time of the Nazis, despite the radical experimentation of the 1920s, such aspirations had hardened into cruel orthodoxy. But in the postwar period, especially after 1960, German Shakespeare in both East and West has once again emerged as a challenge to orthodoxy, both political and aesthetic.

Leaping over the pioneering and widely influential work of Brecht (who remarked that many classical texts are valuable only as raw material), I want to look briefly at the work of two director/adaptors, Peter Zadek and Heiner Müller, one from

West and the other from East Germany. Though neither is a specifically political director, at least not in the sense of Brecht, both reject the cultural management of their respective states and the deadened theatre that results from official orthodoxy. Their weapons include a bizarre and discontinuous scenography, a willingness to break the translated text up into bits or even, in Müller's case, to reduce it to a skeleton, and an insistence on the distance between actor and role, theatre and 'reality'. Zadek's 1977 *Hamlet* was staged in an empty factory in Bochum; Müller's collection of translations and adaptations is entitled *Shakespeare Factory* and his radical stripping and re-working of *Hamlet* was called *Hamletmachine*. If neither is political in the strict sense, each wants to speak to contemporary audiences alert to their industrial surroundings. And Müller's nihilist vision, the result of a deep concern with German 'schizophrenia', defines a political position, especially in relation to the official optimism of East Germany; his *Hamlet/Machine: Shakespeare/ Müller*, which went into rehearsal before the collapse of the Berlin wall and premiered after it, seemed to some an epitaph for the GDR itself, which was, as Müller remarked, not so bad that it did not deserve a decent burial (quoted in Linzer 11).

Zadek's work aims to provoke audiences, especially those who espouse a traditional view of what Shakespeare should look or sound like. Combining circus spectacle, the fun of performance, grotesque comedy, brutal and/or lyrical eroticism, haunting visual imagery, and intensely self-conscious theatricality, Zadek envisions a *Volkstheater* (the term is reminiscent of Schiller) for a new and wider audience (Engle 94-5). To bring in the 'soccer crowd', he discards the plays' sacredness and creates a deliberate distance between character and actor, highlighting performance values and images rather than psychological consistency or esoteric meaning (Engle 103). He sees *Hamlet* as a 'serious comedy' with the play within the play as its centre (Zadek). For the production, designer Peter Pabst divided the concrete performance space, which was surrounded by spectators and lit only by fluorescent lights, into zones: the centre defined by gym mats; at one side a podium for Polonius's room, with armchair, tailor's dummy, and a sideboard with a stuffed hawk on it; here and there a coat-rack, a skeleton, a huge writing desk for the King, and a spinet on which, at the beginning, Ophelia played 'White Christmas';

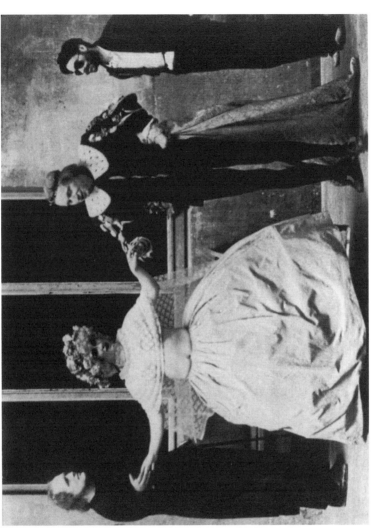

10
Gertrude (Eva Mattes),
with bare midriff and filmy
shawl over painted breasts,
flanked by Hamlet (Ulrich
Wildgruber) and Claudius
(Hermann Lause), is danced
through the opening court
scene of Peter Zadek's
production (1977).

11
The play scene from
Heiner Müller's Berlin
production (1990), showing
projections and screens,
with Hamlet (Ulrich Mühe)
gesturing toward a glum
King and Queen and a stiff
Polonius and Ophelia.

under a paneless window a sofa, 'the place for all twosomes – Polonius and Ophelia, Ophelia and Hamlet, Hamlet and Gertrude, Hamlet and Horatio'. At the edge of the playing space was a huge ornate picture frame with a 'portrait' of Old Hamlet, represented by the young actress who played the Ghost and who watched the entire play through the frame, stepping out of it only to do her part (Canaris 56). Such a doubling of spectatorship is characteristic of Zadek and had the effect here of underlining the theatricality of the enterprise and the involvement of the spectators with the show: the actors in the inner play were identical with the 'actors' who peopled the court so that the whole production became like a play-within-a-play. This also made spectatorship part of the process of coming to know pain or horror through watching, a process with which Hamlet is deeply familiar. *Hamlet*, wrote Zadek, is 'about the kind of theatre that a person needs in order to find, *in a roundabout way*, his true being – his inside, his soul' (my italics).

The costumes, eclectic in the extreme and occasionally shocking, were designed to represent different aspects of the characters at different times. So Gertrude appeared in I.ii with crinolines and bare breasts painted with red bull's eyes – the woman as sexual target; later she was a 'Grande Dame' wrapped in furs, a kind of Bette Davis 'Mama' in gold lamé, a respectable mourner with hat and black veil at the grave-side, and finally an elegant lady with Dior gown, left to die 'like a mannequin ... sitting on a sofa' (Canaris 57). Hamlet, represented throughout as a chatty entertainer, a music hall comic, began as a melancholy clown in white face with dark lipstick smeared around his mouth. In the nunnery scene, he was dressed as a dandy, with red coat, fox fur and the obligatory walking stick; after lugging away the dead Polonius, he wore a bloody butcher's apron. At other times he sported a frock coat and top hat with a flower in his lapel, suggesting his role as master of these theatrical ceremonies (Raab 42, and Canaris 60, 62).

These are not psychologically consistent, unified characters of the kind usually represented on English and American stages, nor were they meant to be. They are defined in terms of images and stance. Distances between actor and character were underlined: Polonius and Hamlet's father were both played by young women, Hamlet was older than his mother, Rosencrantz and Guildenstern were transvestites (one male, one female). But this did not mean that there was no psychology at all; the 'truth' of the character derives from the playing, the way the part is theatricalized, rather than from an inner life represented by an 'invisible' actor. The actress playing Polonius (Rosel Zech), for example, with grey wig and floppy hat, cane and baggy suit, was the clown as old man. But at moments (such as his quiet interruption of the weeping Player and accompanying glance at Hamlet), humour turned to sadness, clownish senility to awareness of truth, the conventional bent back of the old man suddenly carrying the weight of a lifetime (Canaris 59). Such effects are achieved by overtly theatrical means – the actor does not disappear into the character but rather uses *'gestus'*, Brecht's term for the ensemble of presentational practices (bodily movement, facial expression, pitch etc.) by which the character is *shown* to the audience. In Ulrich Wildgruber's Hamlet this led to a presentation of the prince as 'super-conversationalist' (Zadek's phrase) who treats his madness as a theatrical joke, telling the audience his crazy story, sometimes emphasizing the parody with winks and twitches, but elsewhere (as in the second soliloquy) simply wandering through the audience and casually talking to them of the moods of this strange person he is playing (von Becker 9, 8).

A major function of the interplay of images in this kind of production is to visualize the subtext. For example, Ophelia's dreams (of a 'white Christmas'?) quickly turn to nightmares, and this was graphically shown by visual correspondences between nunnery and mad scenes. For the first, she was wearing a beautiful brocade gown with a Victorian look, but when her father lifted her fur stole from her shoulders, the gown was revealed to have no bodice; she stood, a sexual pawn with her breasts bared, as Hamlet entered on the other side of the room. He spoke the 'To be or not to be' soliloquy to her across the wide expanse that separated them. The little colloquy that follows – 'I did love you once' – was soft and sad, but a moment later, when in more conventional productions Hamlet catches sight of the eavesdroppers, Polonius and Claudius entered from different doors, Polonius with a pig mask and Claudius with a horse's skull on his head. Hamlet's tenderness changed abruptly to rage as he brutally attacked Ophelia and then left. The masks reappeared in the mad scene: Claudius and Gertrude were blanked out behind 'faceless ovals', Laertes was a huge pig-faced monster (the actor playing the part was, with deliberate incongruity, 'grossly overweight' (Engle 98)), and Hamlet, dressed as for the nunnery scene, now wore the same pig mask Polonius had worn earlier (Canaris 61). The images marked a suggestive reversal by which Ophelia replaced Hamlet as innocent victim driven mad by oppressive watching, and Hamlet replaced Polonius and Claudius as killer and spy.

Like many another contemporary director and critic, Zadek is generally more interested in the rifts and contradictions in the text and its performance tradition than he is in wholeness and unity. The text he used for *Hamlet* was, like the costumes, eclectic, combining his own translation with a variety of others, including Schlegel's for the soliloquies, though even there he inserted modern references to impertinent officials and stinking smog (Raab 39). His approach is aggressively non-literary, emphasizing always the non-repeatable experience of performance. His disregard for linear narrative, his mélange of styles, and his attempt to create 'a network of correlated situations, a multilayered "scenic text" constantly opening up references' to other visual as well as written texts (Andreas Hofele, quoted in Engle 103) define his aesthetic as distinctly post-modern.

Heiner Müller, like so many other German writers before him, sees Hamlet as a 'very German' character, 'more German than English ... the intellectual in conflict with history' (Müller 15, 50), and emblematized in the split between the two Germanies. His *Hamletmachine*, which was published in 1977 and premiered in French in Paris in 1979, is a short, dense depiction of the schizoid plight of the intellectual under Communism, figured in the intersecting monologues of Hamlet and Ophelia. Hamlet is the despairing intellectual living in what could be Hungary in 1956, his father mysteriously dead, murdered, but honoured by a state funeral; his schizophrenia is registered by his double awareness of himself as the impotent would-be activist and as the actor who refuses any longer to play the role. Scenically, it is represented by a trio of TV sets that are brought onstage as he speaks and tuned to different channels (a motif picked up and amplified by Heyme in 1979) and by the symbolic rending of the author's (i.e. Müller's own) photograph. Müller's Ophelia derives from his interest in terrorism, which he regards ambivalently as heroic and nihilistic: 'I set fire to my prison ... I walk into the street clothed in blood.' In the end, she speaks as Electra, but from deep under water, in a wheelchair and methodically wrapped in gauze by two white-smocked attendants: 'under the sun of torture ... I choke between my thighs the world I gave birth to ... Long live hate and contempt ... When she walks through your bedrooms carrying butcher knives you'll know the truth' (Müller 58). The final line quotes a young woman who tried to assassinate President Ford, an indication of the elusive allusiveness of this text. In an interview in 1979, Müller described the play as 'an effort to articulate a despair so that it can be left behind' (Müller 50). When he staged an amalgam of *Hamletmachine* and his translation of *Hamlet* at the Deutsches Theater in 1990, there was undoubted irony deriving from Marx's axiom quoted in the play, 'The main point is to overthrow all existing conditions': East Berlin had itself ceased to exist before the opening.

The production was over seven hours long, framed by loud-speakers and TV monitors; a radio broadcast of Stalin's funeral could be heard behind the Ghost, and the whole of rotten Denmark was encased in what looked like 'a cube of ice depicted by a stage-high gauze screen' (Guntner 131). In such a world, Hamlet could do nothing; utterly isolated from political action, he was left to cultivate his own interiority in a self-consuming, autistic way, representing the impotence of the East German artist/intellectual. The stage, its machinery all visible (lighting, speakers etc.), displayed a fragmentary collage of cultural history (the design was by Erich Wonder): there were projections of famous paintings, neo-classical arcades, nineteenth-century railway stations; references to the Stalinist legacy of East Germany laced the production; the eclectic costuming evoked both modern and classical drama; and the staging, such as the slow-motion duel of Hamlet and Laertes or the reappearance of Ophelia as Electra at the end, suggested ritual forms of theatre.

This Hamlet, the 'privileged' inheritor of a dead and oppressive tradition, can only refuse roles, can only babble ('I stood at the shore and talked with the surf BLABLA, the ruins of Europe in back of me' – Müller 53). His task of revenge is interpreted as avenging the crimes of his predecessors, including his father. But the sounds of Stalin's funeral which, as much as the Ghost himself, haunt the air raid shelter where the action begins suggest that the old regime has spawned both Claudius and Hamlet – they are a pair, each of them a prisoner of a banal but

inescapable system. This was emphasized late in the performance, during the recital of *Hamletmachine:* King and Prince were
dressed like Didi and Gogo from *Waiting for Godot,* or like
comics from silent film – black suits, bowler hats – and practised
little dance routines, even tossing their hats at each other. Martin
Linzer noted the 'strange ambivalence' in the relationship between Hamlet and Claudius. But if we regard them as historical
twins, the ambivalence seems less strange. Hence the prayer
scene was staged with Hamlet sitting beside his enemy on a
bench, listening to his 'declaration of remorse' as though it were
self-criticism at a party meeting – they are 'comrades' (Linzer 12).

The whole of *Hamletmachine* was inserted into the fourth
act, after Hamlet's last soliloquy, with its echoing 'My thoughts
be bloody or be nothing worth' as a kind of gloss. As Linzer
remarked, 'It becomes clear with the fall of the [Berlin] wall
that the prison did not end there' (10-11). Not only Denmark,
but history itself is a prison. Water drips from the walls at the
start, forming a puddle in the middle of the stage; later, Hamlet
lies in the puddle, hurling 'to be or not to be' at the audience. In
his first scene, he pronounces the famous tag from just before
his death, 'The rest is silence'. Eventually, the stage gets drier
and the light warmer, but it is an ironic warmth. In the last act,
'the floor is covered with red sand from which mirror-like
gravestones emerge; through painted windows we can see a
sunny landscape' (Wille 28). The names of the dead are yet to
be inscribed on the tombs, but in the mirrors the audience can
see itself. The point is clear, perhaps too clear. As Wille suggested,
there is little room for character development, for questions
about motivation, even for family intrigue, when from the beginning the situation is hopeless and foreordained. The very narrowness with which Müller has pinned himself in, however,
may tell us something of the way his own interpretations were
prescribed by his struggle to live an uncompromised artistic
life in the GDR.

Like Zadek, Müller and his actors avoided psychological
realism. Ulrich Mühe's Hamlet was not a character following a
'line' of dramatic development; his mode was artificial, gestic;
he knew he had already failed: 'with a practical grip, he shoulders
the emotionally wounded Ophelia and drags her from the stage' –
there is no room for love (Wille). His Hamlet was '*the* intellectual, his tragedy ... one of mental power/powerlessness, of the

artist's megalomania and vanity' (Linzer 12). Unlike Zadek, Müller emphasized not so much the performance of selfhood as an ideologically marked demonstration of abjection. At the end Fortinbras appeared with golden mask and business suit, personifying perhaps the soaring Deustchmark, and laid a gilded business folder over Hamlet's face (Guntner, 133-4).

Hamlet in the Soviet Union

In Russia, Hamlet remains first of all a person – his individuality itself challenges authority. In 1971, at Moscow's Taganka Theatre, Yuri Lyubimov opened a production that ran in repertory until 1980 (217 performances in all), when the early death of Vladimir Vysotsky, the poet-singer-actor who had played the lead and given the production its special character, brought it to a premature end. Lyubimov had been put in charge of the Taganka in 1964, the year that Kozintsev's film of *Hamlet* appeared. The theatre's beginnings were made possible by the Khrushchev 'thaw', although it soon began to generate a little too much heat for the wan Soviet spring. Eventually becoming an emblem of social and moral opposition to the regime, the Taganka succeeded in feeding the spiritual hunger of oppressed Russians.

In purely theatrical terms, Lyubimov's *Hamlet* was noteworthy for the cinematic montage of the mise-en-scène and the presence of a dominant scenographic image – a ubiquitous, constantly moving curtain (designed by David Borovsky); but far more important was its cultural role and the spiritual power of its leading performer. When he took on Hamlet, Vysotsky was already well known as a troubadour of spiritual freedom – he was 'the living soul and conscience of his time' (Gershkovich 129), much loved throughout the Soviet Union because his songs spoke truth in the oblique ways typical of heavily censored societies. He died during the Moscow Olympics, and people abandoned their stadiums and TV sets to participate in a spontaneous memorial service. Though there had been no announcement of his death in the press, within hours everyone in Moscow knew of it, and thousands gathered near the theatre, where his legendary guitar was displayed, to recite his poems and honour his memory. At the funeral a few days later, mourners jammed the streets all around the Taganka, but only a few were able to file past the coffin before it was whisked away, while someone on a rooftop with a loud voice described the scene to the pressing crowd. 'After Vysotsky's funeral', said Lyubimov, 'I began to respect the people of Moscow' (Gershkovich 111-13).

For all the obvious differences, the scene is reminiscent of David Garrick's brilliant obsequies two hundred years earlier. Those were officially sanctioned, orderly, designed to honour the greatest English actor as a national hero. Vysotsky's were unofficial and disorderly, a sign of repressed desire for freedom in defiance of oppressive authority. But Vysotsky was also a national hero, and, like Garrick, he was especially identified with Hamlet. In the part, he appeared with his guitar. The production began on a bare stage, open to the whitewashed back wall, which was adorned only with a heavy wooden cross. Two silhouetted gravediggers swigged vodka and tossed dirt and skulls out of an open grave downstage (the grave remained throughout). Hamlet, in casual modern dress, approached the grave and, accompanying himself on the guitar, recited Pasternak's 'Hamlet' poem from the banned *Dr Zhivago*:

> The stir is over. I step forth on the boards.
> Leaning against an upright by the entrance
> I strain to make the far-off echo yield
> A cue to the events that may come in my day.

Pasternak's great translation of *Hamlet* defined the character in Russian terms – serious, dedicated, self-sacrificing; he is a witness, even a Christ-like sufferer who 'gives up his will in order to "do the will of him that sent him." *Hamlet* is not a drama of weakness, but of duty and self-denial.' He has been allotted the role of 'judge of his own time and servant of the future' (Pasternak, quoted in Rowe 148). His reality, as the poem suggests, is interwoven with that of the actor, in struggle with himself, putting himself on the line in order to explode 'the misrepresentations which produced moral failure in Soviet life' (Golub 161):

> And yet the order of the acts has been schemed and plotted
> And nothing can avert the final curtain's fall.
> I stand alone. All else is swamped in Pharisaism.
> To live life to the end is not to cross a field.

The visual and symbolic dominance of the Taganka's mobile

curtain was designed to carry the production's distinctively Soviet meaning. Coarsely woven of wool, though appearing like macramé with 'threads hanging in evil bundles', the curtain controlled the action, falling from the ceiling after the opening song, moving around and between the actors,

> like a giant monster … setting the pace, and holding within its folds the symbols and tools of power – black armbands, swords, goblets, thrones edged with knives. It envelops Ophelia, intimidates Polonius, protects Gertrude, supports Claudius and threatens Hamlet. Finally it sweeps the stage clean and moves toward the audience as though to destroy it too. (M. Croyden, quoted in Leiter 145)

More than anything, it was a sign of the prison house, Denmark as gulag. It was also an explicitly theatrical symbol, though slightly displaced since the one direction in which it never moved was the conventional one – up and down. It allowed for powerful lighting effects that extended the analogy between theatre and prison: floor vents would light up to catch clandestine conversations, lights would flicker in the back like signals, shadows would hover and dart on the moving curtain. Encompassing the action within a changing space defined as theatrical by the deployment of an image from theatrical tradition (the curtain) neatly matched the conception of Hamlet as an actor. Hence the images of the theatre, the prison, and the grave, all crucial to Hamlet and *Hamlet*, were adroitly woven together in the production.

The theatrical emphasis did not, however, transform the meaning of the play into an endless succession of mirrored images. Rather, it spoke of the theatre's power to construct for its public a truth that matters. Vysotsky's style of playing fit in with this conception. His strategy was to maintain the distance between actor and role (as in Zadek and Müller though for a different purpose), not blending with the character but expressing his own personal relationship to it (Gershkovich 112). Thus he remained the singer, the troubadour performing the part and communicating his relationship to Hamlet as a way of disclosing his own isolation, of establishing his own poetic voice, and most important of seeking a way to live.[3] He began the run as rather 'nihilistic', but as his conception matured, his Hamlet became more attuned, more a searcher for possible answers to the 'necessary question' that he speaks of in his own poem called 'My Hamlet' (Gershkovich 128-9). The production, like the actor, came to speak for an affirmation of life in the face of curtain and grave, a post-Stalinist theme of 'survival and salvation, rather than the Stalin era's death theme, revenge' (Golub 166).

A year after Vysotsky's death, Lyubimov put together a performance collage entitled *The Poet Vladimir Vysotsky*, which was banned before it opened, though a few public 'dress rehearsals' escaped the censor's fist. Focusing on Vysotsky's place in Soviet culture, the show re-enacted his street songs, his anti-war songs, his evocations of everyday Soviet life, all with an undercurrent of social alienation and a muted desire to speak out. Interspersed throughout were references to and fragments of *Hamlet*, such as a satiric dialogue in which the King and Polonius discussed the strategic 'madness' of Hamlet's 'singing hooliganism' or, as a culmination, a reprise of 'To be or not to be', the cornerstone of Pasternak's and Vysotsky's conception. From a song about Russian baths, the performance shifted without pause to Vysotsky's recorded voice swiftly traversing the soliloquy: 'so a thought turns us all into cowards and our decisiveness withers like a flower ... Thoughts that at first promised success die with a sweep of the hand.' The finale returned to the singer and his songs, producing a double image of hope and defiance against death and loss: 'They've cornered me, cornered me – / But the huntsman isn't left with anything ...' was followed by 'I didn't have time ... to finish living. I won't have time to finish singing ...' At the end the voice faltered, like Hamlet's, into a long silence (Gershkovich 116-26).

The technique of montage that Lyubimov used to put together this tribute to his leading actor was the same as that he used for many of his productions, including *Hamlet*. Learned from Meyerhold and Eisenstein, it is well suited to Shakespearean structure with its alternating scenes and fluid conception of space. Lyubimov broke down the text into short episodes, sometimes cutting scenes off at their emotional peaks and building them around strong physical images – the asymmetrical wooden cross on the back wall, the grave with its real dirt and real skulls, or climactically the duel with the two participants at opposite sides of the stage, striking their weapons violently together to create a harsh soundscape that alternated with moments of silence and rest. The audience was thus encouraged to fill in the silences, to stitch the whole together (Golub 170-1). Such audience participation is crucial to the process that the production invited and sought to capture: to know and understand a certain significant *voice* in a world where to speak is dangerous and to speak out, deadly.

The RSC again – closing the frame

In the kind of international context just sketched, the post-modern flourishes of the Noble/Branagh version with which I began and to which I now want briefly to return may not seem so radical. The daring of a Zadek or Lyubimov has prepared the way for English-language versions of Shakespeare that at least scenically dismember and reassemble the elements of the play in disjunctive ways. But the English *text* remains relatively untouched, even augmented and handled with reverence, as exemplified by Branagh and company. The split between radical scenography and textual conservatism seems to go with the territory – it belongs to English Shakespeare, which lacks the flexibility of mixing different translations, of re-writing the words for contemporary meaning. But it goes without saying that there are also advantages to 'owning' Shakespeare's language.

Dismembering the décor as Noble did, taking us from the curtained Edwardian spaces of the early scenes through the theatrically self-conscious framing of the middle part of the play to, finally, the shattered spectacle of lonely piano, over-turned chairs and withered garlands, links this production to the eclectic, allusive styles of Zadek and Müller, though without their penchant for going to the limit. Noble has no discernible interest in iconoclasm. In fact, the cultural cachet of the lead actor connects this RSC production to the grand tradition of British performances. In the context of the current chapter, there is a link also to Vysotsky and his significance for Russians. But the difference of course is that Branagh is not seen as a rebel or a challenge to authority so much as a highly successful entrepreneur – he embodies aspirations for success rather than for liberation.

A strong and characteristic feature of Noble's production was its emphasis on the domestic, which, as we have seen, has been a dominant aspect of English revivals at least since Irving.

12 Anxious mother (Jane Lapotaire) and confident stepfather (John Shrapnel) try to convince Kenneth Branagh's disdainful young Hamlet to remain at court (RSC, 1992).

Ophelia's bedroom, for instance, with its piano and its nursery air, was the site of her loving farewell to her brother and a tender colloquy with her father as they sat together on the unmade bed. At the top of the scene, Laertes had entered to wake her, and while they chatted she got up, went to her basin and washed herself with a sponge which she playfully threw at her brother when he warned her about Hamlet and the vulnerability of her 'chaste treasure'. Here was a close, teasing family with a sympathetic, if a bit distant, father (David Bradley's Polonius deflected Laertes' move to embrace him with an embarrassed wave). In II.i, Ophelia ran into her father's (Dickensian) office seeking comfort after being confused by Hamlet's strange behaviour. The nunnery scene took place back in the domestic cosiness of her bedroom, the incongruity offset by the powerful image created by Hamlet and Ophelia's playing over and around the little bed. She took her mementoes from a small suitcase which Hamlet later hurled to the floor, scattering the letters and keepsakes which she then desperately sought to gather up. The utter collapse of domestic harmony evident at the end was prefigured here and confirmed by the chilling moment after Hamlet's departure when, ignored by her father and Claudius, she drifted to the piano and began to play. Polonius, his plotting with the King completed, moved to his daughter, closing the keyboard cover gently but decisively, deepening and darkening the sense of irresistible fatherly power over her that had marked their exit in I.iii. Her insidious spiritual disintegration was progressing, and it showed in every move that Joanne Pearce's Ophelia made. When she appeared clown-like, adrift with her piano on a vast and broken stage, dressed in her father's bloodied formal clothes, the effect was to cast a poignant irony over her grief and her shattered domestic hopes (the echoes of Zadek's version – the keyboard, the woman in an oversized man's suit – underline the contrast in concept).

The same emphasis on the domestic permeated the main plot; Hamlet's relation to both father and mother circled around family feeling. Jane Lapotaire's Gertrude displayed an obvious concern for Hamlet throughout: her uncertainty about Claudius's detective methods, her move towards Hamlet when he entered reading (which was cut off by Polonius's officious dismissal), her shrinking from her husband after the closet scene, all these manifested her motherly love. The closet scene itself was embarrassingly hysterical, but the quiet arrival of the Ghost, in a moment strongly reminiscent of Irving, caught the domestic feel especially well. The Ghost, when he entered, seemed much changed. Clad in a white suit of more conservative cut than his brother's, he was quiet and subdued instead of portentous and boring as he had been on the battlements. In a reprise of the scene with Polonius, Laertes and Ophelia, he sat on the edge of the bed, reached out and *almost* touched Gertrude, then clasped hands with Hamlet. The Queen, crouched on the bed beside her son, was aghast, wondering, trying to bring Hamlet back. She stretched out her hand toward Hamlet's, so that the three hands were almost, but not quite, united on the (marriage?) bed, a re-enactment of the complex domestic scene from which both their troubles and their happiness had derived. This symbolic reunion produced a change. Earlier there had been a lot of slightly tense erotic affection between herself and Claudius, such as the kiss they stole during the moment when Polonius went out to fetch the ambassadors in II.ii; but from Claudius's entrance after the closet scene through to her death, she deliberately avoided him – and she died centre stage, alone.

The European productions surveyed in this chapter tend, in contrast with such a domestic emphasis, to interpret the play in cultural or political terms. In so far as they examine family relations, they do so as part of an interrogation of the deployment of social power generally. They read *Hamlet* primarily as a culturally freighted document, to be used as part of an intervention into contemporary life. At the same time, almost all recent productions try to find ways to highlight the intense meta-theatricality of *Hamlet*, to register how it both tells a story by representing actions and characters and tracks the process of representation itself. Many of the European versions, especially from western Europe (Mesguich, Heyme, Zadek), have trained the spotlight on the post-modernist fear/discovery that representation is all there is, that reality is simply a tissue of representations; east European productions, on the other hand, lacking the luxury of such reflexivity, have aimed their representations outward, as a veiled or not-so-veiled social critique to be read by audiences eager for theatrical parallels and resonances appropriate to their day-to-day reality. Noble's version shares the interest in meta-theatricality but steps back from both the dizzying verge of endless reflexivity and social/political critique by insisting on the cultural and personal value of a noble and redemptive prince.

The next production of *Hamlet,* and the next, whether in New York, London, Berlin, Tokyo, or Kuala Lumpur, will undoubtedly move away from what we have so far witnessed in order to meet the exigencies of a new time and place. Different scenographies will tell different stories. In whatever translation, however, it seems likely that the lonely beleaguered self both oppressed and galvanized by the possibilities of theatricality will be one element in the mix. So too will the harsh actualities of political power, the explosive ambiguities of speech, the hesitations as well as the drive of sexual feelings, the perceptions and the pain of madness. *Hamlet* has been in front of audiences for almost four hundred years now, and there is no reason to assume that it will not be performed as many years hence, in states unborn and accents yet unknown.

NOTES

Chapter I

1 The relative authority of 'text' versus performance has long been an issue in Shakespeare studies, but has become a more vexed problem since the advent of 'performance criticism' and the relatively recent emphasis on performance generally; for further discussion, see, for example, Berger, Worthen, and Dawson, 'Impasse' .

2 Guided by practical as well as scholarly considerations, I myself have chosen to use the Riverside Shakespeare text throughout this book. Edited by G. B. Evans, this is a scrupulously careful composite version, based on Q2, prepared by one of the very best Shakespearean editors, and widely available.

3 Interestingly, and rather contradictorily, the Cambridge editor, Philip Edwards, who is aware of all the textual pitfalls, provides good arguments against full conflation and then includes all the passages he has argued Shakespeare revised out.

4 As I will suggest at various points below, the cultural cachet of the actor, whether it is Garrick, Kean, Irving, Olivier, Barrymore, or Branagh, has much to do with the reception of the performance, especially the way the play is made the carrier of personal values and ideas about subjectivity. I should also point out that there were a few exceptions to the general effusiveness, notably Nicholas de Jongh, *Evening Standard*, 21 Dec. 1992.

5 An alternative reading, proposed to me by Barbara Hodgdon, might regard the undone straps as a signal of Hamlet's escape from the bonds of both madness and theatrical representation - it is after all only 'Kenny' whom we all know and love!

Chapter II

1 For over a hundred years, this version, which was never published, was lost to sight. It turned up in the Folger Library in the 1930s where it was discovered by G. W. Stone, who described it in detail and published the final section in his 1934 article. The Folger text consists of a 1747 published version with the many changes in Garrick's autograph, and some leaves in the complicated final parts from another printed text. I have checked the quotations from Stone's reprinting against the original.

2 I have been quoting from the eyewitness commentaries of Mary Stone, who saw Booth play Hamlet, in New York and Boston, six or more times between 1879 and 1884. Her evocative notes, recently discovered and published by Daniel Watermeier, add to the impressive array of material on Booth's Hamlet, 'the most famous impersonation in the history of the American theatre' (Shattuck xiii). Before they came to light, scholars had relied predominantly on an extraordinary document written by a twenty-one-year old clerk (and aspiring writer), Charles W. Clarke, who, captivated by Booth's

Hamlet in 1870, memorized the whole play and went repeatedly to see Booth play it. He then wrote out his impressions in minute detail, producing a manuscript of almost 60,000 words (now in the Folger Shakespeare Library). It should be noted that Charles Shattuck, basing *The Hamlet of Edwin Booth* on Clarke, concentrates on the 1870 performance, although he discusses the whole of Booth's career in the part. Since Stone writes primarily about performances in 1881 and 1883, there are several small differences in business and style, but a remarkable convergence as well, and certainly an identity of interpretation. This is because of the typical approach of nineteenth-century actor-managers, who would fix a part and then play it over and over with a wide variety of supporting actors (in Booth's case often some very poor ones) whose readings would hardly affect the main performance at all; an extreme example of this practice was Booth's highly successful German tour, when he played in English and the rest of the actors spoke their parts in German.

3 The quotations are from an undated clipping pasted into Folger PB 79.

4 Hamlet himself circles such issues in his disquisition on the art of theatre, its holding a 'mirror up to nature' (or 'culture' as we might be more inclined to say now), and even more germane, its power to show 'the very age and body of the time his form and pressure'.

5 For a discussion of Irving and the picturesque in relation to melodrama and theatrical style, see Salter.

Chapter III

1 Information about the details of this production comes largely from a series of very full promptbooks (two of which, now in the Folger Library, I have consulted for this chapter) prepared by Lark Taylor, an actor who played Bernardo, the First Player and Fortinbras. He put together these promptbooks during the various runs of the production, which was directed by Arthur Hopkins and opened in New York in November 1922, was seen again the next year in New York, then went on tour to a number of Eastern cities. In 1825, Barrymore staged the play himself in London using the same basic set and production style, but with a different cast.

2 This can be confirmed by screening a short film that was made in 1932 of two scenes from *Hamlet*, as a kind of test for a full-length feature that was never made. The first Ghost scene and the soliloquy over the praying Claudius reveal Barrymore at his most appealingly histrionic. (There is a print of the film at the Folger.)

3 When the Prince of Wales, with whom he spent many a jolly evening, asked him how he found the energy to play such an exhausting role eight times a week and then revel in an endless round of social occasions, Barrymore is said to have replied, 'My simple recipe is fervour and champagne' (quoted in Morrison 258). His unpredictability onstage was notorious. Whether he was cracking audible jokes to break up his fellow actors, drawing a lifelike face on the dummy used for Ophelia's burial, or, in one of his most famous moments, breaking off his soliloquy to castigate a coughing audience member in blank verse ('Bark! Bark! Bark on! Thou phlegm-beclotted cur!'), working with him was always an adventure. (See Morrison and Webster 301-2).

4 The later promptbook records that in Cleveland at the end of the run, a picture of the Ghost was projected unto Hamlet himself, who was bathed in white light.

5 The verbal and visual details here come from the film mentioned in note 2.

6 The Ghost's invisibility was modified as the production went on, perhaps a surrender to convention. By the time the production reached London, the Ghost seems to have regained all his appearances, though the eerie light and the moment of possession survived the transatlantic crossing.

7 Normally, Birmingham Rep productions opened in Birmingham; this was an exception, perhaps because of its perceived importance. In any event, the 'provincial' origins of company and production probably played a part in giving them the requisite perspective and determination to mount an assault on London sensibilities.

Chapter IV

1 In accordance with Old Vic practice, several performances of this production were devoted to playing the full text. Audiences so inclined could thus see both the full and the cut versions, or either one. Several of the critics remarked on how the full text rounded out both plot and characters, eliminating some of the old puzzles. *The Times* thought the full text gave particular interest and intricacy to the King and Queen, especially the former, who came across as the 'perfect Renaissance villain' (29 April 1930, 12).

2 These were at the Old Vic in 1930, at the New Theatre in 1934 (Gielgud himself directing), at the Empire Theatre in New York in 1936 (directed by Guthrie McClintic – this is the production described in detail by Rosamond Gilder), at the Lyceum and at Elsinore Castle in 1939, and at the Haymarket and on tour in 1944-46.

3 The details that follow are taken mostly from Gilder and refer to the New York production. But the reviews indicate that similar business and a similar approach was used in Gielgud's 1934 version as well. And even in 1944, the scene had approximately the same shape – see Desmond MacCarthy, *New Statesman*, 2 Oct. 1944, 267-8).

4 This production, directed by George Rylands, played in repertory at the Haymarket from October 1944 to August 1945, and was followed by a tour of the Far and Middle East. Gielgud's last performance of Hamlet took place in Cairo, on 7 February 1946.

5 *On Acting* 49. Although this is supposed to be a quotation from psychoanalyst Ernest Jones, whom Olivier had consulted about his planned 'Oedipal' reading of the part, it is hard not to regard it as mostly Olivier's own invention (especially since his memory after almost fifty years was likely to be a bit hazy – it had misled him on the previous page to get the title of Jones's book entirely wrong).

6 Such displays of athleticism became one of his hallmarks as an actor - witness his famous vault at the end of the film *Hamlet*, or, most spectacularly, his extraordinary fall at the end of his *Coriolanus*, where he ended hanging upside down from a parapet by his ankles.

Chapter VI

1 Anne Barton (Righter) had first developed such ideas in her pioneering study of Shakespearean meta-dramatics, *Shakespeare and the Idea of the Play* (London, 1962).
2 For more on this production, see Hortmann. In my final chapter, I deal with another metatheatrical German production, that of Peter Zadek (1977). Also pertinent is Daniel Mesguich's 'deconstructive' French version (also 1977 – see Carlson).
3 Overall, over a thousand lines were cut in the interest of playable speed. The effect of this was to squeeze out the play's characteristic circumlocutions and abstract, sometimes semi-allegorical, idiom.

Chapter VII

1 The water, like the relationship with his father, is warmer than usual, it should be noted, because Laurence has taken his absent brother's position as immediate heir to the family tub.
2 Deep focus, which had been used extensively by Wyler in such films as *The Best Years of our Lives*, allows for both foreground and background to be simultaneously in focus; it requires a great deal of light and, at least in 1947, could work only in black and white. Olivier learned from Wyler how to place his figures within the frame, to give the viewer access to the 'wholeness of the cinematic image', i.e. to everything going on within the frame, without frequent cuts. Like his mentor he reminds us that 'the screen is an *image* of depth, not the real thing' (Affron 93).
3 There may be some influence here of Bergman's wonderful exercise in northern gloom, *The Seventh Seal*; is it too irreverent to be reminded as well of a hilarious parody of such stuff, the little film called *Die Duve*?

Chapter VIII

1 Peter Donaldson made this point in a computer-and-video-enhanced talk he gave at the Shakespeare Association of America in 1993, in which he spoke too of Zeffirelli's preoccupation with looking relations as they connect to family rivalries, and of his use of the 'signature motif' of hands reaching across the screen, in this and other films. I am indebted to Donaldson's talk for stimulating my thinking about this film.
2 Laura Mulvey's influential article, which laid out the groundwork for the theory, has been much debated and revised, but the idea of focusing on the male viewer's position in cinema, and the power that he is afforded, has remained important. Who is looking at whom and under what circumstances has become a way of tracking meanings.
3 This sequence is made possible because the Ophelia scenes, again as in Q1, have also been run together, linking Hamlet's unscripted appearance in Ophelia's room, Polonius's report to the royals on Hamlet's strange behaviour, the 'nunnery' scene (though with all references to the nunnery excised) and then the 'To be or not to be' soliloquy, which here, as in Olivier, follows

the scene with Ophelia instead of preceding it, with the consequence that what Hamlet regards as her treachery seems to trigger his suicidal musings.

4 'The lascivious fervour with which Gertrude kisses Hamlet', writes one critic, seems 'the film's main justification for casting Close, an actress associated with a slightly excessive, slightly jaded sexuality' (*Sight and Sound*, I.i [1992]).

5 The idea of *Hamlet* as action movie is parodied in *Last Action Hero* (1993) where Arnold Schwarzenegger plays Hamlet. The incongruity of the casting is, of course, part of the point (beside Schwarzenegger, Gibson seems like Gielgud), since the film plays with comic relentlessness on the uncertain boundaries between reality and illusion that mark both the texts and performance history of *Hamlet*, even making use of bits of the Olivier film, into which Arnie is ingeniously inserted. Schwarzenegger doesn't turn away like a wimp from the praying Claudius, but flips him through a window ('Hey Claudius, you killed my fodder ... *big* mistake'). In the end, the elaborately meta-cinematic theme of the film transforms movie violence into harmlessness. New York, the emblem of dirty urban reality, riddled with decay, demolition and continual meaningless street crime is contrasted with Hollywood, where, despite the glittery unreality, evil is defeated and tawdriness transformed into social efficacy. The film thus cleverly defends itself and its provenance, making a self-justifying sally into the debate about the social effects of violence on TV and film.

6 For Zeffirelli's interest in loving depictions of male beauty and their association with violence and death, see Donaldson 163-71.

7 Peter Donaldson highlighted this moment in his SAA talk (see note 1), though with a different purpose; he wanted to emphasize 'mediated contact' as a sign of how this film complicates the 'technics of presence'.

Chapter IX

1 A major exception is the *Hamlet Collage* stitched together and directed by Charles Marowitz, in which the text was broken into bits and then reassembled in radically altered ways. Its first performance was in Berlin in 1965. Since then there have developed, among other disintegrative versions, the hilariously reduced 'Fifteen minute *Hamlet*' devised by Tom Stoppard and the exceptionally crude but funny, 'Skinhead *Hamlet*' (Richard Curtis) in which Shakespeare's words are replaced by an array of Anglo-Saxon expletives.

2 For accounts of the French and Czech productions, see Carlson 213-16, and 220-1, and Burian 202-4; for the Heyme version, see Hortmann; the Zadek and Lyubimov productions will be discussed below.

3 'How shall we live?' has been a recurrent motif in Russian understandings of *Hamlet*, and 'To be ...' has frequently been translated as 'To live or not to live'; Spencer Golub suggests that 'the social question of how one lives in an oppressive culture engendered ... the existential question of how one lives at all' (158; see also Rowe 162).

APPENDIX

Major actors and staff for productions discussed in this volume

Sam H. Harris Theatre, New York, November 1922
Director: Arthur Hopkins   Designer: Robert Edmond Jones

Hamlet John Barrymore
Claudius Tyrone Power
Gertrude Blanche Yurka
Polonius John S. O'Brien
Ophelia Rosalind Fuller

Laertes Sidney Mather
Horatio Frederick Lewis
Ghost Reginald Pole
First Player Lark Taylor
First Gravedigger Whitford Kane

Haymarket Theatre, London, February 1925
Director: John Barrymore   Designer: Robert Edmond Jones

Hamlet John Barrymore
Claudius Malcolm Keen
Gertrude Constance Collier
Polonius Herbert Waring
Ophelia Fay Compton

Laertes Ian Fleming
Horatio George Relph
Ghost Courtenay Thorpe
First Player Burnel Lundbec
First Gravedigger Ben Field

Kingsway Theatre, London, August 1925
Director: Henry Ayliff   Designer: Paul Shelving

Hamlet Colin Keith-Johnston
Claudius Frank Vosper
Gertrude Dorothy Massingham
Polonius A. Bromley-Davenport
Ophelia Muriel Hewitt

Laertes Robert Holmes
Horatio Alan Howland
Ghost Grosvenor North
First Player Terence O'Brien
First Gravedigger Cedric Hardwicke

Old Vic, London, May 1930
Director: Harcourt Williams   Designer: Paul Smyth

Hamlet John Gielgud
Claudius Donald Wolfit
Gertrude Martita Hunt
Polonius Brember Wills
Ophelia Adele Dixon

Laertes Francis James
Horatio Gyles Isham
Ghost Harcourt Williams
First Player Eric Adeney
First Gravedigger Henry Wolston

New Theatre, London, November 1934
Director: John Gielgud   Designer: Motley

Hamlet John Gielgud
Claudius Frank Vosper
Gertrude Laura Cowie
Polonius George Howe

Laertes Glen Byam Shaw
Horatio Jack Hawkins
Ghost William Devlin
Ophelia Jessica Tandy

Empire Theatre, New York, October 1936

Director: Guthrie McClintic Designer: Jo Mielziner

Hamlet John Gielgud
Claudius Malcolm Keen
Gertrude Judith Anderson
Polonius Arthur Byron
Ophelia Lillian Gish

Laertes John Emery
Horatio Harry Andrews
First Player Harry Mestayer
First Gravedigger George Nash

Old Vic, London, January 1937

Director: Tyrone Guthrie Designer: Martin Battersby

Hamlet Laurence Olivier
Claudius Francis L. Sullivan
Gertrude Dorothy Dix
Polonius George Howe
Ophelia Cherry Cottrell

Laertes Michael Redgrave
Horatio Robert Newton
Ghost Torin Thatcher
First Player Marius Goring
First Gravedigger Frederick Bennett

Shakespeare Memorial Theatre, Stratford, April 1948

Director: Michael Benthall Designer: James Bailey

Hamlet Robert Helpmann/Paul Scofield
Claudius Anthony Quayle
Gertrude Diana Wynyard
Polonius John Kidd
Ophelia Claire Bloom

Laertes William Squire
Horatio John Justin
Ghost Esmond Knight
First Player Michael Godfrey
First Gravedigger Esmond Knight

Royal Shakespeare Theatre, Stratford, August 1965

Director: Peter Hall Designer: John Bury

Hamlet David Warner
Claudius Brewster Mason
Gertrude Elizabeth Spriggs
Polonius Tony Church
Ophelia Glenda Jackson

Laertes Charles Thomas
Horatio Donald Burton
Ghost Patrick Magee
First Player William Squire
First Gravedigger David Waller

Taganka Theatre, Moscow, 1971

Director: Yuri Lyubimov Designer: David Borovsky

Hamlet Vladimir Vysotsky
Claudius N. Porokhovschikov

Gertrude Alla Demidova

Bochum, Germany, 1977

Director: Peter Zadek Designer: Peter Pabst

Hamlet Ulrich Wildgruber
Claudius Hermann Lause
Gertrude Eva Mattes
Polonius Rosel Zech

Ophelia Ilse Ritter
Laertes Ernst Konarek
Ghost Magdalena Montezuma

Royal Court, London, April 1980

Director: Richard Eyre Designer: William Dudley

Hamlet Jonathan Pryce
Claudius Michael Elphick
Gertrude Jill Bennett
Polonius Geoffrey Chater

Laertes Simon Chandler
First Player Christopher Logue
Ophelia Harriet Walter

Royal Shakespeare Theatre, Stratford, June 1980
Director: John Barton   Designer: Ralph Koltai

Hamlet Michael Pennington
Claudius Derek Godfrey
Gertrude Barbara Leigh-Hunt
Polonius Tony Church
Ophelia Carol Royle

Laertes John Bowe
Horatio Tom Wilkinson
Ghost Raymond Westwell
First Player Bruce Purchase
First Gravedigger Raymond Westwell

Deutsches Theater, Berlin, 1990
Director: Heiner Müller   Designer: Erich Wonder

Hamlet Ulrich Mühe
Claudius Jorg Gudzuhn
Gertrude Dagmar Manzel

Ophelia Margareta Broich
Laertes Michael Kind
Polonius Dieter Montag

Barbican Theatre, London, December 1992
Director: Adrian Noble   Designer: Bob Crowley

Hamlet Kenneth Branagh
Claudius John Shrapnel
Gertrude Jane Lapotaire
Polonius David Bradley
Ophelia Joanne Pearce

Laertes Richard Bonneville
Horatio Rob Edwards
Ghost Clifford Rose
First Player Jonathan Newth
First Gravedigger Richard Moore

Some other significant twentieth-century productions

	Director	*Hamlet*	*Theatre/city*
1900-15	Frank Benson	Frank Benson	London/Stratford
1905-10	H. Beerbohm-Tree	Beerbohm-Tree	His Majesty's
1911-12	K. Stanislavsky/G. Craig	Vasily Kachalov	Moscow Art Theatre
1913	J. Forbes-Robertson	J. Forbes-Robertson	Drury Lane
1926	Leopold Jessner	Fritz Kortner	Berlin
1926	Karel Hilar	Edward Kohout	Prague
1938	Tyrone Guthrie	Alec Guinness	Old Vic
1938	Margaret Webster	Maurice Evans	St James, New York
1945	George Schaefer	Maurice Evans	Columbus Circle, New York
1954	Nikolai Okhlopkov	E. Samoilov	Mayakovsky Theatre, Moscow
1957	Michael Langham	Christopher Plummer	Stratford, Ontario
1958	Glen Byam Shaw	Michael Redgrave	Shakespeare Memorial Theatre
1963/64	Laurence Olivier	Peter O'Toole	National Theatre
1964	John Gielgud	Richard Burton	New York
1968	Joseph Papp	Martin Sheen	New York Public Theatre
1969	Tony Richardson	Nicol Williamson	Roundhouse
1975	Michael Rudman	Sam Waterston	Shakespeare Festival, New York

1975	Buzz Goodbody	Ben Kingsley	The Other Place, Stratford
1976	Peter Hall	Albert Finney	National Theatre
1976	Robin Phillips	Nicholas Pennell/ Richard Monette	Stratford, Ontario
1977	Daniel Mesguich	multiple	Grenoble/Paris
1977	Toby Robertson	Derek Jacobi	Edinburgh Festival
1979	Hansgunther Heyme	multiple	Cologne
1988	Derek Jacobi	Kenneth Branagh	Renaissance Theatre Company
1989	Richard Eyre	Daniel Day-Lewis	National Theatre
1989	Ron Daniels	Mark Rylance	Royal Shakespeare Theatre

Major actors and staff for film versions discussed in this volume

Two Cities Films, GB, 1948
Director: Laurence Olivier

Hamlet Laurence Olivier
Gertrude Eileen Herlie
Claudius Basil Sydney
Ophelia Jean Simmons
Polonius Felix Aylmer

Horatio Norman Woodland
Laertes Terence Morgan
First Player Harcourt Williams
Gravedigger Stanley Holloway

Lenfilm, Soviet Union, 1964
Director: Grigori Kozintsev

Hamlet Innokenty Smoktunovsky
Gertrude Elza Radzin
Claudius Mikhail Nazvanov
Ophelia Anastasiya Vertinskaya

Horatio V. Erenberg
Laertes C. Olesenko
Gravedigger V. Kolpakor
Polonius Yuri Tolubeev

BBC TV, GB, 1980
Director: Rodney Bennett

Hamlet Derek Jacobi
Gertrude Claire Bloom
Claudius Patrick Stewart
Ophelia Lalla Ward
Polonius Eric Porter

Horatio Robert Swann
Laertes David Robb
First Player Emrys James
Gravedigger Tim Wylton
Ghost Patrick Allen

Warner Bros, GB, 1990
Director: Franco Zeffirelli

Hamlet Mel Gibson
Gertrude Glenn Close
Claudius Alan Bates
Ophelia Helena Bonham-Carter
Polonius Ian Holm

Horatio Stephen Dillane
Laertes Nathaniel Parker
First Player Pete Postlethwaite
Gravedigger Trevor Peacock
Ghost Paul Scofield

Some other significant film and TV versions

	Director	Hamlet	Origin
1913	Hay Plumb	J. Forbes-Robertson	Hepworth, GB
1920	Svend Gade	Asta Nielsen	Sweden
1953	George Schaefer	Maurice Evans	NBC, USA
1960	Franz Peter Wirth	Maximilian Schell	West German TV
1964	Philip Saville	Christopher Plummer	BBC/Danmarks Radio
1969	Tony Richardson	Nicol Williamson	Filmways, GB
1970	Peter Wood	Richard Chamberlain	NBC, USA

BIBLIOGRAPHY

Addenbrooke, David, *Royal Shakespeare Company: the Peter Hall Years*, London, 1974.

Affron, Charles, 'The Best Years of Our Lives' in *International Dictionary of Films and Filmmakers*, second ed., ed. Nicholas Thomas, Chicago, 1990, 91-3.

Archer, William, *Henry Irving: Actor and Manager*, London, 1883, rpt St Clair Shores, Michigan, 1970.

Barber, Frances, 'Ophelia', in Russell Jackson and Robert Smallwood, eds, *Players of Shakespeare*, vol. 2, Cambridge, 1988, 137-49.

Barrymore, John, *Confessions of an Actor*, New York, 1926.

Beauman, Sally, *The Royal Shakespeare Company: a History of Ten Decades*, Oxford, 1982.

Berger, Harry Jr, *Imaginary Audition*, Berkeley and Los Angeles, 1989.

Berry, Ralph, *Changing Styles in Shakespeare*, London, 1981.

—, *On Directing Shakespeare: Interviews with Contemporary Directors*, London, 1977.

Bertram, Paul and Kliman, Bernice, eds, *The Three-text Hamlet: Parallel texts of the first and second quartos and the first folio*, New York, 1991.

Brook, Peter, *The Empty Space*, Harmondsworth, 1972.

Bulman, J. C. and Coursen, H. R., eds, *Shakespeare on Television*, Hanover, NH, 1988.

Bulman, James C., 'The BBC Shakespeare and "House Style"' in Bulman and Coursen, 50-60.

Burian, Jarka, '*Hamlet* in postwar Czech theatre' in Kennedy, *Foreign Shakespeare*, 195-210.

Burnim, Kalman A. 'Looking upon His Like Again: Garrick and the Artist' in Shirley S. Kenny, ed., *British Theatre and the Other Arts, 1660-1800*, Washington, 1984, 182-218.

—, *David Garrick, Director*, Pittsburgh, 1961.

Calhoun, Lucia Gilbert, *The Galaxy*, January 1869, rpt in New Variorum *Hamlet*.

Campbell, Kathleen. 'Zeffirelli's *Hamlet* - Q1 in Performance', *Shakespeare Film Newsletter* 16 (Dec. 1991), 7-8.

Canaris, Volker, 'Peter Zadek and *Hamlet*', *Drama Review* 24.1 (March 1980), 53-62.

Carlson, Marvin, 'Daniel Mesguich and Intertextual Shakespeare' in Kennedy, *Foreign Shakespeare*, 213-31.

Chambers, E. K., *The Elizabethan Stage*, 4 vols., Oxford, 1923.

—, *William Shakespeare: a Study of Facts and Problems*, 2 vols, London, 1930.

Child, Harold, 'The Stage History of *Hamlet*' in *Hamlet*, ed. J. Dover Wilson, Cambridge, 1954, lxix-xcvii.

Church, Tony, 'Polonius,' in Philip Brockbank, ed., *Players of Shakespeare*, vol. 1, Cambridge, 1985, 103-14.

Clapp, Henry Austin, *Reminiscences of a Dramatic Critic*, 1902, rpt Freeport, NY, 1972.

Clarke, Charles W., Manuscript on Booth's *Hamlet*, Folger Shakespeare Library, listed in Shattuck, *Shakespeare Promptbooks*, as HAM 86.

Cochrane, Claire E., 'Shakespeare at the Birmingham Repertory Theatre, 1913-1971', unpublished Doctoral Dissertation, University of Birmingham, 1987.

Cockin, Norman, 'Post-War Productions of *Hamlet* at Stratford-upon-Avon, 1948-70', unpublished MA thesis, University of Birmingham, 1980.

Cross, Brenda, ed., *The Film HAMLET: a Record of its Production*, London, 1948.

Crosse, Gordon, unpublished ms. diaries, Birmingham Shakespeare Library.

Dawson, Anthony B., 'The Impasse over the Stage', *English Literary Renaissance* 21.3 (autumn 1991), 309-27.

—, *Watching Shakespeare: a Playgoers' Guide*, London: 1988.

De Grazia, Margreta, *Shakespeare Verbatim: the Reproduction of Authenticity and the 1790 Apparatus*, Oxford, 1991.

Dent, Alan, ed., *Hamlet: the Film and the Play*, London, 1948.

Donaldson, Peter S., *Shakespearean Films/Shakespearean Directors*, Boston, 1990.

Donohue, Joseph W., *Dramatic Character in the English Romantic Age*, Princeton, 1970.

Edwards, Phillip, ed., *Hamlet, Prince of Denmark*, New Cambridge edition, Cambridge, 1985.

Engle, Ron, 'The Shakespeare of Peter Zadek' in Kennedy, *Foreign Shakespeare*, 93-105.

Evans G. B., ed., *Shakespearean Prompt-books of the Seventeenth Century*, vol. IV, Charlottesville, VA, 1966.

—, *The Riverside Shakespeare*, Boston, 1974.

Freedman, Barbara, *Staging the Gaze*, Ithaca, 1991.

Furness, H. H., 'The Hamlet of John Barrymore', *The Drama* (March 1923), 207-08, 230.

—, ed., *Hamlet,* New Variorum edition, 2 vols, Philadelphia, 1905.

Gershkovich, Alexander, *The Theater of Yuri Lyubimov*, trans. Michael Yurieff, New York, 1989.

Gielgud, John, 'The Hamlet Tradition: Notes on Costume, Scenery and Stage Business' in Gilder, 29-81.

—, *Early Stages*, London, 1939.

—, with John Miller and John Powell, *John Gielgud: an Actor and His Time*, London, 1979.

Gilder, Rosamund, *John Gielgud's Hamlet: a Record of Performance*, with 'The Hamlet Tradition' by John Gielgud, London, 1937.

Golub, Spencer, 'The Taganka in the *Hamlet* Gulag' in Kennedy, *Foreign Shakespeare,* 158-77.

Granville-Barker, Harley, *Prefaces to Shakespeare*, Third Series, *Hamlet*, London 1937.

Griffiths, Hubert, *Iconoclastes, or the Future of Shakespeare,* London and New York, n.d.

Guntner, Lawrence, 'Brecht and beyond: Shakespeare and the East German Stage' in Kennedy, *Foreign Shakespeare*, 109-39.

Guthrie, Tyrone, 'Hamlet at Elsinore', *London Mercury* 213 (July 1937), 246-9.

—, *A Life in the Theatre*, New York and London, 1959.

Harwood, Ronald, ed., *The Ages of Gielgud*, London, 1984 .

Hayman, Ronald, *John Gielgud*, London, 1971.

Hazlitt, William, *Hazlitt on Theatre*, ed. William Archer and Robert Lowe, New York, 1957.

Hibbard, George, ed., *Hamlet*, Oxford Shakespeare, Oxford, 1987.

Hillebrand, Harold N., *Edmund Kean*, New York, 1933.

Hodgdon, Barbara, *Henry IV Part Two* (Shakespeare in Performance series), Manchester, 1993.

Holroyd, Michael, *Bernard Shaw*, vol. I, London, 1990.

Hortmann, W., 'Shakespeare in the Federal Democratic Republic', *Shakespeare Quarterly* 31 (1980), 410-11.

Hughes, Alan, *Henry Irving, Shakespearean*, Cambridge, 1981.

Irving, Laurence, *Henry Irving: the Actor and his World*, New York, 1952.

Jackson, Russell, 'Another Part of the Castle: Some Victorian Hamlets' in Werner Habicht et al., ed., *Images of Shakespeare*, Newark, 1988.

Jones, Ernest, *Hamlet and Oedipus*, London, 1949 (orig. pub. 1923 in essay form).

Jorgens, Jack J., *Shakespeare on Film*, Bloomington, 1977.

Kemble, Frances Ann, *Records of a Girlhood*, New York, 1879.

Kennedy, Dennis, ed., *Foreign Shakespeare*, Cambridge, 1993.

—, *Harley Granville-Barker and the Dream of Theatre*, Cambridge, 1985.

—, *Looking at Shakespeare: a Visual History of Twentieth Century Performance*, Cambridge, 1993.

Kliman, Bernice W., 'The BBC *Hamlet*, a Television Production', *Hamlet Studies* 4.1-2 (1982), 99-105.

—, *Hamlet: Film, Televison and Audio Performance*, London and Toronto, 1988.

Kott, Jan and Mirsky, Mark, 'On Kozintsev's *Hamlet*', *Literary Review* 22.4 (summer 1979), 385-407.

Kozintsev, Grigori, *Shakespeare: Time and Conscience*, trans. Joyce Vining, New York, 1966.

Leiter, Samuel L., ed., *Shakespeare Around the Globe: a Guide to Notable Postwar Revivals*, Westport, CT, 1986.

Lewes, George Henry, *On Actors and the Art of Acting*, 1875, rpt New York, 1957.

Lichtenberg, Georg, 'Letters from England' in *Lichtenberg's Visits to England*, trans. and ed. Margaret Mare and W. H. Quarell, Oxford, 1938, 1-41.

Linzer, Martin, 'Die Welt ist aus den Fugen', *Theater der Zeit* 45.5 (1990),10-12.

McMillin, Scott, 'The Moon in the Morning and the Sun at Night: Perversity and the BBC Shakespeare' in Bulman and Coursen, 76-81.

Mander, Raymond and Mitchenson, Joe, *Hamlet through the Ages: a Pictorial Record from 1709*, London, 1952.

Manvell, Roger, *Shakespeare and the Film*, London, 1971.

Mazer, Cary M., *Shakespeare Refashioned: Elizabethan Plays on Edwardian Stages*, Ann Arbor, 1981.

Mills, John A., *Hamlet on Stage: the Great Tradition*, Westport, CT, 1985.

More, Hannah, *The Letters of Hannah More*, ed. R. B. Johnson, London, 1925.

Morrison, Michael A., 'John Barrymore's *Hamlet* at the Haymarket Theatre, 1925', *New Theatre Quarterly* 27 (August 1991), 246-60.

Müller, Heiner, *Hamletmachine and Other Texts for the Stage*, ed. and trans. Carl Weber, New York, 1984.

Mulvey, Laura, 'Visual Pleasure and Narrative Cinema', *Screen* 16 (1975), 6-18.

Neve, Brian, *Film and Politics in America*, London and New York, 1992.

O'Connor, Garry, ed., *Olivier: In Celebration*, London, 1987.

Odell, George, *Shakespeare from Betterton to Irving*, New York, 1920.

Olivier, Laurence, *Confessions of an Actor*, London, 1982.

—, *On Acting*, London, 1986.

Palmer, John, '*Hamlet* in Modern Dress', *Fortnightly Review*, 2 Nov. 1925, 675-83.

Pennington, Michael, '*Hamlet*' in Philip Brockbank, ed., *Players of Shakespeare*, vol. 1, Cambridge, 1985, 115-28.

Playfair, Giles, *The Flash of Lightning: a Portrait of Edmund Kean*, London, 1983.

Price, Cecil, *Theatre in the Age of Garrick*, Oxford, 1973.

Raab, Michael, *Das Widerspenstigen Zahmung: moderne Shakespeare-Inszenierungen in Deutschland und England*, Rheinfelden, 1985.

Rhode, Eric, 'Screened Culture', *Encounter* (Nov. 1965), 61-5.

Roach, Joseph, 'Garrick, the Ghost and the Machine', *Theatre Journal* 34.4 (Dec. 1982), 431-40.

—, *The Player's Passion: Studies in the Science of Acting*, Newark, 1985.

Rothwell, Kenneth, '"The Shakespeare Plays": *Hamlet* and the Five Plays of Season Three', *Shakespeare Quarterly* 32.3 (1981), 395-401.

Rothwell, Kenneth and Melzer, Annabelle, *Shakespeare on Screen: an International Filmography and Videography*, New York, 1990.

Rowe, Eleanor, *Hamlet: a Window on Russia*, New York, 1976.

Rowell, George, *Theatre in the Age of Irving*, Oxford, 1981.

Russell, Edward R., *Arrested Fugitives*, London, 1912.

Salter, Denis, 'Henry Irving, the "Dr. Freud" of melodrama', in James Redmond ed., *Melodrama*, Cambridge, 1992.

Senelick, Laurence, *Gordon Craig's Moscow Hamlet: a Reconstruction*, Westport, CT, 1982.

Shakespeare, William, *Hamlet: First Quarto, 1603*, Shakespeare Quarto Fascimiles, Oxford, 1965.

Shattuck, Charles H., *The Hamlet of Edwin Booth*, Urbana IL, 1969.

—, *The Shakespeare Promptbooks: a Descriptive Catalogue*, Urbana, IL, 1965.

Showalter, Elaine, 'Representing Ophelia: women, madness, and the responsibilities of feminist criticism' in Patricia Parker and Geoffrey Hartmann, eds, *Shakespeare and the Question of Theory*, London, 1985.

Silviria, Dale, *Laurence Olivier and the Art of Film Making*, Rutherford, NJ, 1985.

Sinfield, Alan, 'Royal Shakespeare: theatre and the making of ideology', in Jonathan Dollimore and Alan Sinfield, eds, *Political Shakespeare*, Manchester and Ithaca, 1985, 158-81.

Smith, Helen R., *David Garrick 1717-1779: a Brief Account*, London, 1979.

Sprague, A. C., *Shakespeare and the Actors: the Stage Business in his Plays (1660-1905)*, Cambridge, MA, 1944.

—, *Shakespearian Players and Performances*, Cambridge, MA, 1953.

Sprague, A. C. and Trewin, J. C., *Shakespeare's Plays Today: Some Customs and Conventions of the Stage*, London, 1970.

Stahl, E. L., *Shakespeare und das deustche Theater*, Stuttgart, 1947.

Stein, Elizabeth P., ed., *Three Plays by David Garrick*, New York, 1926.

Stone, G. W., 'Garrick's Long Lost Alteration of *Hamlet*', *PMLA* 49 (Sept. 1934), 890-921.

Stone, Mary Isabella, *Edwin Booth's Performances*, ed. Daniel Watermeier, Ann Arbor, 1990.

Styan, J. L., *The Shakespeare Revolution*, Cambridge, 1977.

Taylor, Lark, 'My Season With John Barrymore in *Hamlet*' (1923), unpublished ms. in Vanderbilt University Archives.

—, Promptbooks for John Barrymore's *Hamlet*, 1922-23, Folger Library.

Terry, Ellen, *The Story of My Life*, New York, 1909.

Trewin, J. C., *Shakespeare on the English Stage 1900-1964*, London, 1964.

—, *Five and Eighty Hamlets*, London, 1987.

Tynan, Kenneth, *Tynan on Theatre*, Harmondsworth, 1964.

Urkowitz, Steven, '"Well-sayd olde Mole": Burying Three *Hamlets* in Modern Editions' in Georgianna Ziegler, ed., *Shakespeare Study Today*, New York, 1986.

Von Becker, Peter, 'Shakespeare heute - Shakespeare harmlos?', *Theater Heute* (November 1977), 6-9.

Vosper, Frank, 'Shakespeare in Modern Dress - The Actor's Point of View', *Theatre World* (Oct. 1925).

Ward, David, 'The King and *Hamlet*', *Shakespeare Quarterly* 43.3 (fall 1992), 280-302.

Warren, Roger, 'Shakespeare in Performance 1980', *Shakespeare Survey* 34 (1981), 149-60.

Webster, Margaret, *The Same Only Different*, London, 1969.

Wells, Stanley, *Royal Shakespeare: Four Productions at Stratford-upon-Avon*, Manchester, 1977.

Wells, Stanley and Taylor, Gary, *William Shakespeare: a Textual Companion*, Oxford, 1987.

Werstine, Paul, 'The Textual Mystery of Hamlet', *Shakespeare Quarterly* 39.1 (spring 1988), 1-26.

Wille, Franz, 'Mühe hat's gemacht', *Theater Heute* (May 1990), 25-8.

Williams, Harcourt, *Four Years at the Old Vic*, London, 1935.

—, *Old Vic Saga*, London, 1949.

Williams, Simon, 'Actorial Representations of the Self in the Romantic Age: Edmund Kean and Ludwig Devrient', *New Comparison: a Journal of Comparative and General Literary Studies* 9 (spring 1990), 103-16.

Williamson, Audrey, *Old Vic Drama*, London, 1948.

Willis, Susan, *The BBC Shakespeare Plays: Making the Televised Canon*, Chapel Hill, 1991.

Wilson, Michael S., 'Garrick, Iconic Acting, and the Ideologies of Theatrical Portraiture', *Word & Image* 6.4 (Oct.-Dec. 1990), 368-94.

Woods, Leigh, *Garrick Claims the Stage: Acting as Social Emblem in Eighteenth Century England*, Westport, CT, 1984.

Worthen, W. B., 'Deeper Meanings and Theatrical Technique: the Rhetoric of Performance Criticism', *Shakespeare Quarterly* 40.4 (winter, 1989), 441-55.

Zadek, Peter, 'Um nichts - um Hekuba', *Theater Heute* (November 1977), 8.

Zeffirelli, Franco, *The Autobiography of Franco Zeffirelli*, New York, 1986.

Zitner, Sheldon P., 'Wooden O's in Plastic Boxes', in Bulman and Coursen, 31-41.

INDEX